CONTRACT
ADMINISTRATION
MANUAL
for the
DESIGN
PROFESSIONS

ALAN N. CULBERTSON
DONALD E. KENNEY, P.E.

CONTRACT ADMINISTRATION MANUAL for the DESIGN PROFESSIONS

How to Establish, Systematize, and
Monitor Construction Contract Controls

McGRAW-HILL BOOK COMPANY
New York St. Louis San Francisco Auckland Bogotá Hamburg
Johannesburg London Madrid Mexico Montreal New Delhi
Panama Paris São Paulo Singapore Sydney Tokyo Toronto

Library of Congress Cataloging in Publication Data

Culbertson, Alan N.
  Contract administration manual for the design professions.

  Includes index.
  1. Building—Contracts and specifications.
I. Kenney, Donald E.   II. Title.
TH425.C84   1983   624'.068'5   82-12692
ISBN 0-07-014894-5

1 2 3 4 5 6 7 8 9 0   DOC/DOC   8 9 8 7 6 5 4 3 2

ISBN 0-07-014894-5

The editors for this book were Joan Zseleczky and Chet Gottfried,
the designer was Elliott Epstein, and the production supervisor
was Terry Leaden. It was set in Melior by Bi-Comp, Incorporated.

Printed and bound by R. R. Donnelley & Sons Company.

To Sharon and Joyce,
for their love—and their patience.

CONTENTS

This volume is intended as a manual for working construction contract administrators and as a primer for students in the design professions and public administration contemplating careers related to construction contract administration. We know of no other book like it, and we hope its readers will conclude that it fills a definite need in the successful completion of construction projects.

Contract administrators are known by many names. We regard "contract administrators" as a functional category which includes all persons employed or retained (directly or indirectly) by the project owner to promote construction in accordance with one or more written agreements—called the contract, or contract documents—between the owner and the party or parties obligated to construct the project, i.e., the contractor or contractors. Thus defined, contract administrators may have the title of consulting engineer, architect, owner's project manager or project engineer, or even construction manager. Whatever the title, the contract administrator's function is to increase the probability that the project is built by the contractor or contractors in substantial compliance with the contract documents.

But to define contract administrators according to function is not to justify the function itself: in short, why have contract administrators at all? The answer is to be found in the number of participants in the construction process, the cross-purposes at which they work, and their sophistication in achieving their respective goals. The owner, for example, customarily seeks the best possible project at the lowest possible cost. The contractor shares, in most cases, the owner's desire for a final "product" of high quality; however, a contractor who becomes caught in an irreconcilable conflict between providing that level of quality and realizing what he believes to be a reasonable profit will usually choose to pursue the profit. This is not to say that the owner and the contractor are at war, but merely to observe that the potential for a conflict of purposes exists in most construction projects. Subcontractors and suppliers hold goals similar to those of the contractors. The fact that most participants are operating with large sums of borrowed money adds intense pressure to the pursuit of their differing purposes. Given this pressure, the formidable talents of the participants, and the complexity of major construction projects, there is a definite need for some participant to keep the contract documents— and the performance of the various participants in relation to the contract documents—in clear focus. Enter the contract administrator.

The function of the contract administrator is to increase the probability that the project will be constructed substantially as designed, i.e., in substantial compliance with the contract documents. The contractual *duty* to so construct the project continues to rest exclusively with the contractor; the contract administrator's role is to promote the successful performance of that duty. This is one critical distinction between contract administration and construction management: the responsibilities of most construction managers exceed those of most contract administrators. In other words, the construction manager usually places himself, contractually speaking, *between* the owner and the contractor, usually accepting some *shared* responsibility for construction in substantial compliance with design, whereas the contract administrator most often plays the role of monitor, reporting to the owner but communicating with the contractor only within the bounds of authority granted by the owner. The contract administrator is not a *party* to the contract between the owner and the contractor, but is a *participant* in the construction process. Although much of the discussion set forth in this book applies to construction managers, the focus will remain upon contract administrators.

The reader will note that the construction obligation of the contractor is one of *substantial* compliance. It seems safe to say that no construction project has ever been built exactly as designed; thus the question is, How much deviation from the absolute plans and specifications is acceptable? Thousands of court cases have been tried to answer the question, with the general consensus that nominal deviations (such as changes in brands of pipe of equal quality) are of no consequence, that minor deviations (such as construction of a building slightly but not critically smaller than designed) are to be redressed through financial adjustments among the parties, and that substantial deviations (such as construction of facilities which fail to perform at critical levels identified in design) are to be reconstructed at the expense of the party responsible. In short, the courts have recognized that construction is as much an art as a science and that the attainment of something less than perfection is to be accepted by the owner.

The typical scenario for the development of contract documents should be mentioned here. Usually, the owner becomes aware that it has a short- or long-term need for upgraded or additional facilities but requires assistance to define its needs more clearly and to determine the most cost-effective way to meet those needs. The owner often retains a consulting engineer or architect to provide such services. Upon defining the needs precisely and designing solutions, the consultant customarily submits for the owner's approval plans, specifications, and provisions governing the relationship to exist between the owner and the party or parties to be hired to construct the project designed by the consultant. These plans, specifications, and other provisions are cumulatively called the contract documents, or contract. Once the contractor has been selected (either through bidding or through direct procurement) and the contract documents have been executed, the time for commencement of construction will have been fixed, and the need for contract administration services will have become paramount. Some owners perform such services themselves, some retain their design consultants, and some retain firms which are engaged solely in contract administration. In any event, it is important that the duties of the contract administrator be documented thoroughly at the outset.

It is axiomatic that contract administration begins with a thorough working knowledge of the contract documents. It is also clear that contract administrators are intelligent people who have been placed in critical positions because they presumably have the talents necessary to bring expensive and complex projects to successful conclusions; others rely upon them to *control* those projects.

Yet most practicing contract administrators will admit that at some point in most projects the feeling of control is lost. The reason given may be that the contractor has become uncooperative or that the contract administrator has fallen behind in the paperwork. The true reason is often that the seeds of loss of control in the middle of the project were sown with the contract administrator's failure to establish the necessary controls at the outset and to adhere to them faithfully as the project progressed. Whatever the reason, the feeling that the project is out of control adds immense pressure to the contract administrator's life. Most veterans in the field can name colleagues whose health and standing declined with their failure to keep up with the work.

The theme of this book is that construction projects *can* be effectively controlled with relative ease *if* the proper controls are established at the outset, systematized for manageability, and monitored religiously.

Traditional lecture and textual presentations for contract administrators have identified selected pitfalls and offered general explanations of what to do to avoid them; this book provides a detailed, integrated *method* to control the project successfully from beginning to end. The method has three distinct but logically sequential stages:

Stage 1: Organized learning of the project, definition of responsibilities of each participant, and understanding of project construction costs (*establishment of controls*)

Stage 2: Organization of contract administration resources to follow the discharge of those responsibilities (*systematization of controls*)

Stage 3: Efficient and effective use of the systems to monitor the actual performance of the participants (*monitoring of controls*)

These stages comprise the three major parts of the book. Each stage—and each subpart of each stage—is heavily dependent upon every other stage and subpart: to neglect *any* subpart would substantially increase the risk of loss of control.

We offer this "cookbook" approach with two notes of caution. The first is that the wide variety of types of construction contracts may require thoughtful application of the method to specific contract provisions. For example, a simple lump-sum, or fixed-price, contract fixes the total contract price except in the event of a change in the scope of the work. It provides the owner with the best possible indication of final project cost and places with the contractor both the possibility of substantial profit and the risk of most unknown and unknowable contingencies. A different prototype is the unit-price contract, in which the contractor is paid for work performed at a predetermined rate for predefined units. Unit prices provide less certainty to the owner as to final project cost but also reduce the prospect of windfalls to the contractor; for his part, the contractor's focus is on productivity, the risk of the unknown having been substantially reduced. A third prototype is the time-and-material contract, in which the owner pays for the labor, materials, overhead, and profit at predetermined rates. Here the risk of low productivity rests with the owner, whereas the contractor's profit is assured. These prototypes are frequently combined to create contracts best suited to unique physical and economic conditions.

We have chosen to illustrate the principles and techniques discussed in this book with examples of lump-sum contracts with some unit prices, a combination which will permit the widest scope of work in a given project and which is sufficiently common as to be readily adapted by readers to their specific needs.

The second note of caution follows directly from the first. The technical, legal, and business features of any construction contract are at the least mutually dependent and at the worst inseparable. Successful contract administrators will know and admit the limits of their knowledge and will seek the assistance of experts in the interpretation and—if necessary—the legal enforcement of the contract. Each contract is unique, and contract administrators should employ all available assistance to resolve any ambiguities as to the proper contractual roles of the various participants. Above all, the contract administrator's difficult task is to represent the owner's interests effectively by monitoring and influencing the activities of the contractor without jeopardizing those interests by intruding upon prerogatives reserved to the contractor. An overzealous contract administrator is a disservice to both his client and himself.

How can readers obtain the greatest benefit from this book? They should read *every chapter, in order, several times.* As we stated earlier, the book is the discussion of a method and a manual for the development of a complex skill: the step-by-step approach we offer cannot be mastered in a piecemeal or haphazard manner. There is simply too much substance in each chapter to be mastered in one reading, however diligent. In short, both the *practice* of contract administration and the *study* of contract administration must be organized for the best results. The difference between reading this book methodically and reading it casually will be the difference between time invaluably spent and time wasted.

Once contract administrators have completed their reading, they can strengthen their understanding by employing the techniques promptly in their next new project. In our judgment, the reader will master the method more rapidly and completely by starting fresh with a new project than by attempting to infuse it into a project already in progress. The mutual reinforcement of study and practice should make each succeeding application of the method faster and easier than the last.

Present and future contract administrators can make a significant contribution to society by doing their jobs well. We hope this book will aid in that endeavor and provide greater satisfaction for contract administrators along the way.

In writing this book, we have attempted to eliminate, wherever possible, references to gender. Remaining pronouns of gender are meant to be generic, for contract administration is an area with opportunities for both men and women.

ACKNOWLEDGMENTS

We acknowledge the valuable contributions of Beverly B. Hawk and Chet Gottfried in the preparation of the manuscript for this book.

Several of the illustrative materials of this book were adapted from the service products of the authors' employer, O'Brien & Gere Engineers, Inc., of Syracuse, New York, from projects undertaken for the County of Onondaga, New York, Department of Drainage and Sanitation, John J. Hennigan, Jr., P.E., Commissioner.

CONTRACT ADMINISTRATION MANUAL
for the
DESIGN PROFESSIONS

PART ONE

ESTABLISHMENT OF CONTRACT CONTROLS

Contract administration begins with the contract documents. In their original form, however, the contract documents are of little value to the contract administrator: they are simply too voluminous and too complex to permit full understanding—let alone control—of the project. Part 1 will be concerned at the outset with breaking the contract documents down—first by abstracting the contractual responsibilities of each participant and second by determining the construction components of the project. (The word "participant" is used to denote any person or entity involved significantly in the construction of the project. Thus it includes persons and entities, such as the contract administrator, who are not legal "parties" to the contract.) In dissecting the contract documents, the contract administrator will become thoroughly knowledgeable about the construction details of the project. Once the responsibilities and construction components have been abstracted and tabulated, contract administrators can approach their projects from a perspective similar to that of the contractor in order to "build the jobs in their minds." Such an approach will enable them to judge realistically the proposed construction schedules and lump-sum breakdowns submitted by contractors.

Armed with the tools provided in Part 1, contract administrators will have remade the contract documents to suit their special needs and will be well equipped to control the project within the limits of authority granted by the owner.

CHAPTER 1

DIVISIONS OF RESPONSIBILITY

Readers are urged to begin their scrutiny of this manual with a thorough reading of the Preface.

From the perspective of the contract administrator, three dimensions of each construction project must be controlled: quality, time, and cost. Control of these three dimensions depends upon effective allocation of responsibilities among participants and their performance of the duties which will discharge those responsibilities. If the contract has been drawn properly, nearly all the responsibilities will appear in clear form in that instrument. The contract should answer in detail such questions as what is to be built, where, when, and how. The first major task of contract administrators is to gain an understanding of the responsibilities of the respective participants; performance of this task will enable them to assess accurately the performance of each participant against the requirements of the contract.

But few, if any, construction contracts contemplate all situations which may arise in the course of a project. Accordingly, the arrangement defined in the contract for the project must when unforeseen situations arise be viewed in the context of normal construction practices in the geographical area in question; in such situations, local custom supplements the contract. Before resorting (or recommending resort) to local custom, however, the contract administrator will do well to consult the owner and its legal counsel for authoritative interpretation of the contract and instruction as to how to resolve the matter at hand.

With this knowledge of local custom and the contract documents in hand, the contract administrator is prepared to begin controlling the project.

The construction contract between the owner and the contractor is the all-important document in any construction project, for it alone allocates the rights and responsibilities of these two parties and their respective agents. Once the contractor has been selected and has met preliminary legal requirements, the contractual relationship between the owner's contract administrator and the contractor is the key to the success of the project. To protect adequately the owner's interests, the contract administrator's knowledge and control of the contract must equal—and preferably exceed—the contractor's; otherwise, the contract administrator and his client, the owner, will be at the mercy of the contractor who has done the homework during the bid and mobilization stages. The way to gain the necessary familiarity with the contract is to define the responsibilities of each party and its agents such that responsibilities can be effectively monitored, recorded, and known to be properly discharged. This is *not* to say that the contract administrator's relations with the contractor are—or should be—adversarial; on the contrary, the best projects are almost always constructed in an atmosphere of harmony and mutual respect. The point here is that such harmony and mutual respect are the product of similar degrees of careful preparation by the two participants.

This chapter provides a simple, but effective, technique by which the responsibilities set forth in the contract may be understood, refined, and tabulated according to who is required to act to discharge those responsibilities. Once the technique has been mastered and implemented, the contract administrator will have an effective device for monitoring the progress of each participant in discharging each of his responsibilities during the project.

EXTRACTING CONTROL RESPONSIBILITIES

The value of following *faithfully* the techniques described below cannot be overstated. The time and expense of setting up the control procedures which follow will be returned manyfold in savings to the owner and peace of mind for the contract administrator.

The First Step:
Reviewing the Contract

The first step is to read the contract—the *entire* contract—*two times*. The temptation to gloss over any section is to be avoided at all costs.

First Reading   The first reading is for general understanding:

- Understanding how the parts of the contract *documents* fit together, i.e., which parts supersede other parts in the event of inconsistencies, which parts deal with which subjects, and which parts are affected by addenda

- Understanding the general role of each participant, i.e., how and where the responsibilities of the participants are set forth and how the responsibilities of the owner and contract Administrator—as set forth in the *contract*—square with their respective responsibilities as set forth in the contract administrator's *agreement for services*

- Understanding—really, confirmation—that there is no glaring error in the contract which would impair the success of the Project

Second Reading   The second reading is intended to provide a more detailed understanding and to catch anything major that was missed during the first reading. It should occur at least a day after the first reading to avoid fatigue and boredom. During the second reading, any impressions should be noted in the margins. The importance of this rereading should not be underestimated: most contracts simply have too much substance for any reader, however diligent, to absorb in one sitting. The urge to "quit reading and get on with the project" should be suppressed because, for the contract administrator, this is the most important stage of the project!

The Second Step:
Extracting Control Responsibilities

Third Reading   The second step of the technique is to read the contract a final time in order to identify certain key responsibilities, called "control responsibilities." This third reading is intended to render the contract documents effectively usable by contract administrators in administering the project. They should read the contract from cover to cover, noting responsibilities allocated to each participant with highlighter markers in various colors and paper clips in various sizes. One color of marker and one size of paper clip should be used to denote each responsibility of a given participant. If, for example, the only participants are the owner, the engineer, and the contractor, each should be assigned a marker color and paper-clip size. Next to a responsibility of the engineer, an engineer-sized paper clip should be affixed at that location on the page, and the responsibility should be highlighted in the engineer's color; the same procedure should be followed for the other participants.

Identification of Control Responsibilities   But not all responsibilities of all Participants require the attention of the contract administrator. The contract administrator is interested in refining from that aggregate only those responsibilities which either:

1. Require *positive action* (i.e., require something to be done) by some participant

2. Require *interaction* by two or more participants

3. Necessitate the *keeping of records* to properly record its discharge

These control responsibilities are the only types of responsibilities with which the contract administrator need be concerned at this point, and they should be ever-present in his mind during the third reading. This is the second step in the technique for allocating contractual responsibilities.

When the contract administrator comes to a line, paragraph, or section of the contract which denotes or connotes a control responsibility, it should be marked with the appropriately colored highlighter and an appropriately sized paper clip. Examples of typical control responsibilities follow:

Examples of Action Being Required by Some Participant   The typical construction contract requires the contractor to notify the engineer prior to the commencement of work by the contractor through a statement in the contract such as:

> The Contractor shall notify the Engineer, in writing, of his intention to enter upon the site of the work at least five days in advance of such entry.

This statement requires positive action (i.e., requires something to be done) by the contractor and thus constitutes a control responsibility.

During the review of the contract for the purpose of noting control responsibilities, this statement should be highlighted with the color coded to define a responsibility of the contractor and a paper clip, the size coded to define a responsibility of the contractor, should be placed on that page. This contractual provision necessitates positive action on the part of the contractor which must be discharged prior to the contract administrator allowing the contractor to enter the site; evidence that the contractor has performed this duty should be on file in order to document the fact that the contractor has, in fact, discharged this responsibility.

A second example of a single-party responsibility is a typical statement in the contract that:

> Control lines and elevations will be established in the field by the Engineer.

This statement should be highlighted in the color coded to denote a responsibility of the engineer, and a paper clip of the size coded to denote the responsibility of the engineer should be placed on the page. This duty must be performed by the engineer to allow the contractor to proceed with construction activities.

Example of a Single Responsibility Not Required to Be Noted Most contracts contain a provision similar to the following:

> The Contractor shall not permit or cause any hindrance to, or interference with, any individual, municipal department, public service corporation, or other company or companies in protecting its or their mains, pipes, poles, or other structures, nor in shifting, removing, or replacing the same. The Contractor shall allow said individual, company, or companies to take all such measures as they may deem prudent to protect their structures.

This statement imposes a responsibility on the contractor, but no positive action is required. Since no positive action is required, it should not be highlighted.

Examples of Interaction by Two or More Participants Involved in the Contract Which Should Be Noted The prime example of interaction required by two or more participants involved in the contract which should be noted is the contractual procedure by which *changes* to the contract are to be undertaken.

The specific verbiage in a contract to provide for changes is usually lengthy; an example will not be quoted, at this point, but is included in the comprehensive example which appears at the end of this chapter. For our present purposes it is enough to say that the contract statement related to changes should be highlighted and the page or pages, paper-clipped. Since the primary action among the participants involved must be that of the engineer, the color highlighter marker and paper-clip size coded to denote the engineer's responsibility should be used.

Another example of multiparticipant duties would be a statement, in the contract, such as:

Upon execution and delivery of the Contract and the delivery of the required performance and labor and material bonds and insurance certificates and policies by the Contractor to the Owner, and the approval thereof by the Owner's attorney, the Contractor will be notified by the Engineer to proceed with the work of the Contract.

This statement requires: (1) the contractor to provide the documents listed; (2) the owner and its attorney to (a) approve the documents, (b) advise the engineer the documents are acceptable, and (c) advise the engineer to notify the contractor to proceed; and (3) the engineer to notify the contractor.

The statement should be highlighted and the page upon which it appears should be paper-clipped in the color and paper-clip size coded to a contractor's responsibility since his is the initiating action.

Example of a Responsibility Which Will Necessitate Records   A simple statement, such as "One copy of all concrete test reports shall be submitted directly to the Engineer by the Testing Laboratory for review," in the contract can connote voluminous record-keeping responsibilities should the project have a large quantity of concrete work.

This statement should be highlighted and paper-clipped to refer to the participant whose action will initiate the reports. Should the contract require that the contractor engage the services of the testing laboratory, the contractor's highlighter color and paper-clip size should be used; on the other hand, if the owner is to engage the laboratory directly, the owner's marking devices should be employed.

The Third Step:
Control Responsibility Summary Sheets

Completion of this marking, the second step in the technique—even with its coded markings and paper clips—brings the contract administrator only to the point of having a scattered aggregate of key duties of project participants. These key duties (control responsibilities) must now be organized to facilitate administration. The first part of this overall organization process is the *third* and final step in this chapter, namely, the tabulation of control responsibilities on "Control Responsibility Summary Sheets."

A word of caution is in order here. Procedures employed to reach this point have involved mere analysis and notation of textual materials prepared by engineers and reviewed by the owner's attorneys. The tabulation process, however, contemplates the *transfer* of contractual provisions from the contract documents to summary sheets. It is *critical* that the substance of those provisions not be altered in the transfer, for alterations—and subsequent misinterpretation by the contract administrator—would create a new noncontractual arrangement to which no other participant had agreed and could create enormous liability for the contract administrator. Contract administrators must never forget that their role is to carry out effectively the terms and conditions of a contract already in place, not to change the terms of that foundation document in the course of their administration.

The Control Responsibility Summary Sheet should have seven columns whose headings should be (1) contract citation, (2) description, (3) contractor responsibility, (4) owner responsibility, (5) engineer responsibility, (6) contract administrator responsibility, and (7) interaction responsibility. Figure 1-1 illustrates a blank Control Responsibility Summary Sheet.

The first column should note the section of the contract which defines the responsibility, and the second column should describe the responsibility in detail sufficient so as *not* to require reference back to the contract to define it. Checkmark the third column if the responsibility is a *single* responsibility of the contractor; the fourth column, a single responsibility of the owner; the fifth column, a single responsibility of the engineer; the sixth column, a single responsibility of the contract administrator; and the seventh column, an interaction responsibility of *two or more* participants. Once an entry has been made in the seventh column, the participant which must act first, second, and, if necessary, third or fourth, sequentially, should be identified by placing a number "1" under the third, fourth, fifth, or sixth column; the party which must take action after the first party's action should be so noted by placing a number "2" under that party in the third, fourth, fifth, or sixth column, and so forth.

In more complex arrangements with more participants, additional columns may be required; however, the principles of the Control Responsibility Summary Sheets would remain unchanged.

All responsibilities which were highlighted during the contract responsibility review should be transferred to the Control Responsibility Summary Sheet as described above. The Control Responsibility Summary Sheet should then be transmitted to the engineer's design group for its concurrence in the division of control responsibilities between the design group and the contract administrator in columns 5 and 6.

SUMMARY

In this chapter, contract administrators have identified the general areas of their duties in the project by reducing the contract, a com-

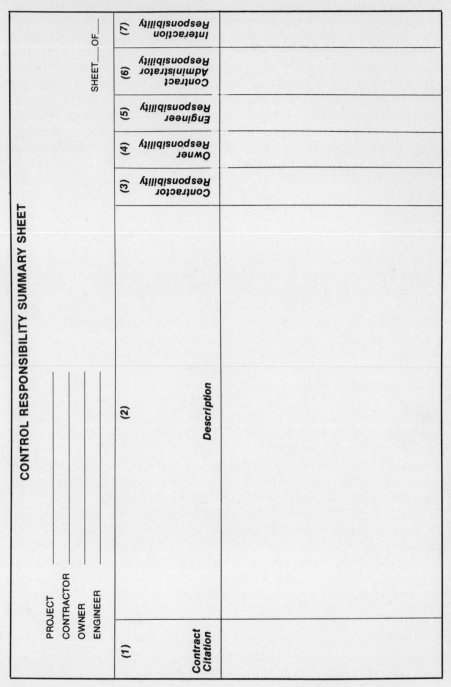

FIGURE 1-1 Control Responsibility Summary Sheet.

prehensive legal document, to Control Responsibility Summary Sheets, a manageable administrative tool, through careful use of the technique. They have (1) studied the contract systematically, (2) abstracted from the contract those responsibilities (called control responsibilities) of primary concern, and (3) consolidated them for administrative convenience in the form of Control Responsibility Summary Sheets. The result of their faithful use of this three-step technique is that they have created the key device to control the quality of their respective projects.

COMPREHENSIVE ILLUSTRATION

A comprehensive illustration of the technique involves the detailed discussion of selected provisions from a typical construction contract. For the purposes of this book, an underlining system, rather than highlighting the applicable verbiage, will be utilized as follows:

1. A single line under particular verbiage will indicate a control responsibility of the contractor.
2. Two lines will indicate a control responsibility of the engineer.
3. Three lines will indicate a control responsibility of the owner.
4. A broken line will indicate a control responsibility of the contract administrator.

One further clarification is necessary prior to beginning the detailed explanation of the technique. Most contracts for construction projects are generated by the consultant engineer or architect. Hence these contracts will usually refer to the "engineer" as being the entity to whom submittals, requests, and approval must be submitted and obtained by the contractor. The contract documents usually do not differentiate between the contract administrator and the design engineer.

We will assume in the review of the contract documents for the purpose of establishing control responsibilities that all design-related responsibilities are those of the design engineer—or "engineer"—and that all field-related responsibilities are those of the contract administrator. This is the usual division of responsibilities when the contract administrator is an employee of the same firm as the consultant engineer.

Should the contract administrator not be the employee of the same firm as the design engineer, he must examine his agreement with the owner regarding these services to determine the exact extent of his responsibilities and coordinate his responsibilities with those of the design engineer in order that both participants are clear as to which belong to each.

SAMPLE PROVISION G-1.01

COMMENCEMENT AND COMPLETION OF WORK: TIME OF ESSENCE

The Contractor shall complete the Work within the time specified in the Bid. The Contractor shall notify the Engineer, in writing, of his intention to enter upon the Site of the Work at least five days in advance of such entry.

Time is of the essence of this Contract.

Explanation of Control Responsibility Marking

The foregoing sample provision requires the positive action of the contractor to write to the contract administrator (field-related responsibility). Hence that one sentence—*not* the entire sample provision—defines a control responsibility of the contractor.

SAMPLE PROVISION G-1.02

RATE OF PROGRESS

The rate of progress of the Work shall be as nearly uniform as practicable and shall be such that all Work under the Contract will be completed within the time specified, or before such later date to which the time of completion may have been extended by the Owner.

The Contractor shall within ten days following the execution of this Contract prepare and submit to the Engineer for approval, two copies of a practical and feasible Work schedule showing the order and date on which the several salient features (including equipment) will be started and completed.

The Work schedule shall be in the form of a critical path or bar graph.

Explanation of Control Responsibility Marking

Positive action by the contractor is required to prepare and submit the work schedule. Hence one line has been drawn under the applicable verbiage requiring this positive action.

The review of the work schedule is a field-related item: the contract administrator must approve the work schedule. This requires the positive action of the contract administrator. A broken line under the applicable verbiage indicates his control responsibility.

SAMPLE PROVISION G-2.01

CLAIMS

If the Contractor claims (1) that any Work he has been ordered to do is extra work or (2) that he has performed or is going to perform extra work or (3) that any action or omission of the Owner or the Engineer is contrary to the terms and provisions of the Contract, he shall:

a. Promptly comply with such order;

b. File with the Owner and the Engineer within fourteen working days after being order to perform the work claimed by him to be extra work or within fourteen working days after commencing performance of the extra work, whichever date shall be the earlier, or within fourteen working days after the said action or omission on the part of the Owner or the Engineer occurred, a written notice of the basis of his claim and a request for a determination thereof;

c. File with the Owner and the Engineer, within thirty calendar days after said alleged extra work was required to be performed or said alleged extra work was commenced, whichever date shall be earlier, or said alleged action or omission by the Owner or the Engineer occurred, a verified detailed statement, with documentary evidence, for the items and basis of his claim;

d. Produce for the Owner's examination, upon notice from the Owner, all of his subcontractors' (of any tier) books of account, bills, invoices, payrolls, subcontracts, time books, progress records, daily reports, bank deposit books, bank statements, checkbooks, and canceled checks showing all of his actions and transactions in connection with, or relating to, or arising by reason of, his claim, and submit himself, persons in his employment, and persons in his subcontractor's employment for examination under oath by any person designated by the Owner to investigate any claims made against the Owner under the Contract, such examination to be made at the offices of the Owner or the Owner's agent;

e. Proceed, prior to and subsequent to the determination of the Owner with respect to any such disputed matter, with the performance of the Contract diligently and in accordance with all instructions of the Owner and the Engineer.

The Contractor's failure to comply with any or all of the foregoing provisions of this Section shall be deemed to be: (1) a conclusive and binding determination on his part that said order, work, action, or omission does not involve extra work and is not contrary to the terms and provisions of the Contract; and (2) a waiver by the Contractor of all claims for additional compensation or damages as a result of said order, work, action, or omission.

No person shall have power to waive or modify any of the foregoing provisions. In any action against the Owner to recover any sum in excess of the sum certified by the Owner to be due under or by reason of the Contract, the Contractor must allege in his complaint and prove at the trial compliance with the provisions of this Section.

Nothing in this Section shall in any way affect the Owner's right to obtain an examination before, or a discovery and inspection in, any action that might be instituted by, or against, the Owner or the Contractor.

Explanation of Control Responsibility Markings

It is quite likely that a claim will develop during the course of the construction project. It is, therefore, a good idea to define the control responsibilities which will develop should claims be made.

Paragraph b Positive action on the part of the contractor is required should he feel he has a claim. Applicable verbiage is underlined to note this.

Paragraph c The underlined verbiage imposes further positive action on the part of the contractor.

Paragraph d Positive action of the owner is required in the form of written notice to the contractor, and the contractor's subsequent positive action is required if the owner desires the data.

Paragraph e This requires the owner or the contract administrator to give the contractor instructions as to how to proceed in matters related to a claim. Hence it requires the positive action of either or both.

SAMPLE PROVISION G-2.02

NO CLAIMS AGAINST INDIVIDUALS

No claim whatsoever shall be made by the Contractor against any officer, agent, or employee of the Owner for, or on account of, anything done or omitted to be done in connection with the Contract.

Explanation of Control Responsibility Markings

No positive action is required on the part of any of the entities involved in the contract. No documentation is required. No recordkeeping will be required. Hence this is not a control responsibility and need not be marked.

SAMPLE PROVISION G-3.01

BREAKDOWN OF LUMP SUM ITEMS

At least ten days prior to the submission of his first application for a progress payment, the Contractor shall present to the Engineer for his approval a detailed schedule showing the breakdown of all lump sum bid prices in the Contract. Such schedule shall contain the amount estimated for each part of the Work and a quantity survey for each part of the Work. Work to be performed by subcontractors shall be separately identified. Upon request of the Engineer, said schedule shall be apportioned by the Contractor for labor and for materials.

Explanation of Control Responsibility Markings

Positive action is required of the contractor in the first instance; subsequent interaction is required of the contract administrator. Thus the section should be marked in the color denoting contractor and contract administrator responsibilities, respectively, and an appropriately sized paper clip should be affixed to the page.

SAMPLE PROVISION G-3.02

CURRENT ESTIMATES

The Owner will establish dates during the respective months of the Project on which the Owner will accept applications for payment (current estimate) and consider same (current estimate) for payment.

At least ten days before each date set for consideration for payment, the Contractor shall submit to the Engineer for review an application for payment, filled out and signed by the Contractor and covering the Work completed as of the date of the application, in satisfactory form and supported by such data as the Owner and Engineer may reasonably require.

The Engineer will, within ten days after receipt of each application for payment, either indicate in writing his recommendation of payment and present the application to the Owner or return the application to the Contractor, indicating in writing his reasons for not recommending payment. In the latter case, the Contractor shall make the necessary corrections and resubmit the application.

The Engineer's recommendation of any payment request shall constitute his advice to the Owner: that to the best of his knowledge, information, and belief, based on the Engineer's on-site observations of the Work in progress and on his reliance upon application for payment and supporting data, the Work has progressed to the point indicated; that the quality of the Work is in substantial compliance with the Contract Documents (subject to any subsequent tests and qualifications stated in his final review); and that the Contractor is entitled to the payment of the amount recommended. However, by recommending any such payment, the Engineer shall not thereby be deemed to have represented that he made exhaustive or continuous on-site inspections to check the quality or quantity of the Work, that he has reviewed the means, methods, techniques, sequences, and procedures of construction, or that he has made any examination to ascertain how or for what purpose the Contractor has used the monies paid or to be paid to him on account of the Contract price.

Where Work has been included in the current estimate recommended by the Engineer for payment, and where such Work is later found to be defective, and where such defective Work has not been corrected, the Engineer will recommend to the Owner that the value of such uncorrected Work be deducted from the amount due or to become due the Contractor.

The Engineer may decline to act upon requests for monthly payment if lists of vendors and subcontractors, work schedules, instruction manuals, and breakdowns of lump sum bid items necessary for orderly prosecution of the Work, are not submitted as required.

Explanation of Control Responsibility Markings

First Paragraph   Positive action is required by the owner to establish dates at which it will accept applications for payment.

Second Paragraph   Positive action on the part of the contractor is required in the submittal of the application for payment, and positive action on the part of the contract administrator is required to review the application for payment.

Third Paragraph   The positive action of the contract administrator required in the second paragraph is defined, and, if necessary, the further positive action of the contractor, required.

Fourth Paragraph   No control responsibilities are present.

Fifth Paragraph   Although a control responsibility is imposed on the contract administrator should he inadvertently pay the contractor for defective work, this situation is not thought apt to occur. We choose not to note this as a contract responsibility.

Sixth Paragraph   This paragraph allows the contract administrator to choose whether or not he will act. Since action is optional, we choose not to note it as a control responsibility.

SAMPLE PROVISION G-3.03

TITLE TO MATERIALS, EQUIPMENT, AND SUPPLIES

The Contractor warrants and guarantees that he will have good title to all materials, equipment, and supplies delivered to the Site for use in the Work.

Title to all materials, equipment, and supplies to be sold by the Contractor to the Owner pursuant to this Contract or to be installed or incorporated into the Project shall immediately vest in the Owner upon delivery of such materials, equipment, and supplies to the Site and prior to their installation or incorporation into the project. Such materials, equipment, and supplies shall then become the sole property of the Owner subject to the right of the Owner to reject the same as hereinafter provided. The Contractor shall mark or otherwise identify all such materials, equipment, and supplies as the property of the Owner. The Contractor, at the request of the Owner, shall furnish to the Owner such confirmatory bills of sale and other instruments as may be required by it, properly executed, acknowledged, and delivered, confirming to the Owner title to such materials, equipment, and supplies free of encumbrances. In the event that, after title has passed to the Owner, any of such materials, equipment, and supplies are rejected as being defective or otherwise unsatisfactory, title to all such materials, equipment, and supplies shall upon such rejection re-vest in the Contractor, and the Contractor shall then replace the rejected material, equipment, and supplies with acceptable material, equipment, and supplies at no additional cost to the Owner.

Nothing in this Section is intended, or shall be construed, as relieving the Contractor from his obligations under this Contract, and the Contractor shall have the sole continuing responsibility to install the materials, equipment, and supplies purchased or furnished in accordance with the provisions of this Contract, to protect the same, to maintain them in proper condition, and to forthwith repair, replace, and make good any damage thereto or loss thereof, without cost to the Owner until such time as the work covered by the Contract is accepted by the Owner.

The Contractor warrants and guarantees that no materials, equipment, or supplies delivered to the Site for use in the Work will have been acquired by the Contractor (or any other person performing work at the Site or furnishing materials, equipment, or supplies for the project) subject to an agreement under which an interest therein or an encumbrance thereon is retained by the seller (or otherwise imposed by the Contractor for such other person).

Explanation of Control Responsibility Markings

Second Paragraph   Positive action of the contractor is required to mark the materials, equipment, and supplies as the property of the owner. Other actions by the contractor are contingent upon the request of the owner and are, hence, not to be defined as control responsibilities.

Should the contract administrator know of the owner's desire to have the confirmatory bills of sale on record, he would, of course, note this to be a control responsibility.

SAMPLE PROVISION G-3.04

PAYMENTS FOR MATERIALS DELIVERED TO SITE

In making estimates of the value of the Work done and materials incorporated in the Work, the Contractor may, subject to the approval of the Owner or as required by law, include in the current estimates the delivered cost, as modified below, of equipment and non-perishable materials which have been tested for adequacy and which have been delivered to the Site and adequately protected from fire, theft, vandalism, the effect of the elements, and any damage whatsoever, or similarly placed in approved storage facilities adjacent thereto. Such materials and equipment shall at all times be available for inspection by the Engineer and the Owner.

No progress payment shall, however, be made for said material and equipment until each of the following conditions has been fulfilled:

a. The Contractor shall have furnished to the Engineer invoices establishing the value of the said materials and equipment with an indication of the amount the Contractor agrees to pay the vendor. Such invoices shall be furnished at least ten days in advance of the date of preparation of monthly estimates as established by the Engineer.

b. The Engineer shall have inspected said material and equipment and recommended payment therefor.

c. The Contractor shall have furnished to the Owner the fire insurance policies, as provided in this Contract and with the broad form extended coverage endorsement, for said material and equipment in an amount equal to one hundred percent of the value thereof and which policies shall be maintained, at the sole cost and expense of the Contractor, until said material and equipment has been incorporated into the Project.

Within sixty days of the submission to the Owner of any progress payment, including payment for said materials and equipment, or within thirty days of the date of payment to the Contractor by the Owner, whichever is longer, the Contractor shall furnish to the Engineer satisfactory evidence that the funds included in the progress payment for said materials and equipment have been paid to the vendors supplying such items. Satisfactory evidence shall be: a canceled check in the correct amount and including identification of the invoice or invoices paid; a letter or telegram, from the vendor and signed by his properly authorized employee, stating the amounts and invoices that have been paid; or a receipted invoice.

Should the above evidence of payment not be furnished, the Engineer will recommend the deduction of any funds included in previous estimates for such materials and equipment for which said evidence has not been furnished from the current estimate or subsequent current estimates.

Any payment made for materials and equipment delivered will not relieve the Contractor of any responsibility for furnishing all the necessary equipment and materials required for prosecution of the Work in the same manner as if such payments had not been made.

Explanation of Control Responsibility Markings

First Paragraph   It will be assumed the owner will allow the contractor payment for the materials and equipment specified once they are delivered to the site. Hence the first paragraph requires positive action of the contractor in the protection of those delivered items.

Paragraph a   Positive action of the contractor is required to submit to the contract administrator invoices establishing the value of the items.

Paragraph b   Positive action of the contract administrator is required to inspect the items.

Paragraph c   Positive action of the contractor in the submittal of fire insurance policies on the items is mandated.

Second Paragraph   Positive action of the contractor is required to furnish to the contract administrator evidence of payment on the items.

Third Paragraph   Positive action of the contract administrator is required to deduct funds previously paid for inventoried materials and equipment should the contractor not furnish evidence of payment within the time stipulated.

SAMPLE PROVISION G-3.05

OWNER'S PAYMENT OF MONTHLY ESTIMATES

The Owner will, within thirty days of presentation to him of an approved application for payment (current estimate), pay the Contractor ninety-five percent of the amount of such estimate, retaining five percent of the amount until Substantial Completion of all Work covered by the Contract. All applications for payment shall be in a form satisfactory to the Owner.

Acceptance by the Contractor of the monthly payment shall constitute his warranty that he will pay each of his subcontractors and vendors all monies due them as required by the laws of New York State, or other applicable State and Federal Laws and Regulations.

Explanation of Control Responsibility Markings

First Paragraph Positive action of the owner is required to pay the contractor within the time stipulated.

Second Paragraph Although this item requires the positive action of the contractor to pay his subcontractors and vendors, the contract only requires his *warranty* to do so. Hence the contract administrator need not require documentation.

SAMPLE PROVISION G-4.01

ASSIGNMENT

The Contractor shall not assign, transfer, convey, or otherwise dispose of this Contract, or any portion thereof, or of his right, title, or interest therein, or his power to execute such Contract, to any other person or corporation without the previous consent in writing of the Owner.

The provisions of this Section shall not hinder, prevent, or affect an assignment by the Contractor for the benefit of creditors made pursuant to law, nor is it intended to prohibit subcontracting a portion of the Work of the Contract in accordance with the provisions of law and this Contract.

Explanation of Control Responsibility Markings

It will be assumed that the contractor will subcontract a portion of the contract. Hence positive action of the contractor to request such subcontracting is required, as is the owner's consent.

SAMPLE PROVISION G-4.02

SUBCONTRACTS

In the event that the Contractor desires to subcontract any part of the Work, he shall first submit to the Engineer a statement showing the character and amount of the Work to be subcontracted and the party to whom it is proposed to subcontract the same. Submission of said statement shall be 30 days prior to the time the Contractor plans to actually employ the proposed subcontractor. If requested by the Engineer, the Contractor shall also furnish a statement as to the proposed subcontractor's experience, financial ability, or other qualifications for properly performing the Work proposed to be subcontracted.

The Contractor warrants that all subcontractors selected by him are financially able, sufficiently experienced, and otherwise qualified to perform the work of their subcontracts.

The Contractor shall be solely responsible for the acts or defaults of subcontractors and of such subcontractors' officers, agents, and employees each of whom shall, for this purpose, be deemed to be the agent or employee of the Contractor to the extent of his subcontract.

The Contractor shall be fully responsible for the administration, integration, coordination, direction, and supervision of all of his subcontractors.

No subcontractor shall be permitted to work at the Site until he has furnished evidence to the Owner of the insurance required by this Contract.

The Contractor shall execute with each of his subcontractors and all subcontractors shall execute with their sub-subcontractors a written agreement which shall bind the latter to the terms and provisions of this Contract insofar as such terms and provisions are applicable. The Contractor and all subcontractors and sub-subcontractors shall promptly, upon request, file with the Owner a conformed copy of such agreements, from which the price and terms of payment may be deleted.

If, at any time during the progress of the Work to be performed, the Owner decides that any subcontractor of any tier is incompetent, careless, or uncooperative, the Engineer will notify the Contractor accordingly and immediate steps will be taken by the Contractor for cancellation of such subcontract. Such termination, however, shall not give rise to any claim by the Contractor or by such subcontractor for loss of prospective profits on work unperformed or work unfinished, and a provision to that effect shall be contained in all subcontracts.

No provisions of this Contract shall create or be construed as creating any contractual relation between the Owner and any subcontractor or sub-subcontractor or with any person, firm, or corporation employed by, contracted with, or whose services are utilized by the Contractor.

The divisions or sections of the Contract Documents are not intended to control the Contractor in dividing the Work among subcontractors or to limit the Work performed by any trade.

The Owner reserves the right to limit the total amount of subcontracts to sixty percent of the total contract price.

Explanation of Control Responsibility Markings

First Paragraph It is likely the contractor will desire to subcontract a portion of the work; hence his positive action is required as noted in the first sentence. It is also likely that the contract administrator and the engineer will not have a firsthand knowledge of the proposed subcontractors; hence the contract administrator and the engineer may require the contractor to submit the proposed subcontractor's qualifications for review.

Fifth Paragraph Positive action of the subcontractor (in submission of insurance certificate) is required.

Sixth Paragraph It is likely the owner will desire a copy of the subcontract; hence positive action of the contractor is required.

Seventh Paragraph It is unlikely that a subcontractor will be expelled from the project. We therefore opt not to regard this paragraph as requiring the positive action of the contractor.

SAMPLE PROVISION G-5.01

OWNER'S CHANGES IN THE WORK

a. The Owner at any time without notice to any Surety may make changes in the Work of the Contract by making alterations therein, by making additions thereto, or by omitting Work therefrom, and no such action shall invalidate the Contract, relieve or release the Contractor from any guarantee under the Contract, affect the terms or validity of any bond, relieve or release any Surety, or constitute grounds for any claim by the Contractor for damages or loss of anticipated profits. All Work required by such alterations, additions, or omissions shall be executed under the terms of the Contract.

b. Other than in an emergency endangering life or property or pursuant to a Field Order, the Contractor shall not make any change in the Work nor furnish any labor, equipment, materials, supplies, or other services in connection with any change except pursuant to, and after, receipt of a written authorization from the Owner in the form of a Change Order, Modification, or Proceed Order. The Contractor shall not be entitled to any increase in the Contract price or extension of the Contract time, and no claim therefor shall be valid, unless such written authorization has been so issued to the Contractor.

c. The Engineer may authorize minor changes in the Work which do not alter the character, quantity, or cost of the Work as a whole. These changes may be accomplished by a Field Order, or Clarification. The Contractor shall carry out such Field Orders promptly and without any adjustment of the Contract price or Contract time.

Explanation of Control Responsibility Markings

Paragraph c   It is likely the contract administrator will issue a field order or clarification during the course of the project. If he does, his positive action is required.

SAMPLE PROVISION G-5.02

ADJUSTMENTS IN PRICE

Any increase or decrease in the Contract price resulting from changes in the Work ordered by the Owner as in this section provided shall be determined as follows:

a. By such applicable unit prices, if any, as set forth in the Contract; or

b. If no such unit prices are so set forth, then by unit prices or by a lump sum mutually agreed upon by the Owner and the Contractor; such unit prices or lump sum being arrived at by estimates of reasonable value prepared in general comformance with the outline set forth in (c) below.

c. If no such unit prices are so set forth and if the parties cannot agree upon unit prices or a lump sum, then determination shall be made as the sum of the following amounts for all Work necessary for the changes:

(1) Cost of materials delivered to the job site for incorporation into the Contract Work.

(2) Wages paid to workmen and foremen and wage supplements paid to labor organizations in accordance with current labor agreements.

(3) Premiums or taxes paid by the Contractor for workmen's compensation insurance, unemployment insurance, FICA tax, and other payroll taxes as required by law.

(4) Sales and use taxes paid as required by law.

(5) Allowances for necessary use of construction equipment (exclusive of hand tools and minor equipment), as approved by the Engineer.

(6) An amount for overhead.

(7) An amount for profit.

Construction equipment rental rates shall be in accordance with those published in that issue of the Associated Equipment Distributors (AED) Rental Guide, current at the time the work is done. In the event that rental rates for equipment used in the performance of extra work are not listed in the AED Rental Guide, rental rates will be approved for payment which are consistent with those prevailing in the construction industry in the area of the Work. Monthly, weekly, or daily rates shall apply, prorated to the actual time the equipment is in use; the classification of monthly, weekly, or daily rate to be used shall be determined by the length of time the piece of equipment under consideration was in use on the total project under Contract plus either the time used in the performance of the extra work or the time used in the performance of the extra work plus additional subsequent time used on the total project under contract. Gasoline, oil, and grease required for operation and maintenance will be paid for at the actual cost. When, in the opinion of the Contractor as approved by the Engineer, suitable equipment is not available on the Site, the moving of said equipment to and from the Site will be paid for at actual cost.

The Contractor shall submit evidence satisfactory to the Engineer to substantiate each and every item included in an estimate prepared pursuant to G-5.02(b) or a determination pursuant to G-5.02(c).

The amounts allowed for overhead and profit for a change resulting in an increase in Contract price may be less than, but shall not exceed, the applicable percentages as follows:

(a) For work done directly by the Contractor, the sum of overhead amount plus profit amount shall not exceed 20 percent of the cost.

(b) For work done by subcontractors of any tier, the sum of total overhead amounts of the subcontractors and Contractor, plus total profit amounts for the subcontractors and Contractor, shall not exceed 25 percent of the cost.

Overhead is defined as all expense not included in the amounts outlined in G-5.02(c)(1) through G-5.02(c)(5), including administration, superintendents, insurance not outlined in G-5.02(c)(1) through G-5.02(c)(5), material used in temporary structures, additional premiums placed upon the labor and performance bonds of the Contractor, and small hand tools.

Where Work necessitated by the change involves overtime, no overhead or profit will be allowed on the premium portion of overtime pay.

Explanation of Control Responsibility Markings

First Paragraph It is likely that changes to the project will be authorized by the owner. If so, positive action will be required.

Third Paragraph The contractor's positive action is required as noted.

SAMPLE PROVISION G-5.03

PROCEED ORDER

If the Owner and the Contractor cannot agree upon an equitable adjustment of the Contract price prior to performance of the change in the Work, a Proceed Order will be issued authorizing the change, and Contractor shall proceed with the work thereof by the most economical methods. Upon completion of the change in the Work and a determination of the adjustment in the Contract price, a Change Order will be issued.

Explanation of Control Responsibility Markings

It is probable that a proceed order will be required during the course of the project. If so, it will require the positive action of the contract Administrator to issue it.

SAMPLE PROVISION G-6.01

LISTING OF ITEMS

Following execution of the Contract by the Contractor and following the issuance of notice to proceed, the Engineer will submit to the Contractor a list of equipment, materials, and other items for which shop drawings, samples, or shop drawings and samples will be required. This listing shall not be construed to be all-inclusive and may be added to, or deleted from, as may be required in the opinion of the Engineer.

Explanation of Control Responsibility Markings

The design engineer, not the contract administrator, must initiate positive action since the review of shop drawings and submittals is normally a design function rather than a field function.

SAMPLE PROVISION G-6.02

ACCEPTANCE OF MANUFACTURERS OR VENDORS

The Contractor, with such promptness and in such sequence as to cause no delay in the Work, shall submit to the Engineer the name of the manufacturer or vendor for each item on the list or addition to the list submitted. No awards shall be made by the Contractor, and no work under any item shall proceed, until acceptance of the manufacturer or vendor has been given by the Engineer. Such acceptance will be only on the basis of the manufacturer's or vendor's experience and reputation and will not imply that the shop drawings or samples for the item will be acceptable. Review of shop drawings for an item will depend upon full compliance with the Contract Documents as demonstrated by material submitted.

Explanation of Control Responsibility Markings

Positive action is required of the contractor in submitting the names of vendors and manufacturers. Positive action is required by the design engineer in accepting or rejecting those vendors and manufacturers.

SAMPLE PROVISION G-6.03

SHOP DRAWING SUBMITTAL REQUIREMENTS

Shop drawings and data shall be submitted to the Engineer by the Contractor for each item on the latest revised list determined from Section G-6.01 above. Submittals shall be made sufficiently in advance of the Work to permit proper review, necessary revisions, and resubmittals.

Shop drawings shall present complete and accurate information relative to all working dimensions, equipment weights, assembly, and section views, and all necessary details pertaining to coordinating the work of the Contract, lists of materials and finishes, parts lists and the description thereof, lists of spare parts and tools where such parts or tools are required, and any other items of information that are required to demonstrate detailed compliance with the Contract Documents. Drawings for electrical equipment shall include elementary and interconnection diagrams.

Each shop drawing submitted shall be presumed to have been reviewed by the Contractor before being submitted to the Engineer. The Contractor's submittal of a shop drawing shall constitute his representation that the Contractor has determined and verified all quantities, dimensions, field construction criteria, materials catalog numbers, and similar data and that he has reviewed or coordinated each shop drawing with the requirements of the Work and the Contract Documents.

Unless otherwise permitted in specific cases, all data shall be transmitted to the Engineer by the Prime Contractor.

Each shop drawing submitted shall indicate the following:

1. Project name and contract number

2. Manufacturer of the equipment

3. Notation as to whether original submittal or resubmittal

4. Date received by Contractor from manufacturer or vendor

5. Date submitted to Engineer

Each shop drawing submittal shall be accompanied by a transmittal letter indicating the item or items submitted, with particular reference to latest revised list of equipment, materials, and other items described in G-6.01 above. The transmittal letter shall also indicate whether the submittal constitutes a complete set of drawings for the item, a partial set of drawings for which additional submittals are to be expected by the Engineer, or a partial set of drawings to complete a previous submittal. In any case, the Contractor shall indicate by the transmittal letters when the submittals for an item are intended to be complete.

Unless otherwise stated in the Special Provisions, the Contractor shall submit at least four copies of drawings, catalog data, and similar items for review. This number includes one for return to the Contractor noted as "Reviewed" or request for amendment. If the Contractor desires more than one copy returned to him, he shall submit with the initial and any subsequent transmittals the additional number desired up to a maximum of three copies. If the Engineer requires additional copies, he will so inform the Contractor upon return of the material noted as "Reviewed."

Explanation of Control Responsibility Markings

Positive action of the contractor is required in the submission of shop drawings. The remainder of the sample provision notes the details of these submittals; and although the details could meet the definition of a control responsibility, they need not be recorded as such.

SAMPLE PROVISION G-6.04

ENGINEER'S REVIEW OF SHOP DRAWINGS

The Engineer's review of shop drawings is for general compliance with the Contract Documents only and is not a complete check on the method of assembly, erection, or construction. Such review shall in no way be construed as permitting any departure whatsoever from the Contract Documents, except where the Contractor has previously requested and received written approval of the Engineer for such departure.

Review of shop drawings by the Engineer will be limited to completed submittals except where review of a partial submittal is specifically requested by the Contractor and where such review of a partial submittal is necessary for timely completion of the Work of the Contract. Where shop drawings of related items are necessary for review of a particular submittal, the Engineer will so inform the Contractor, who will promptly submit such shop drawings of said related items.

Drawings and similar data will be reviewed and stamped by the Engineer as follows:

1. "Reviewed," if no change or rejection is made. All but four copies of the submitted data will be returned.

2. "Reviewed and Noted," if minor changes or additions are made but resubmittal is not considered necessary. All but four copies of the submitted data will be returned and all copies will bear the corrective marks.

3. "Resubmit," if the changes requested are extensive or if retransmittal of the submittal to another Contractor is required. In this case, the Contractor shall resubmit the items after correction, and the

same number of copies shall be included in the resubmittal as in the first submittal. One copy of the first submittal will be retained by the Engineer and two copies will be returned to the Contractor unless the Contractor has requested the return of additional copies as set forth above. All other copies will be destroyed.

4. "Rejected," if it is considered that the data submitted cannot, with reasonable revision, meet approval or when the data submitted are not sufficiently complete to establish compliance with the Plans and Specifications. Only two copies will be returned unless additional copies have been requested; two copies will be retained by the Engineer and all others will be destroyed.

Explanation of Control Responsibility Markings

First Paragraph   Should the contractor request a departure from general compliance with the contract documents, his positive action is required.

The design engineer's positive action is required to either accept or reject the contractor's proposed deviation. The remainder of the sample provision merely details the procedures for the engineer's review of shop drawings.

SAMPLE PROVISION G-6.05

RESUBMITTALS

Any changes, other than those indicated as requested, made in drawings or other data shall be specifically brought to the attention of the Engineer upon resubmittal. Changes or additions shall not be made in, or to, "Reviewed" data without specific notice to the Engineer.

If, after reasonable correction and resubmittal of the shop drawings for an item of equipment, acceptance is not given, the Contractor shall submit the name of another manufacturer or vendor to supply the item required in accordance with G-14.02. Should progress of the Work be delayed by the changing of the manufacturer or vendor, such a cause will not be considered an extenuating circumstance beyond the control of the Contractor, and charges for delay, if otherwise applicable, will be levied.

Explanation of Control Responsibility Markings

Positive action of the contractor is required in the first paragraph and, if it becomes necessary, in the second paragraph. (Section G-14.02 is irrelevant to this discussion and therefore does not appear.)

SAMPLE PROVISION G-6.06

SAMPLES

The Contractor shall, when specified in the Special Provisions, Materials and Performance Sections, or Payment Items, submit to the Engineer for review typical samples of materials and appliances. The samples shall be properly identified by tags and shall be submitted sufficiently in advance of the time when they are to be incorporated into the Work, so that rejections thereof will not cause delay. A letter of transmittal from the Contractor requesting approval shall accompany such samples.

The procedures set forth in Section G-6.04 and G-6.05 above for shop drawings shall be used for processing samples.

Explanation of Control Responsibility Markings

Positive action of the contractor is required in the submittal of samples as noted.

SAMPLE PROVISION MP-1.01

TESTS FOR SEWERS

Tests to be made for leakage and infiltration of water into sewers shall be made prior to making connections with other sewers, pipes, or drains unless otherwise permitted by the Engineer.

The initial 100 feet of sewer constructed shall be tested for leakage prior to backfilling before the Contractor will be allowed to continue laying additional sewer pipe. Other intermediate leakage tests during construction shall be made as required by the Engineer. Upon completion of the work of any sewer, it shall be tested for watertightness and

CONTROL RESPONSIBILITY SUMMARY SHEET

PROJECT — 96-in. Outfall Tunnel
CONTRACTOR — ABC Construction, Inc.
OWNER — Springfield Sewer Authority
ENGINEER — XYZ Engineer's, Inc.

(1) *Contract Citation*	*(2)* *Description*
G-1.01	The contractor shall advise the engineer of his intent to enter the site 5 days in advance
G-1.02	The contractor shall submit for approval a work schedule within 10 days
G-2.01	Written notice of claim
G-3.01	Lump-sum breakdown procedure
G-3.02	Current estimates procedure
G-3.03	The contractor shall mark materials, equipment, and supplies as property of the owner
G-3.04	Payment for materials delivered to the site—procedure
G-3.05	Payment of monthly estimates
G-4.01	Assignment of contract
G-4.02	Subcontracts procedure
G-5.01	Field orders and/or clarifications
G-5.02	Adjustment of contract price for changes
G-5.03	Proceed orders
G-6.01	Listing of equipment, materials, and other items for which shop drawings are required
G-6.02	Acceptance of proposed manufacturers or vendors
G-6.03	Shop drawing submittals
G-6.04	Engineer's review of shop drawings
G-6.05	Shop drawing resubmittals
G-6.06	Sample submittals
MP-1.01	Leakage tests

FIGURE 1-2   Sample of completed Control Responsibility Summary Sheet.

SHEET___OF___

(3) Contractor Responsibility	(4) Owner Responsibility	(5) Engineer Responsibility	(6) Contract Administrator Responsibility	(7) Interaction Responsibility
X				
1			2	X
1	3		2	X
1			2	X
2	1		3	X
X				
2	1		3	X
	X			
1	2			X
1	3		2	X
			X	
2	1			X
			X	
		X		
1		2		X
X				
1		2		X
X				
X				
1			2	X

shall meet the requirements set forth below before final acceptance of the work of the Contract.

Tests shall be made by filling the sewer with water and measuring the quantity of leakage from the sewer. The head of water during the tests shall be maintained at least 2 feet above the highest section of the work being tested. Where work being tested has been constructed in water bearing soils, leakage tests may, at the discretion of the Engineer, be made by measuring the quantity of infiltration into the sewer.

The allowable leakage or infiltration per 24 hours per inch of diameter per 1000 feet of sewer tested shall not exceed the following quantities for various types of sewer pipe:

Asbestos-cement pipe with rubber ring joints	25 gallons
Concrete pipe with rubber & steel joints	25 gallons
Concrete pipe with rubber gasket joints	25 gallons
Clay pipe with rubber gasket joints	25 gallons
Cast iron pipe	25 gallons

All localized or spurting leaks of any volume detected in sewers or in floors or walls of appurtenant structures shall be permanently stopped. Should any leaks, defective joints, or defective construction be found, they shall be promptly made good, and should any defective pipes or specials be discovered, they shall be removed and replaced with sound pipes or specials in a satisfactory manner at the Contractor's expense.

Explanation of Control Responsibility Markings

This sample provision requires the contractor to perform a leakage test on sewers constructed for the project. The contract administrator must document that the tests have been taken and that they were successfully completed.

THE COMPLETED CONTROL
RESPONSIBILITY SUMMARY SHEET

Upon completion of the review of the contract to determine the control responsibilities within it, the contract administrator should then note these responsibilities on a Control Responsibility Summary Sheet, as in Figure 1-2.

CHAPTER 2

THE CONTRACT DRAWINGS AS A CONTROL DEVICE

In Chapter 1, procedures were explained for developing a clear under-standing of the *textual* parts of the contract, then transferring those parts of the contract which are of special interest to the contract ad-ministrator, i.e., control responsibilities, to Control Responsibility Summary Sheets for easier reference. However, not all control respon-sibilities are to be found in the text of the contract.

This chapter will be concerned with the *pictorial* parts of the contract—the contract drawings. The objectives will be (1) to transfer further control responsibilities from the drawings to the summary sheets, (2) to develop a thorough knowledge of the construction details of the project, (3) to note and correct any errors or ambiguities which may appear in the drawings, and (4) to form a general impression of the construction sequence of the project. This chapter will also provide the base for establishing the two remaining key contract controls—cost control and schedule control—to be discussed in the succeeding chap-ters of Part 1.

There can be no shortcuts here. If the contract administrator finds the tasks set forth below to be unduly burdensome, it must be observed that the time invested in establishing these basic control devices will be repaid—with substantial dividends—later in the project.

EXTRACTING CONTROLS FROM THE CONTRACT DRAWINGS

The method for analyzing contract drawings is similar to that employed for analyzing the textual parts of the contract. Like the method set forth in Chapter 1, the contract drawing review method has three steps. Also, as in the preceding chapter, the scheme of the drawing review method is to tear the contract drawings apart, then reassemble selected components of the drawings in a form better suited to the needs of the contract administrator, verifying the details of the drawings in the process. Just as careful adherence to the method described in Chapter 1 left the contract administrator with a thorough working knowledge of the contractual provisions, diligent application of the method set forth in this chapter will leave him comfortable with project design.

The contract administrator will need a *complete* set of the contract drawings and a set of colored pencils (preferably yellow, red, blue, and green). He should take great care to verify that he has the latest versions of any revised drawings; the price (in wasted time) to be paid for reviewing incorrect or incomplete drawings will be substantial.

The First Step:
Review of the Contract Drawings

The point of beginning for review of the contract drawings is the general drawings, since they will provide an overall view of the project. The first step in reviewing the general drawings is to read all the notes which appear on each drawing. If a given note appears to be correct *and* requires *no* positive action (see section G-1.02 in Chapter 1) of any participant, the entire note should be highlighted in yellow. If, on the other hand, the note appears to be correct but *does* require positive action by some participant, the entire note should be highlighted in yellow *and* circled in red. If the note appears to be erroneous or if the contract administrator finds the note in any way unclear, the entire note should be circled in red but should *not* be highlighted in yellow. Table 2-1 summarizes this marking procedure.

TABLE 2-1 Marking Codes for the Contract Drawings

	Highlight in yellow	Circle in red
Note correct but no positive action required	x	
Note correct and positive action required	x	x
Note incorrect		x
Note unclear		x

After reading and marking all the notes on a given drawing, the second task is to review the drawing itself. During this part of the review, every line and work *except dimensions* which appears to be *correct* should be highlighted, or traced, as the case may be, in yellow. Items which seem incorrect or unclear should be circled in red but not marked in yellow. The need for thoroughness in this task cannot be overstated: with the exception of dimensions, everything—the north arrow, the outlines of structures, the dimension arrows, the border, and the title block—should be marked. Thus when the contract administrator's review of the first general drawing is complete, every line, letter, and mark on that sheet, except dimensions, should be either marked in yellow or circled in red, or, in the case of some notes, both.

The contract administrator should employ the same two-task procedure for each general drawing, then for each detailed drawing, until all contract drawings have undergone this first review.

The contract administrator should next conduct an extensive review with the design professional of all drawing items circled in red. Each item so marked must ultimately be clarified for the benefit of the contractor or explained by the designer to the satisfaction of the contract administrator.

The next matter which the contract administrator should address is the transfer of the substance of any notes requiring positive action by any participant (i.e., those marked in yellow and circled in red) to the Control Responsibility Summary Sheets developed in Chapter 1. As in the case of the textual transfers of that chapter, it is *critical* that the substance of the notes not be altered in the transfer, for alterations would create a new noncontractual arrangement to which no other participant had agreed and could create enormous liability for the contract administrator. The contract administrator must constantly bear in mind that his role is to carry out effectively the terms and conditions of a contract already in place, not to make unilateral modifications to that document in the course of administration.

During the transfer of notes marked in yellow and circled in red to the summary sheets, the contract administrator should refer to those items in the drawings which were initially marked as incorrect or unclear and were discussed with the design professional. Those items which were discussed and satisfactorily explained should be circled in green outside the red circle. Any of these explained items which require positive action of any participant should then be transferred to the summary sheets.

Items which were discussed with the design professional and were found to be in error or in need of clarification should be circled in blue outside the red circle. The design professional should then issue the appropriate document of correction or clarification; under no circumstances should the contract administrator attempt to change or clarify the design unless his firm is also the design professional's or unless his written agreement with the owner expressly and unequivocally requires it, as the potential liability for assuming design responsibility would far outweigh any short-term benefits. As the appropriate documents are issued, the appropriate drawing items should be circled in green outside the blue circles. Any of these items which require positive action of any participant should then be transferred to the summary sheets.

Upon completion of this first review, every line, work, and mark (except dimensions) on the drawings should be either (1) marked in yellow or (2) within a green circle.

The Second Step:
Review of the Contract Drawing Dimensions

The second review of the contract drawings involves a checking of dimensions. The procedure for checking dimensions closely parallels that employed for the other details of the drawings: the marking procedures are identical. As in the first review, the point of beginning should be the general drawings. The contract administrator should verify each dimension in a given drawing against other dimensions in that drawing, then against dimensions in other drawings.

If this twofold verification leads the contract administrator to conclude that a given dimension is correct, it should be highlighted in yellow. If, on the other hand, he concludes that the dimension is incorrect or unclear, it should be circled in red; if it is later found to be correct, it should then be circled in green outside the red. Each dimension ultimately determined to be erroneous or unclear after discussion between the contract administrator and design professional should be resolved by a correcting or clarifying document issued by the appropriate participant, i.e., the one responsible under the contract or some other agreement for generating such documents. Once the error or ambiguity has been resolved, the correct dimension should be noted on the drawing and circled in green outside the red.

At the completion of the second review, every original line, letter, number, and mark should be either highlighted in yellow or circled outermost in green. At this point, the contract administrator has, through two painstaking but essential reviews of the contract drawings, (1) identified important additional control responsibilities and transferred them to the summary sheets, (2) identified and resolved errors and ambiguities in the drawings, and (3) developed a thorough working knowledge of the details of construction of the project.

The Third Step:
Developing a Probable Construction Sequence

The purpose of the third review of the contract drawings is to permit the contract administrator to form a general impression of the construction *sequence* of the project. Development of this broad perspective is utterly dependent upon the working knowledge of the construction details—and the confidence in their accuracy—which grew out of the first and second reviews. Conversely, this broad perspective can be developed only in an atmosphere free from concern over the details which were learned and verified earlier. Thus having studied the trees, the contract administrator is well equipped to examine the forest.

The third review is essentially a conceptual exercise. The contract administrator's task is to chart general *hypothetical* alternative construct sequences which could be followed were *he* the contractor for the project; the goal is to cause himself to approach the project as the contractor might.

Relatively little writing will be required; mere lists of possible sequences of major project components will suffice. For example, Table 2-2 sets forth a typical scenario.

TABLE 2-2 Construction Sequence Sheet

Item no.	Description	Before item no.	Concurrent with item no.	After item no.
1.	Clearing and grubbing	All	None	None
2.	Site grading	—	3	1
3.	Siltation basins	4	2	1
4.	Outside piping	6	5	3
5.	Foundation excavation	6	4	3
6.	Footings	—	None	4

But to term this sequence building a conceptual exercise is not to diminish its importance, for these sequences will form the base in succeeding chapters for explaining establishment of cost control and schedule control, the two remaining control devices essential to successful contract administration—and thus successful projects.

SUMMARY

In this chapter, the contract drawings were dissected to (1) abstract additional control responsibilities, (2) identify and resolve errors and ambiguities, (3) acquaint the contract administrator with the construction details of the project, and (4) permit informed speculation as to probable construction sequences, thereby providing the bases for establishment of cost and schedule controls. Chapters 3 through 7, the remainder of Part 1, will explain those two procedures in detail.

COMPREHENSIVE ILLUSTRATION

The comprehensive illustration of this chapter involves contract drawings which contemplate the construction of a tunnel under railroad tracks and uses the techniques described in the foregoing text to review the notes on each drawing, to review the drawing itself (except for dimensions), to review dimensions, and to establish a preliminary construction sequence for the project.

SITE PLAN

Figure 2-1 provides a general site plan. Following the drawing is our commentary concerning proposed markings.

Commentary

The first step is to review the drawing notes, and the "General Notes" should be highlighted in yellow.

· Note 1, first sentence: It is not certain that all control is shown; therefore, the sentence should be left unmarked until it can be confirmed or corrected.

· Note 1, second sentence: This is acceptable and should be highlighted in yellow.

· Note 2: This appears to be acceptable and should be highlighted in yellow. Each section cut will subsequently be checked on all drawings for confirmation.

· Note 3: The intent of the note seems clear, but the note is improperly written. It should provide, "All elevations refer to plant datum. Plant datum equals U.S.G.S. datum plus 0.41 ft." The correction should be entered in red, and the note should be circled in red.

· Note 4: Since the arrows on the drawing are not "otherwise noted," the note seems acceptable and should be highlighted in yellow.

· Note 5: This warning to the contractor appears acceptable and should be highlighted in yellow.

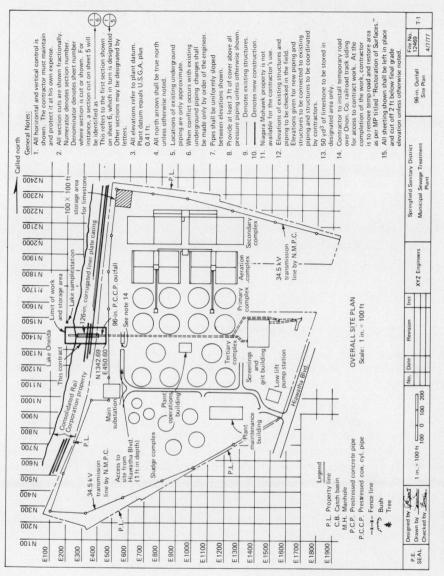

FIGURE 2-1   Site plan for 96-in. outfall.

45

- Note 6: This note appears acceptable; however, the comma between the word "piping" and the word "changes" did not appear. A red comma should be inserted between these words, and the note should be circled in red.

- Notes 7 through 11: These appear acceptable and should be highlighted in yellow.

- Note 12, first sentence: This note is acceptable and should be highlighted in yellow.

- Note 12, second sentence: Unless the word "coordinated" is defined in the contract documents, the meaning of this sentence requires clarification; it should be circled in red.

- Note 13: It probably can be assumed that "yd^3" means cubic yards, but, if so, a confirming abbreviation should appear in the contract documents. Also, the correctness of the note depends on the existence of the "designated area" somewhere on site; until the existence of this "area" is confirmed, the note should be left unmarked.

- Notes 14 and 15: These appear acceptable and should be highlighted in yellow.

General Review of the Drawing

The contract administrator should begin reviewing the drawing with the easiest items. Items such as the border, the drawing number, the title blocks, the signature block, and the revision block appear to be acceptable and should be highlighted in yellow.

Next, the measurements of the scale should be compared to the grids. They appear to be the same and should be marked in yellow.

The title "Overall Site Plan" is not the same as the drawing title "Site Plan." The word "overall" should be circled in red; the following words "site plan" should be highlighted in yellow. The scale is correct and should be highlighted in yellow. The contract administrator should next examine the grid, measuring the spacing of the grid to the scale. Since these appear to be acceptable, all vertical and horizontal grid lines should be highlighted in yellow.

The grid begins at the upper left-hand corner of the drawing. The "called north" arrow points to the right. Therefore, north coordinates should increase in number from left to right, and east coordinates should increase in number from top to bottom of the drawing; it appears that they do. The contract administrator should confirm that the grid coordinates increase in those directions uniformly without skipping any numbers; they do. Thus the "called north" arrow and all grid numbers should be highlighted in yellow.

The contract administrator should next address the legend. The word "legend" is spelled correctly and should be highlighted in yellow. The abbreviation "P.L." stands for property line and should be highlighted in yellow. The contract administrator should examine the drawing for the P.L. abbreviations. They appear to denote the property lines around the site and, accordingly, should be highlighted, together with the property lines themselves, in yellow.

The next item in the legend is "C.B.," which appears to denote catch basin. The absence of catch basins in the drawing in question supports an inference that the note applies to other drawings. Accordingly, the C.B. reference in the legend should be left unmarked at present but should be marked in yellow once the contract administrator encounters catch basins in other drawings.

"M.H." is given as the symbol for manhole; however, as in the case of catch basins, no manholes appear in this drawing. Thus the entry in the legend should remain unmarked but should be marked when manholes are encountered.

"P.C.P." is given to indicate prestressed concrete pipe. Given the absence of prestressed concrete pipe in this drawing, the entry in the legend should be treated as catch basins and manholes were treated.

The next entry in the legend indicates that "P.C.C.P." stands for "prestressed conc. cyl. pipe." In construction parlance, this means prestressed concrete cylinder pipe. This item should be circled in red, and the designer should be reminded not to abbreviate the *meaning* of any abbreviation.

The contract administrator should then proceed to the north 14+00 grid and highlight both the abbreviation "P.C.C.P." and the pipe it denotes in yellow.

The remaining three legend items should remain unmarked at present as there are no such entries in the drawing.

The contract administrator should next consider those lines in the drawing which have yet to be addressed. The contractor will observe in the upper right-hand corner of the drawing a shaded area described as "Storage area for limestone" and will note that this area relates to note 13. The shaded area itself, the description, the arrow going from the description to the shaded area, and note 13 should all be highlighted in yellow.

Contiguous to the storage area are straight lines with intermittent circles. Further to the left, they are described as a 34.5 kV transmission line owned by "N.M.P.C." The lines and description should be highlighted in yellow.

The next matter for consideration concerns the heavy black lines on the upper part of the drawing near grid north 14+00. The contract administrator will recall that note 10 indicated these lines denote new construction. The one description on the drawing pertaining to these lines is "limit of work and storage area." This description would seem to be acceptable, although the drawing also provides for "Storage area of limestone." We chose to overlook this discrepancy and to highlight the heavy lines and the note in yellow.

The contract administrator will note a description pertaining to the heavy lines and labeled "This contract." This note seems unacceptable given the existence of a storage area outside the lines and comprising a part of "This contract"; it is also clear from note 14 that a temporary road will be installed beyond the area marked by the heavy lines. The description should be changed to read "Main area of work for this contract" and circled in red.

The coordinate "N1342.69/E450.60" appears at the lower left-hand corner of the rectangle formed by the heavy black lines. The coordinate seems correct and should be highlighted in yellow as should coordinate "N1442.69/E450.60."

The contract administrator should proceed to the description "126-in. corrugated liner plate casing." The description and the lines referenced seem to be correct; they should be highlighted in yellow. The same treatment should be given to the description "Lake sample station."

The contract administrator should next proceed immediately downward from the heavy black line to the words "See note 14." He will also note the caption "Access to site from Hiawatha Blvd." These items indicate both the necessity and location of the temporary road and the contractor's access to the site. They appear to be correct and should be highlighted in yellow.

Although the site plan remains partly unmarked at this point, the marking process is sufficiently complete to illustrate the process.

TUNNEL PLAN AND PROFILE

The next drawing for consideration is Figure 2-2, entitled "Tunnel Plan and Profile" and detailed to provide in-depth project information. The contract administrator should again conduct his review of the drawing.

Commentary

Again, the first step is to review the notes. The three notes seem to be in order and should be highlighted in yellow.

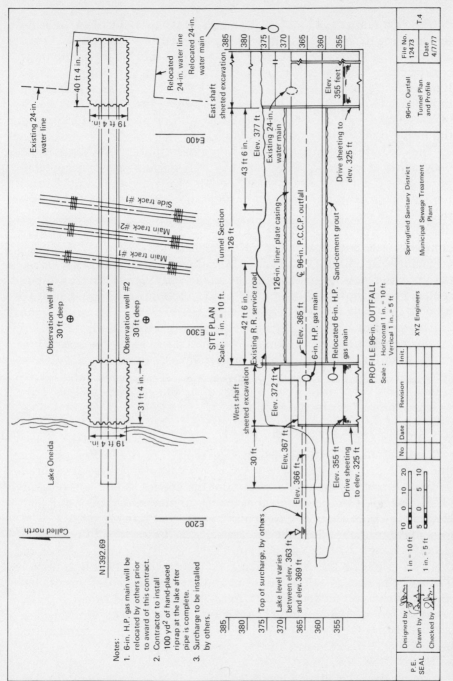

FIGURE 2-2 Tunnel plan and profile for 96-in. outfall.

The following items should be considered in order and, as they appear to be correct, highlighted in yellow:

- Border

- Drawing number

- Title blocks

- Revision block

- Signature block

- Scale block

- Profile—96-in. outfall

On the left and right sides of the profile are scales representing vertical elevations. They begin at 355 and proceed to 385 in 5-ft increments. These measurements are consistent with the vertical scale, but the numbers should be preceded by the abbreviation for elevation (Elev.). The contract administrator should write "Elev." in red in front of each number, then highlight the number itself in yellow.

The contract administrator should then proceed to the following items, in order, and highlight them in yellow:

- Elev. 366 ft indicated to be the "Top of surcharge" and the line indicating this top of the surcharge

- The item "Surcharge fill (by others)"

- "West entrance portal—sheeted excavation"

The contract administrator will note the entries "Elev. 372 ft" and "Elev. 367 ft." It would appear that the top of the sheetpiling is stepped to these two elevations. It would also appear that if the lake level were near maximum elevation, the lower-step sheetpiling should be higher than 369 ft, not 367 ft as noted. Thus "Elev. 367 ft" should be circled in red, and "Elev. 372 ft" should be highlighted in yellow. The upper step of the sheetpiling at 372 ft should be highlighted in yellow; the lower step at "Elev. 367 ft" should be circled in red.

Going down the line indicating the west side of the sheetpiling, the contract administrator will observe the item "Drive sheeting down to Elev. 352 ft." This item and the line representing the sheetpiling should be highlighted in yellow.

The top of excavation within the sheetpiling is indicated to be at "Elev. 355 ft," but the item is unclear. The contract administrator should add, in red, "Bottom of excavation" immediately above "Elev. 355 ft" and also add a red arrow pointing to the bottom of the excavation. He should highlight "Elev. 355 ft" and the lines indicating the bottom of the excavation in yellow and should do the same for the breakline in the sheetpiling. The contract administrator might next proceed up the vertical lines indicating the eastern section of sheetpiling in the western cofferdam, highlighting them in yellow. There is no note calling the top of this elevation of sheetpiling. However, the *east* cofferdam states an elevation of 377 ft. The contract administrator should write in red at the top of the west cofferdam sheeting "Elev. 377 ft?" (It will be assumed that the sheetpiling will be revised to the 377-ft elevation in data generated from this drawing in the future.)

Inside the cofferdam are two notes: "Existing 6-in H.P. gas main" and "Relocated 6-in H.P. gas main" (at the 358-ft elevation). This supports an inference that it will be necessary for a contractor to lower the gas main. Both items should be highlighted in yellow. (It will be recalled that note 1 calls for this work to be done by others prior to the award of this contract.)

The long dimensioning arrow on the top of the profile to the right of the west cofferdam, entitled "Tunnel section," seems acceptable and should be highlighted in yellow. The item "Existing R.R. service road" seems correct and should be highlighted in yellow.

As he moves down and to the right on the drawing, the contract administrator will note the item "126-in. liner plate casing." This supports an inference that the tunnel is to be excavated and a liner plate is to be installed subsequently—a normal construction procedure. The item and the liner plate should be highlighted in yellow.

The contract administrator will note the item "$\mathcal{C}$, 96-in. P.C.C.P. outfall," indicating placement of a 96-in.-diameter pipe inside the 126-in.-diameter liner plate configuration. This seems reasonable; accordingly, both the item and the pipe itself should be highlighted in yellow.

The nearby item calling for the centerline elevation of a 96-in. P.C.C.P. to be "Elev. 365 ft." conforms with the grids on both sides of the profile and should be highlighted in yellow.

On the lower part of the tunnel section appears the item "Sand-cement grout" with an arrow pointing to the space between the tunnel liner plate and the P.C.C.P. pipe. This would seem to indicate installation of a sand-cement grout between the liner plate and the pipe after placement of the pipe. This seems reasonable, and both should be highlighted in yellow.

This process should be continued through the drawing, with the contract administrator either accepting the notations and highlighting them in yellow or taking exception and circling them in red. After the completion of this procedure for each drawing, the drawing would be checked against all other related drawings for inconsistencies.

DEVELOPING A TENTATIVE CONSTRUCTION SEQUENCE

From these comprehensive reviews of Figures 2-1 and 2-2, the contract administrator can now envision a tentative construction sequence. One such sequence would be the following:

1. Mobilization (not shown anywhere but must occur before contractor can start work)
2. Installation of temporary road crossing (note 14, Figure 2-1)
3. Relocation of water main around east shaft
4. Driving of sheetpiling, west shaft
5. Driving of sheetpiling, east shaft
6. Observation wells
7. Excavation of west shaft
8. Excavation of east shaft
9. Dewatering
10. Excavation and installation of tunnel liner plates
11. Installation of 96-in.-diameter P.C.C.P.
12. Grouting of space between 96-in. P.C.C.P. and liner plate
13. Backfilling of shaft
14. Installation of riprap
15. Cleanup and demobilization

   The contract administrator's next task would be to assemble all items circled in red on the drawings, transmit them to the engineer, and request that he either clarify them to the satisfaction of the contract administrator (so that the contract administrator may subsequently communicate these clarifications to the contractor) or revise his drawings to eliminate ambiguities and errors.

   This approach to the design professional must be undertaken in a professional and tactful manner. It cannot, however, be avoided: if the contract administrator has encountered uncertain or erroneous detail in the design, it is fair to expect that the contractor will encounter similar problems when he undertakes construction of the project.

Once each matter circled in red has been resolved to the satisfaction of the contract administrator, all clarifications and changes should be issued at the earliest time to the contractor, and each completed item should be circled in green.

CHAPTER 3

THE PRELIMINARY COST ESTIMATE

The theme of Part 1 is the establishment of basic approaches to permit the contract administrator of a construction project to control its conformance to design and its cost. Toward that end, Chapter 1 illustrated procedures for analyzing the *text* of the contract, then reassembling selected provisions in more usable form on Control Responsibility Summary Sheets. Chapter 2 set forth procedures for using the contract *drawings* to further control responsibilities, learn the project, verify drawing details, and form a general impression of possible construction sequences. By the time the contract administrator has mastered the procedures laid out in these chapters, he should have a comprehensive understanding of the project and of the responsibilities of the respective participants.

COST

Each construction project has three dimensions—time, quality, and cost—and all are primary concerns of the contract administrator. This chapter will be concerned primarily with *cost*. Once time has been determined, the goal, simply stated, is the best possible project at the least possible cost. There are many means by which overall project cost can be controlled during the competitive or noncompetitive selection of contractors. But few of these are available by the time of the contract administrator's entrance upon the scene: advertisements for bid or requests for proposal have gone out, bids or proposals have been received, and one or more contractors have been selected. Thus the contract administrator whose agreement for services requires him to administer payments to the contractor is left with the difficult tasks of conserving the owner's funds, treating the contractor fairly, and promoting construction as contemplated in the contract.

To strike the proper balance between prudence and parsimony, the contract administrator must understand both the pricing elements of the project and the payment mechanisms of the contract. He must establish the cost of each labor and material component of the project. He must know how interim payments are to be made to the contractor. And, above all, he must know how to correlate any interim payments to the contractor's completion of the project components. The contract administrator's principal tools in "measuring the money" will be the preliminary cost estimate, the control procedure described in this chapter, and the preliminary cash-flow curve discussed in detail in Chapter 5.

Construction contracts vary widely in their provisions for payment to contractors. It is, however, possible to classify such contracts according to the extent to which they place risk with the owner or the contractor. Of greatest risk to the owner are the "time-and-material" contracts, which pay the contractor for (1) the actual cost of materials and equipment installed, (2) the actual cost of labor to make these installations, (3) a percentage of the foregoing costs, to cover overhead, and (4) another percentage of those costs, for profit. In such arrangements, the contractor's risks are negligible, and the owner carries the risks of price escalations and a contractor's low rate of productivity. At the other end of the risk spectrum is the "lump-sum" contract. In a pure lump-sum arrangement, the contractor agrees to construct the project as described in the contract documents for one all-encompassing price. The risks of low productivity rates and rising prices are allocated to the contractor, not the owner. Between the extremes of the time-and-materials and lump-sum contracts lie innumerable variations, including the "lump-sum contract with unit prices." In such a contract, items which cannot be quantified in design are segregated from all other items. As such unquantifiable items are actually incorporated into the project, payment is made to the contractor at predetermined prices per unit. All other items are included in a lump-sum package.

To discuss the *type* of payment provisions, however, is to say nothing of the *timing mechanisms* of payment. It has been found to be in the interest of both the owner and the contractor that payments be made to the contractor *during* construction. From the contractor's standpoint, an obvious benefit is that periodic payments permit minimization of borrowings and interest; less obvious, however, is the indirect corresponding benefit to the owner of a lower contract price where the contractor quotes a reduced price in contemplation of such interim payments. Interim payments provide an important means to control both the progress and the quality of the project through reimbursement to the contractor for materials obtained in advance of their need to be incorporated into the project and through nonpayment for work which fails to meet the standards of the contract.

In most cases, the responsibility for establishing, systematizing, and monitoring control procedures by which interim payments are made falls to the contract administrator. His function is to determine the extent to which the contractor's efforts during a given period of time have increased the value of the project and to recommend that the owner make a corresponding payment to the contractor. The device used to make that determination in lump-sum contracts is called a "lump-sum breakdown."

It is clearly in the financial interest of the contractor that interim payments be maximized; it is clearly in the interest of the owner that such payments not exceed the value of the work completed. In this setting, the task of the contract administrator is to determine the value of the contractor's efforts to the project during a given period as accurately as possible in the interests of fairness to *both* owner and contractor.

The ability of most contractors to promote their interests in "pricing out" a contract, i.e., allocating values to project components, presents a formidable challenge to the contract administrator. For the contractor, the ability to price out is more than a matter of the degree of his prosperity: his ultimate survival rests upon his success in obtaining payment equal to, or exceeding, a significant part of the value he adds to the project during a given period. Most contract administrators will not attain the sophistication of successful contractors in pricing out construction contracts; however, with careful study and application of the control procedure set forth in this chapter, the reader can become sufficiently knowledgeable to keep interim payments reasonably correspondent to the growth in the value of the project.

The purpose of this chapter is explanation of a cost estimating procedure through which the contract administrator can determine the approximate price of each significant labor and material component necessary to construct the project. The procedure will permit him to develop a thorough understanding of the "cost" dimensions of the project while he generates a preliminary cost estimate, one of the two documents through which he will be able eventually to *control* the costs of the project to the owner.

DEVELOPING THE PRELIMINARY COST ESTIMATE

Cost Estimating Guides

The method to be employed by the contract administrator in generating his preliminary cost estimate is much the same as that employed by many Contractors in their preliminary pricing operation. Both the contract administrator and the contractor will accumulate pricing data for ultimate tabulation on standard summary sheets to facilitate analysis. Also, both will probably begin their search for pricing data by use of one or more "cost estimating guides," periodic compilations of averages for standard labor and material components of construction projects. In accumulating these data, however, the contractor enjoys one advantage over the contract administrator: he alone has the opportunity to supplement information obtained from the cost estimating guide with actual price quotations from prospective vendors and suppliers, and he alone is privied to his productivity rates demonstrated in previous projects. Notwithstanding this disadvantage, the contract administrator's preliminary cost estimate should provide sufficient accuracy to determine the authenticity of the contractor's allocations of the contract price and requests for interim payment.

There are a number of excellent cost estimating guides available. If contract administrators are not already familiar with at least one, they should obtain several and browse through them as soon as possible. It is important that the guide the contract administrator ultimately decides to use contain average productivity rates as well as labor and material prices.

The Preliminary Schedule and Cost Control Summary Sheet

Having acquired a general understanding of cost estimating guides and an intimate knowledge of the textual (see Chapter 1) and pictorial (see Chapter 2) sections of the contract, the contract administrator is now ready to generate a Preliminary Schedule and Cost Control Summary Sheet. Figure 3-1 depicts a sample sheet. The sheet is comprised of sixteen columns; the completion of some of which will be left to Chapter 4.

- The first column, entitled "Item No.," is intended merely to identify the line item on the horizontal line. Each item will be numbered consecutively down the left-hand side of the sheet.

- The second column, entitled "Description," requires that the contract administrator characterize the construction activity in question. The

PRELIMINARY SCHEDULE AND COST CONTROL SUMMARY SHEET

Item No.	Description	Quantity	Unit	Estimating Guide Data					Adjusted Total Cost $[(9) \times$ factor$]$	Productivity Rate	Productivity Unit	Duration (Days)	Before	Concurrent With	After
				Unit	Material Price	Labor Price	Total Price $[(6) + (7)]$	Total Cost $[(3) \times (8)]$							
(1)	(2)	(3)	(4)	(5)	(6)	(7)	(8)	(9)	(10)	(11)	(12)	(13)	(14)	(15)	(16)

FIGURE 3-1 Preliminary Schedule and Cost Control Summary Sheet.

description should be brief but clear, e.g., "Administration building, excavation" or "Laboratory building, structural steel."

- The third column, entitled "Quantity," and the fourth column, entitled "Unit," require that the contract administrator calculate, by reference to the contract drawings, the unit of measurement for the item described and the quantity of said units required for the project. Standard abbreviations should be used.

- The fifth column, entitled "Unit," the sixth column, entitled "Material Price," the seventh column, entitled "Labor Price," and the eighth column, entitled "Total Price," call for a mere transfer of data from the cost estimating guide to the appropriate column. The Unit and Estimating Guide Data Unit columns are purposely juxtaposed in order that the contract administrator may verify that his proposed units and those contemplated by the cost estimating guide are identical. If they are not, one or the other must be adjusted before the contract administrator can continue; it is suggested that the contract administrator's proposed unit is by far the easier of the two to adjust.

- The ninth column, entitled "Total Cost," is a "multiplication product" column to be completed by multiplying the number of units stated for a given item in the third column by the estimating guide unit total cost in the eighth column.

- The tenth column, entitled "Adjusted Total Cost," also a multiplication product column, is to be completed by multiplying the dollar amount shown for a given column item in the ninth column by the ratio of the contractor's lump-sum price divided by the total of the preliminary cost estimate shown in column 9 for that item.

- The eleventh column, entitled "Productivity Rate," and the twelfth column, entitled "Productivity Unit," are to be completed by direct transfer of data from the cost estimating guide for the item in question.

- The thirteenth column, entitled "Duration (Days)," is to be completed by dividing the quantity shown in the third column for a given item by the productivity rate shown in the eleventh column for that item and by converting the dividend into days, if necessary.

- The fourteenth, fifteenth, and sixteenth columns, entitled "Before," "Concurrent With," and "After," respectively, will be addressed in Chapter 4.

The Preliminary Cost Estimate

With these brief descriptions of column functions in mind, the contract administrator can now make his preliminary cost estimate for a given project by completing the first thirteen columns of the Preliminary Schedule and Cost Control Summary Sheet. Columns 1 through 10 are directly concerned with generation of the preliminary cost estimate. Columns 11 through 16 are concerned with generation of the preliminary schedule; however, the contract administrator will realize a time savings by completing columns 11 through 13 at this time inasmuch as completion of columns 1 through 13 involves use of a cost estimating guide and common calculation. A general word concerning completion of the Preliminary Schedule and Cost Control Summary Sheet is in order here. Judgment on the part of the contract administrator becomes important in arranging the *sequence* of the items on the sheet. That having been said, however, a contract administrator's lack of experience, and therefore lack of judgment, will not prevent him from completing the sheet: it will merely require that he allocate additional time to the task, i.e., that he be prepared to rearrange line items as necessary. Some of this ordering of construction tasks was discussed during the third step in the review of contract drawings (see Chapter 2). That exercise having been completed, the contract administrator should have a reasonable idea of the overall project sequence. Assistance is also available from most cost estimating guides, which are organized in the normal construction sequence.

In compiling the preliminary cost estimate, the focus of the contract administrator should be placed squarely upon the items of construction to be incorporated into the project, including excavation, site, utilities, roadways, reinforcing steel, and concrete. The cost estimating guide provides data concerning overhead costs, construction equipment costs, and other similar considerations vital to the contractor, but at this point such considerations are to be *disregarded* by the contract administrator.

The data listed in the preliminary cost estimate will ultimately be utilized in generating a cost control system for the project. At this point, the contract administrator's task is to include items of construction only to the extent that their installed quantities can later be monitored and measured. Examples of such items of construction to be included in the preliminary cost estimate follow:

Item	Unit of Measurement
Site clearing	Acre

Foundation excavation	Cubic yard
Site drainage	Linear foot
Bituminous concrete roads	Square yard in place (not detailed by items such as base course, base course compaction, tack, binder course, and surface course)
Concrete	Cubic yard in place (not detailed with items such as form work, reinforcing steel, concrete, form stripping, and finishing; on large projects, however, reinforcing steel might be a separate item)

The list of possible items is endless. The contract administrator should start on the first item of work he envisions to be performed, calculate the quantity of that item to be incorporated into the project (based upon his speculation at the conclusion of Chapter 2 concerning project sequence), then proceed through the contract drawings until all major components of the project have been described and quantified on the Preliminary Schedule and Cost Control Summary Sheet.

The next step is to obtain from the cost estimating guide the units, material costs, labor cost, total cost, and the productivity factor which most clearly describe the item of work. Those figures should then be entered on the sheet.

The final step in completing the sheet is to complete the remainder of the first thirteen columns by the simple calculations previously described. The contract administrator should bear in mind that the dollar amounts which appear in the ninth column, Total Cost, are to be totaled at the bottom of the sheet. The contractor's lump-sum bid price is then to be divided by this total. Each Total Cost item is then to be multiplied by the ratio derived by the division, and the product of the multiplication for that item is to be entered in the Adjusted Total Cost for that item. These mathematical operations distribute unknown markups for the contractor's overhead and profit uniformly throughout the preliminary cost estimate. This distribution of unknowns may not be identical to that of the contractor, but it is the most equitable method through which an accounting of unknowns can be obtained quickly.

SUMMARY

This chapter has provided the contract administrator a means to allocate the contractor's lump-sum bid price among the various labor and materials components of the project. This is a necessary first step in assuring that interim payments to the contractor do not exceed the value added to the project during a given period.

Before setting out to give an example of how the preliminary cost estimate for a project is generated, however, we believe that the philosophy related to the preliminary cost estimate must be stated. There is no one correct cost estimate. There is no incorrect cost estimate. There are only different estimates. People with analytical training are in the habit of finding the one numerically correct answer to a problem. This is not the goal in generating the preliminary cost estimate. The goal is to think about, record, and assign a reasonable price to each component of the project which the contract administrator, as an estimator, envisions to be required. Contract administrators have neither the detailed data nor, in all likelihood, the expertise available to them that a professional estimator working for a contractor has. They should not attempt to pretend that they have such abilities by delving into infinite detail. Nor should they become upset upon finding that the cost data available is not exactly applicable to their needs. The goal, once again, is to think about what must be done and how it can be done, then assigning an average cost to each of these items. The contract administrator's proficiency in this task will grow markedly with experience.

COMPREHENSIVE ILLUSTRATION

A comprehensive illustration of the techniques for generating the preliminary cost estimate will involve the tunnel project described in Chapter 2. Development of the preliminary cost estimate will begin with an expansion of the projected construction sequence developed at the close of Chapter 2 and an assignment of cost to each detail through use of a cost estimating guide. The previously developed projected construction sequence could be expanded as follows:

1. MOBILIZATION

Mobilization includes all preparations required of the contractor to enable him to commence the administrative and physical work at the project. Administrative items would include insurance, bonds, shop drawings, and samples; physical requirements would include transportation of equipment and materials to the site, establishment of field offices, and construction or placement of equipment trailers, change shacks for workers, and telephone, power, and sanitary facilities. It is probable that the contractor, in computing his bid price for the project, would itemize each and every such requirement and assign a price to each. However, such detail is not required for the purposes of the contract administrator. Most cost estimating guides provide for mobilization costs as a percentage of project costs. The contract administrator should postpone development of any actual amounts for mobilization until he totals the rest of his cost estimates; he should then add a reasonable percentage for mobilization costs. This cost may vary from 2 to 12 percent of the project cost, depending on the size and type of the project.

The contract administrator should prepare a Preliminary Schedule and Cost Control Summary Sheet and note as his first item on the sheet "Mobilization." Under the Quantity column for this first item, he should enter "L.S.," the abbreviation for lump sum and an indication that no units are to be calculated for this item.

2. TEMPORARY ROAD

The temporary road was the second item envisioned in the preliminary construction sequence in Chapter 2. The first step is to scale the drawing to obtain the quantity of material required for the temporary road: scaled length = 40 ft; scaled width = 20 ft; specified depth = 1 ft. Thus the *area* of run-of-bank gravel required is 89 yd^2. Reference to a cost estimating guide for gravel roads 1 ft in depth provides the following data:

Equipment and crew	One bulldozer and operator
Estimating guide	
Unit	Square yard
Material price	1.25
Labor price	0.22
Total price	1.47
Productivity	1800
Productivity unit	Square yards per day

Hence on the Preliminary Schedule and Cost Control Summary Sheet, the following items should be noted:

Item number	2
Description	Temporary road
Quantity	89

Unit   Square yard

Estimating guide
 Material price $1.25
 Labor price $0.22
 Total price $1.47

Productivity   1800 (1800/yd^2 per 8 working hours)

Productivity unit Square yards per 8 working hours

3. WATERLINE RELOCATION

The next construction item envisioned to occur is the relocation of the 24-in.-diameter waterline. The reader will recall that this relocation is required to provide space to dig the east shaft for the tunnel. The relocated length of pipe is scaled from the drawings to be 105 lin ft. A note on Figure 2-1 states that 3 ft of cover is required over the top of all buried pipe. Relocation of the pipe, of course, contemplates the digging of a new trench, installation of the pipe, covering of the pipe, tying of the new line to the old, and removal of the inactive portion of the old line. After entering the item number and description on the summary sheet, it will be necessary to estimate the cost of each of these five parts.

a. *Excavation.* The depth of excavation will be 2 ft to below the top of the pipe plus 3 ft of cover required over the top of the pipe plus 2 times the pipe's thickness. For the purposes of the contract administrator, the pipe thickness, which is negligible, can be ignored. Thus the depth of excavation will be 5 ft. Similarly, the contract administrator can reasonably estimate the width of the excavation for the 2-ft-diameter pipe at 3.5 ft. The total excavation is, therefore,

$$\frac{105 \text{ lin ft} \times 5 \text{ ft} \times 3.5 \text{ ft}}{27 \text{ ft}^3/\text{yd}^3} = 68 \text{ yd}^3$$

After reference to the cost estimating guide, the contract administrator would enter the following data on his Preliminary Schedule and Cost Control Summary Sheet:

Item number   3a

Description   Excavation

Quantity   68

Unit   Cubic yard

Estimating guide

 Unit   Cubic yard

 Material price   0

Labor price	$1.30
Total price	$1.30
Productivity	20
Productivity unit	Cubic yards per day

b. *Pipe Installation.* The contract administrator next seeks to obtain the cost of installing 105 lin ft of 24-in.-diameter waterline. This information should be obtained from the guide, then entered on the Preliminary Schedule and Cost Control Summary Sheet under item number 3b. The following data was obtained from the guide:

Item number	3b
Description	Pipe installation
Quantity	105
Unit	Linear foot
Estimating guide	
Material price	$15.75
Labor price	$3.00
Total price	$18.75
Productivity	120
Productivity unit	Linear feet per day

c. *Tie-In.* The tie-in of the new pipe will require that the old line be shut down temporarily and drained, that the section to be abandoned be cut out, and that the new section be welded in place. Reference to the cost estimating guide reveals that a welder can weld about 50 lin ft of pipe (with 3 passes) in one 8-hour day at a cost of approximately $330. In the tunnel illustration, it appears that only 6 ft of pipe need to be welded and cut; however, the length of time required to shut down and drain the existing line is unknown. In such a case, the contract administrator is without alternative but to hazard an educated guess based upon his experience; our experience leads us to place the cost of cutting, welding, shutdown, and drainage of line at $500. Thus the entry on the Preliminary Schedule and Cost Control Summary Sheet should appear as follows:

Item number	3c
Description	Tie-in
Quantity	Lump sum
Unit	Allowance

Estimating guide
    Unit   —

    Material price   —

    Labor price   —

    Total price $500

Productivity

Productivity unit   Lump sum per day

d. *Backfill.* The quantity of backfill will be the quantity of excavation less the volume of the pipe. The volume of the pipe is calculated at 12.2 yd^3; since the total volume of excavation was 68 yd^3, the volume of backfill will be 55.8 yd^3. After consulting the cost estimating guide, the contract administrator might make the following entry in the Preliminary Schedule and Cost Control Summary Sheet:

Item number   3d

Description   Backfill

Quantity   55.8

Unit   Cubic yard

Estimating guide
    Unit   Cubic yard
    Material price   — (The material will have been left over from excavation.)
    Labor price $3.55
    Total price $3.55

Productivity   20.6

Productivity unit   Cubic yards per day

e. *Removal of Bypassed Line.* Much of the time for this item was accounted for under item 3c: the cost of tie-in included waiting, cutting, and welding. One might assume that the old pipe could be removed during the waiting period and that the item could be eliminated from the Preliminary Schedule and Cost Control Summary Sheet; accordingly, the contract administrator should make no entry for this item.

4. DRIVING OF SHEETPILING, WEST SHAFT

The top elevation of the sheetpiling was assumed to be changed to 377 ft, and the bottom elevation is given as 325 ft; therefore, the length of the sheetpiling is 52 ft. The *perimeter* of the west shaft is twice 31 ft 4 in. plus twice 19 ft 4 in., or 101 ft 4 in., or 101.33 ft;

therefore, the *surface area* of the sheetpiling is 52 ft × 101.33 ft², or 5269.1 ft².

The guide shows the following for sheetpiling, including wales and struts:

Unit	Square foot
Equipment and crew	1 crane, 1 vibratory hammer, 1 supervisor, 4 pile drivers, 2 operators, and 1 oiler

Estimating guide

Material price	$6.85
Labor price	$1.50
Total price	$8.35
Productivity rate	1200
Productivity unit	Square feet per day

The contract administrator should note the following data on the Preliminary Schedule and Cost Control Summary Sheet:

Item number	4
Description	Sheetpiling, west shaft
Quantity	5269.1
Unit	Square foot

Estimating guide

Unit	Square foot
Material price	$6.85
Labor price	$1.50
Total price	$8.35
Productivity	1200
Productivity Unit	Square feet per day

5. SHEETPILING, EAST SHAFT

The top elevation of the sheetpiling in the east shaft is 377 ft. The bottom elevation of the sheetpiling in the east shaft is 325 ft. The length of the sheetpiling in the east shaft is, therefore, 52 ft. The perimeter of the east shaft is twice 40 ft 4 in. plus twice 19 ft 4 in., or 119.33 ft. The area of the sheetpiling in the east shaft is, therefore, 119.25 ft × 52 ft, or 6205.2 ft².

The data from the cost estimating guide is the same as for the west shaft. The contract administrator should enter the following data onto the Preliminary Schedule and Cost Control Summary Sheets:

Item number	5
Description	Sheetpiling, east shaft
Quantity	6205.2
Unit	Square foot
Estimating guide	
Unit	Square foot
Material price	$6.85
Labor price	$1.50
Total price	$8.35
Productivity	1200
Productivity unit	Square feet per day

6. OBSERVATION WELLS

Figures 2-1 and 2-2 show that two observation wells at 30 ft in depth, each, are required. The cost estimating guide gives the following data:

Item number	6
Description	Observation wells
Quantity	60
Unit	Linear foot
Equipment and crew	Well-digger operator and laborer
Estimating guide	
Material price	$5.50
Labor price	$5.50
Total price	$11.00
Productivity	40
Productivity unit	Linear feet per day

The contract administrator should enter this data onto the Preliminary Schedule and Cost Control Summary Sheets.

7. EXCAVATION, WEST SHAFT

From the drawings, one will observe that the depth of excavation is

22 ft and that the area of excavation is 605.6 ft², so that the volume of Excavation is

$$\frac{22 \text{ ft} \times 605.6 \text{ ft}^2}{27 \text{ ft}^3/\text{yd}^3} = 493.5 \text{ yd}^3$$

The cost estimating guide's data results in the following additions to the Preliminary Schedule and Cost Control Summary Sheets:

Item number	7
Description	Excavation, west shaft
Quantity	493.5
Unit	Cubic yard
Estimating guide	
Unit	Cubic yard
Material price	$0.76
Labor price	$0.64
Total price	$1.40
Productivity	280
Productivity Unit	Cubic yards per day

8. EXCAVATION, EAST SHAFT

Calculations taken from the drawings result in 635.2 yd³ of excavation being required in the east shaft. Cost estimating guide data will be the same as for the west shaft.

9. DEWATERING

The cost estimating guide indicates that continuous dewatering will cost $750 per day. Since the number of days in which such dewatering will be required has yet to be determined, the following entry should be made in the Preliminary Schedule and Cost Control Summary Sheet, with the number of days left blank:

Item number	9
Description	Dewatering
Quantity	
Unit	24 hours per day
Estimating guide	
Unit	24 hours per day
Material price	—
Labor price	—

Total price $750

Productivity   —

Productivity unit   —

10. TUNNELING

As in the case of waterline relocation, it will be necessary to divide the tunneling operation into its components. The following division of item 10 seems reasonable. It should be noted that tunneling operations usually are undertaken on a three-shift, 24-hour-a-day basis.

a. *Cutting and Bracing of Portals:* The drawings indicate that the excavated tunnel will be 126 in. in diameter. Hence at each portal, it will be necessary for the contractor to cut

$$\frac{\pi \times 126 \text{ in.}}{12 \text{ in. per lin ft}}$$

or 32.98 lin ft, of sheetpiling. The portal will then have to be stiffened with bracing—perhaps 50# of steel per lin ft of the circumference of the opening. The cost estimating guide might provide a material cost of $90 per ton for structural steel bracing. Thus the contract administrator might compute the cost of bracing as follows: 33 lin ft × 50 lb/lin ft = 1650 lb × 2 portals = 3300 lb ÷ 2000 lb/ton = 1.65 tons × $90/ton = $148.50 for material.

Our best estimate as to labor cost for this item is that it will take 4 laborers 2 days for each portal, but, to provide a margin of safety, we suggest a projected cost of $200 per day per laborer (including equipment). Thus the labor cost could be computed as follows: 4 laborers × 2 days × 2 portals = 16 worker days at $200 per worker day = $3200 for labor plus $150± for steel = $3350±.

This information should be recorded on the Preliminary Schedule and Cost Control Summary Sheet.

b. *Tunnel Excavation:* The tunnel is to be 10.5 ft in length and 126 in. in diameter. Therefore, the volume of excavation is computed at 404.1 yd³. The cost estimating guide indicates that a laborer can excavate 3 yd³ of clay per 8-hour day at a unit labor cost of $24.25 per yd³. This information should be entered on the Preliminary Schedule and Cost Control Summary Sheet.

c. *Mucking Operation:* The cost estimating guide indicates that 1 laborer can load 8 yd³ of clay onto a truck in 8 hours at a cost of $12.55 per yd³. These data should also be entered on the sheet.

d. *Muck Removal:* Assuming that two laborers will be required to push the muck cars to the shaft, an operator and crane would lift the muck car to the surface, and a truck (with driver) will remove the muck from the site, labor costs will be as follows:

Laborers (2)	$200 per 8-hour day
Crane and operator	$490 per 8-hour day
Truck and driver	$220 per 8-hour day
	$910 per 8-hour day = $2730 per 24-hour day

It would seem reasonable to add $270 per day for such items as cars, rails, and related items, making the total cost per 24-hour day $3000. Assuming 2 laborers excavated 3 yd³ per shift each for 3 shifts per day, the total excavation in one 24-hour period would be 18 yd³. Since the total tunnel excavation is 404.1 yd³, approximately twenty-three 24-hour days will be required for muck removal.

e. *Liner Plate Installation:* As the excavation progresses, liner plates will be installed to prevent the clay from entering the tunnel. These plates come in various widths, lengths, and thicknesses: they are usually bolted through holes in the internal flanges. Assuming that the contractor will use 1-ft- by 2-ft- by ⅜-in.-thick plates with 2-in. flanges, each plate will weigh between 30 and 35 lb. It might further be assumed that while mucking was in progress, two laborers could bolt the two plates together and could place the plates at the rate of excavation without getting into the way of the mucking laborers. If the tunnel work is to progress at a rate of 5.5 lin ft per 24-hour day, 6 plate-installation laborers (i.e., 2 laborers per shift) would be required. Thus unit labor would be computed as follows: 6 laborers at $100 per day = $600 per day ÷ 5.5 ft per day = $109.09 per foot.

As in the case of labor costs for liner plate installation, material costs for such installation must be estimated. A reasonable approach might be to project 126 lin ft × π × 10.5 ft = 4156.33 ft² × $4 per ft² = $16,625.32 ÷ $126 = $131.95 per ft. Thus the total cost of the sheeting per linear foot would be labor ($109.09) + material ($131.95), or $241.04. These data should be entered on the sheet.

f. *Tunnel Ventilation:* The volume of the tunnel has been calculated at 404.1 yd³, or 10,910.7 ft³. If 12 air changes per hour were required, air exchange capability of 2182 ft³ per minute would be required. The guide indicates that a 2960 ft³ per minute fan costs approximately $350; however, the cost of the fan in relation to other items is negligible and should be ignored.

11. INSTALLATION OF 96-in. CONCRETE PIPE

The total length of the pipe is computed as follows:

East shaft	40.33 ft
Tunnel	126.00 ft
West shaft	31.33 ft
Extension to lake	30.00 ft
Total	<u>227.66 ft</u>

The cost estimating guide provides the following information:

Estimating guide unit   Linear foot

Equipment and crew   Crane, operator, oiler, supervisor, and 4 laborers

Estimating guide

Material price	$110
Labor price	$ 38
Total price	$148

Productivity   20

Productivity Unit   Linear feet per day

These data should be entered on the Preliminary Schedule and Cost Control Summary Sheet.

12. GROUT

The next step projected by the contract administrator is the grouting of space between the outside of the pipe and the inside of the liner plate. The volume inside the liner pipe has been estimated at 104.1 yd^3. The volume of the pipe has been estimated at 254.3 yd^3. Thus the space to be grouted is approximately 150 yd^3. According to the cost estimate guide, the cost of such grouting would be as follows:

Estimating guide unit   Cubic yard

Equipment and crew   1 supervisor and 5 laborers

Estimating guide

Material price	$35
Labor price	$7.50
Total price	$42.50

Productivity 150

Productivity unit Cubic yards per day

These data should be entered on the sheet.

13. BACKFILLING OF EAST AND WEST SHAFTS

The volume of the west shaft is 493.5 yd^3 and the volume of the east shaft is 635.2 yd^3, for a total of 1128.7 yd^3. From that total must be subtracted the volume of 61.33 lin ft of 96-in. pipe, i.e., 123.8 yd^3, resulting in a required volume of backfill of 1004.9 yd^3. The cost estimating guide provides the following data:

Estimating guide unit Cubic yard

Crew 1 laborer

Estimating guide

  Material price — (material present from excavation)

  Labor price $8.30

  Total price $8.30

Productivity 24

Productivity Unit Cubic yards per day

These data should be entered.

14. INSTALLATION OF RIPRAP

The area of riprap is estimated to be 100 yd^2. Based upon this estimate, the following data is obtainable from the guide:

Estimating guide unit Square yard

Crew 2 laborers

Estimating guide

  Material price $9

  Labor price $15.40

  Total price $24.40

Productivity 50

Productivity unit Square yards per day

15. CLEANUP AND DEMOBILIZATION

The contract administrator should merely estimate this to be in the order of 5 days at a total cost of $3000 based upon his experience.

The contract administrator should now return to item 9 (dewatering). The number of days required for dewatering can now be estimated as follows:

During grouting	1 day
During pipe installation	12 days
During tunneling	26 days
Total	39 days

This information should be entered on the sheet.

The contract administrator should next return to item 1 (Mobilization), noting that the total estimated cost, *excluding* mobilization, is $301,629. Assuming a 4 percent factor for mobilization and allowing for a mobilization period of 4 weeks, the contract administrator can derive a total mobilization cost of $12,065. Thus the estimated project cost is now determined by the contract administrator as $301,629 plus $12,065, or $313,694.

This total estimated cost must now be applied to the actual bid price for the project. If the low bid price were $445,000, that price divided by the contract administrator's total estimated cost would produce a dividend of 1.419. This would mean that the contract administrator's estimate was 41.9 percent lower than the bid price. This disparity can be explained by the failure of the contract administrator's estimate to include markups for overhead, profit, and contingencies, as well as the contract administrator's errors in estimating. A 20 percent contingency would seem reasonable given the method used to propose the estimate. If he adds a 20 percent contingency, 10 percent overhead, and 5 percent profit consecutively, the contract administrator arrives at the total price of $438,297—quite close to the $445,000 bid price. Thus without knowing the contractor's actual profit percentage, the contract administrator can ascertain, in approximate terms, whether his estimate is within the realm of reason.

The contract administrator's next task is to multiply each item in his total estimated cost by the factor 1.419. The products of these multiplications should be entered in column 10 of the Preliminary Schedule and Cost Control Summary Sheet. Figure 3-2 is a completed Preliminary Schedule and Cost Control Summary Sheet based upon the foregoing data.

PRELIMINARY SCHEDULE AND COST CONTROL SUMMARY SHEET

Bid price ~ or average of all bids

Item No. (1)	Description (2)	Quantity (3)	Unit (4)	Estimating Guide Data					Adjusted Total Cost [(9)× factor] (10)	Productivity Rate (11)	Productivity Unit (12)	Duration (Days) (13)	Before (14)	Concurrent With (15)	After (16)
				Unit (5)	Material Price (6)	Labor Price (7)	Total Price [(6)+(7)] (8)	Total Cost [(3)×(8)] (9)							
1	Mobilization	L.S.	—	—	—	—	—	12,065	17,115	Allow					
2	Haul Road	89.	yd^2	yd^2	1.25	0.22	1.47	131	186	1800	yd^2/day				
3	Waterline relocation														
3a	Excavation	68.	yd^3	yd^3	0	1.30	1.30	88	125	20	yd^3/day				
3b	Pipe installation	105	lin ft	lin ft	15.75	3.00	18.75	1,969	2,793	120	lin ft^2/day				
3c	Tie-in	L.S.	Allow	—	—	—	—	500	709	Allow	—				
3d	Backfill	55.8	yd^3	yd^3	6.85	3.55	3.55	198	281	20.6	yd^3/day				
4	Sheetpiling, west shaft	5269.1	ft^2	ft^2	6.85	1.50	8.35	43,998	62,415	1200	ft^2/day				
5	Sheetpiling, east shaft	6205.2	ft^2	ft^2	6.85	1.50	8.35	51,813	73,501	1200	ft^2/day				
6	Observation wells	60	lin ft	lin ft	5.50	5.50	11.00	660	936	40	lin ft^2/day				
7	Excavation, west shaft	493.5	yd^3	yd^3	0.76	0.64	1.40	691	980	280	yd^3/day				
8	Excavation, east shaft	635.2	yd^3	yd^3	0.76	0.64	1.40	889	1,251	280	yd^3/day				
9	Dewatering	39	24-h day	24-h day	—	—	750.00	29,250	41,493	—	—				
10	Tunnel														
10a	Cut & brace portals	4	Worker day	Worker day	37.50	800.00	837.50	3,350	4,752	Allow	—				
10b	Excavation	404.1	yd^3	yd^3	—	24.25	24.25	9,799	13,901	Allow	—				
10c	Mucking	404.1	yd^3	yd^3	—	12.55	12.55	5,071	7,194	Allow	—				
10d	Muck removal	23	24-h day	24-h day	—	—	3000.00	69,000	97,882	Allow	—				
10e	Liner plate	126	lin ft	lin ft	109.09	131.95	241.04	30,371	43,084	Allow	—				
11	Install 96-in. pipe	227.67	lin ft	lin ft	110.00	38.00	148.00	33,695	47,800	20	lin ft/day				
12	Grouting	150	yd^3	yd^3	35.00	7.50	42.50	6,375	9,043	150	yd^3/day				
13	Backfill shafts	1004.9	yd^3	yd^3	0.76	8.30	8.30	8,341	11,832	24	yd^3/day				
14	Riprap	100	yd^2	yd^2	9.00	15.40	24.40	2,440	3,461	50	yd^2/day				
15	Cleanup & Demobilization	L.S.	—	—	—	—	3000.00	3,000	4,256	Allow	—				

Total cost, excluding mobilization $301,629

Say 4% for mobilization = $301,629 × 0.04 = $12,065

$$\frac{\$301,629}{+12,065}$$

Total estimated project cost = $313,694

Adjusted cost factor = bid price ÷ total estimated project cost = $\dfrac{\$445,000}{\$313,694} = 1.419$

FIGURE 3-2 Sample of a partially completed Preliminary Schedule and Cost Control Summary Sheet.

CHAPTER 4

THE PRELIMINARY SCHEDULE

In Chapter 3, the contract administrator was concerned with developing a preliminary cost estimate for the entire project and learning the relative prices of the various components of the project. Although the component prices derived may bear only a general resemblance to the actual allocation of prices by the contractor, they are nonetheless useful to the contract administrator as a first step in determining how much value will be added to the project—and thus how much of the owner's capital will be required for interim payments—in each phase of construction.

To do the job effectively, however, the contract administrator must know not only the *relative worth* of each component and its *sequence* in the construction process but also the *timing* of its incorporation into the project: he must know the approximate date of the components' incorporation into the project. This chapter will deal with establishment of a preliminary schedule to answer these questions at a *theoretical* level. As in the case of the preliminary cost estimate, the preliminary schedule may bear only a general resemblance to the actual construction schedule developed and submitted by the contractor: the actual schedule is the sole responsibility of the contractor, subject, of course, to the overall construction period or periods delineated in the contract. By creating his own model schedule, however, the contract administrator will be better able to judge the validity of the contractor's schedule in negotiating the lump-sum payment breakdown (to be discussed in Chapter 5) and will also further familiarize him with the timing and general construction problems inherent in the project.

The purpose of this chapter is to explain a method by which the contract administrator may exert indirect control over the *timing* of construction by:

1. Determining the amount of time required to incorporate each component described in the Preliminary Schedule and Cost Estimate Summary Sheets

2. Using the construction sequences previously developed to create a schedule by which the project *could* be constructed

3. Gaining insight into the construction problems inherent in the project

4. Beginning development of mechanisms for judging the validity of the contractor's proposed lump-sum breakdown for interim payment purposes

The idea is to arrive at a workable schedule even though in all likelihood it will not be the one actually employed.

DEVELOPING THE PRELIMINARY SCHEDULE

Completing the Preliminary Schedule and Cost Control Summary Sheet

The point of beginning in constructing the preliminary schedule is the Preliminary Schedule and Cost Control Summary Sheet. The reader will recall that completion of the first thirteen columns of this sheet was discussed in Chapter 3. Although columns 11 through 13 did not relate directly to the subject of that chapter—the preliminary cost estimate—they were nevertheless completed because they, like the first ten columns, involved reference to the cost estimating guide. Thus, at this point, the Productivity Rate and Productivity Unit columns should be complete.

The contract administrator's attention is directed once again to columns 3, 4, 11, 12, and 13. The duration of each item should be completed by dividing the Quantity column entry by the productivity rate entered, the dividend representing the duration contemplated by the cost estimating guide to be required to construct or install the line item.

The focus now shifts to the last three columns of the Preliminary Schedule and Cost Control Summary Sheet, headed "Before," "Concurrent With," and "After." During the third review of the contract drawings, explained in Chapter 2, the contract administrator was encouraged to list alternative feasible construction sequences for the project in question. The immediate task before him now is to complete columns 14, 15, and 16 using the best of those alternative sequences revised as necessary to reflect his cumulative knowledge of the project. If he diligently applied the control procedures set forth in prior chapters, the contract administrator should encounter little difficulty in completing these columns; if the exercise does prove difficult, he may wish to retrace his steps through the early chapters in order to gain the familiarity so necessary to successful project control. In Chapter 3, it was pointed out that the line items should be arranged in the general sequence of the project as envisioned by the contract administrator. It was further pointed out that lack of experience on the part of the contract administrator in arranging this sequence would not guarantee failure in the exercise; rather, the price of inexperience would be additional time required to complete the exercise. That having been said, the contract administrator's first task in completing columns 14, 15, and 16 should be a comprehensive review of the sequence of the line items listed in the preceding chapter; any items which he believes to be out of place should be rearranged at this time. Once satisfied with the general sequence of line items, the contract administrator should begin by placing a zero in the After column of the first line item. The After column for the second line item should be completed by entry of the number "1," representing the first line item, which in the contract administrator's judgment should precede the second line item. The contract administrator should then proceed through all line items, numbering the After column entries to reflect the logical progression of the project.

In completing the After column, the contract administrator may find that some line items logically follow others and that other line items stand independently. In other words, he may find some line items could be started concurrently. In such cases, the Concurrent With column should be completed, and any entry previously made in the After column should be deleted. Once every line item contains at least one line-item number entry in its After or Concurrent With column, the total theoretical sequence of construction for the project will have been noted. With this information in hand, the contract administrator should now work backward to complete the Before column. Although this exercise will produce information that is, in fact, redundant, it has the value of highlighting construction constraints imposed by other line items and providing a cross-check of the numbering undertaken in columns 15 and 16. Once this exercise is complete, there should be at least one number entry in column 14, 15, or 16 for each line item; there may be multiple entries for some line items.

Plotting the Preliminary Schedule

With all columns of the Preliminary Schedule and Cost Control Summary Sheet now accounted for, the contract administrator should start the actual plotting of the "Preliminary Schedule Sheet." The size of the paper required for the sheet will depend upon the number of line items and the projected duration of the project, but, generally speaking, the larger the paper, the better. The paper should be divided horizontally into ¼-in. lines, one such line for each line-item entry on the Preliminary Schedule and Cost Control Summary Sheet. The Preliminary Schedule Sheet should then be divided vertically, as follows, beginning at the left-hand edge of the paper:

1. A ¼-in. column, entitled "Item No"

2. A 3-in. column, entitled "Description"

3. A series of ¼-in. columns, each column representing 1 *working* day

Once these organizational tasks have been completed, the Preliminary Schedule Sheet will be ready to accommodate transfer of data from the Preliminary Schedule and Cost Control Summary Sheet.

The contract administrator should enter the number and the description of each line item from the Preliminary Schedule and Cost Control Summary Sheet in the appropriate space on the Preliminary Schedule Sheet. Once this has been done, he should refer to the After column. Beginning with the item for which a zero appeared in the After column, he should (1) plot the theoretical duration of that line item from the column for that line item which is located immediately to the right of the Description column on the Preliminary Schedule Sheet and (2) outline one square (representing 1 working day) for each day of theoretical duration for that item. Also, it is quite important that he record the adjusted price (from column 10 of the Preliminary Schedule and Cost Control Summary Sheet) within the space outlined. The contract administrator should then proceed to that line item in whose After column the item number just plotted appears. Beginning in the column representing the first day after the first item plotted ended, the contract administrator should plot the duration of the second item as he did the first, noting the adjusted price for that second item in the space outlined. This procedure should be followed religiously for each item appearing on the Preliminary Schedule and Cost Control Summary Sheet. As he encounters line items with entries in the Concurrent With column, the contract administrator should begin plotting such items in the column representing the same working day in which he plotted the other line items with which the one in question is concurrent. Once all line items have thus been plotted, the contract administrator will have created a theoretical bar chart schedule for the entire project.

Some aspects of the preliminary schedule may require considerable thought. For example, if the specified contract completion date were to be overrun, with the contemplated construction of an item of 100 units that has a productivity rate of 1 unit per day, the contractor might be required to use two or more crews in order to complete the project within the specified time limits. In such a case, the contract administrator should simply note his assumption of "2 crews" within the outline, or "bar," for the given item and only 50 days, not 100 days, would be required. The contract administrator is cautioned, however, not to attempt in his Preliminary Schedule Sheet the degree of sophistication employed by a contractor in balancing total personnel for a given project. The contract administrator should use multiple crews only when they are required to complete the project within the overall time limitations imposed by the contract itself.

SUMMARY

Chapter 4 has explained the means by which the contract administrator can determine the theoretical *timing* of commencement and completion of components of the project by the contractor. Such timing is important because it will enable the contract administrator to negotiate the lump-sum breakdown with the contractor from a position of knowledge and strength. In the next chapter, dealing with the preliminary cash-flow curve, the information developed in Chapters 3 and 4 will be combined to produce a cash-flow projection which can be adjusted to reflect negotiations with the contractor and thus keep the owner's disbursement of interim payments consistent with the value actually added to the project by the contractor during those interim payment periods.

COMPREHENSIVE ILLUSTRATION

A comprehensive illustration of the techniques discussed in this chapter follows. The numbered items below correspond to those construction items identified in the illustration for Chapter 2 and carried forward onto the Preliminary Schedule and Cost Control Summary Sheet of Chapter 3.

1. MOBILIZATION

In Chapter 3, it was explained that mobilization encompasses administrative and physical tasks required of the contractor prior to his starting actual work on the project. Since the cost estimating guide offered little assistance in calculating the time required for such tasks, we suggested an estimate of 4 weeks. Accordingly, the contract administrator should insert the number "20" (representing 20 working days) in the Duration column of the Preliminary Schedule and Cost Control Summary Sheet for this item.

2. HAUL ROAD

The temporary road requires 89 yd^2 of run-of-bank gravel to be installed by a bulldozer. According to the cost estimating guide, a bulldozer can spread and compact 1800 yd^2 per day. Thus the required duration for this construction item is approximately 0.05 working days (i.e., less than ½ hour). However, experience teaches that given the delays inherent in any major construction project, it is wise to round off all durations to the next full day. Thus in the case of the temporary road, the duration should be entered as "1," indicating that a full day will be required for the operation.

3. WATERLINE RELOCATION

By dividing the Quantity column by the Productivity Rate column for each of the four subitems for which entries were made in the waterline relocation component, the contract administrator will derive the following durations:

a. Excavation, 3.4 days (rounded to 4)

b. Pipe installation, 0.875 days (rounded to 1)

c. Tie-in, 1 day (arbitrary allowance)

d. Backfilling, 2.7 days (rounded to 3)

e. No entry

The question remaining to be resolved is, How much time will be required for the entire waterline relocation component? It would seem reasonable to excavate for 3 days, begin laying pipe on the fourth day during completion of excavation, tie in the two areas, and begin backfilling at the same time in other areas.

If these separate tasks were to be conducted in a series, the waterline relocation component would require 9 working days; by "paralleling" as noted above, the contractor could save 2 working days. Accordingly, the contract administrator should complete the Duration column for the four items, but should bracket his entries and note "7" as the duration for the entire component.

4. SHEETPILING, WEST SHAFT

The duration of this component is calculated at 4.4 days, rounded to 5.

5. SHEETPILING, EAST SHAFT

The duration of this activity is estimated at 5.17 days, rounded to 6.

6. OBSERVATION WELLS

The duration of this activity is estimated at 1.5 days, rounded to 2.

7. EXCAVATION OF WEST SHAFT

The duration of this activity is calculated at 1.8 days, rounded to 2.

8. EXCAVATION OF EAST SHAFT

The duration of this activity is calculated at 2.3 days, rounded to 3.

9. DEWATERING

Consideration of this item should be deferred.

10. TUNNEL

a. *Cutting and Bracing of Portal.* It was estimated that this activity would require 2 days for each of the two portals; the contract administrator should enter "4" in the Duration column.

b. *Excavation.* The duration of this activity is calculated at 22.5 days, rounded to 23.

c. *Mucking.* The duration of this activity is calculated at 16.9 days, rounded to 17.

d. *Muck Removal.* Arbitrary allowance for 23 days.

e. *Liner Plate.* Arbitrary allowance for 23 days. The mucking, muck removal, and liner plate installation are constrained by the excavation which will take 23 days. In calculating an overall duration for item 10, it seems safe to assume a duration of 2 days for cutting and bracing plus 23 days for excavation plus 1 day for remaining mucking, muck removal, and liner plate installation. The inherent assumption is that the second portal can be cut and braced during excavation. This reasoning process produces a duration of 26 days for the total tunnel component: the contract administrator should place a bracket around the five subitems and write "26" in the Duration column.

11. INSTALLATION OF PIPE

The duration of this activity is calculated at 11.4 days, rounded to 12.

12. GROUTING

The duration of this activity is calculated at 1 day.

13. BACKFILLING OF SHAFTS

The duration of this activity is calculated at 41.9 days, rounded to 42. Inasmuch as 42 days appears exceptionally lengthy given the other durations, it is proposed to make the calculation using two crews, one in each shaft to cut down the total duration period. Since the east shaft is the larger of the two, its duration should control. Thus the overall duration of the project should be entered at 26.5 days, rounded to 27.

14. INSTALLATION OF RIPRAP

The duration of this activity is calculated at 2 days.

15. CLEANUP AND DEMOBILIZATION

Arbitrary allowance of 5 days.

The one item which remains for consideration is dewatering. The contract administrator should now realize that dewatering will be necessary during tunneling, grouting, and installation of pipe. These items total 39 days, and "39" should be entered in the Duration column for dewatering.

PRELIMINARY SCHEDULE AND COST CONTROL SUMMARY SHEET

The contract administrator's next task is to complete the three "sequence" columns of the Preliminary Schedule and Cost Control Summary Sheet. The first item for consideration is mobilization. In the interest of simplicity, it should be assumed that mobilization in this project must be completed prior to commencement of other construction components. Thus in the Before column of the sheet on the mobilization components line, the word "all" should be entered.

The next construction component is the construction of the temporary road. Although it would be possible to begin driving of sheetpiling for the west shaft at the same time as construction of the temporary road was commenced, it seems likely that the contractor would be reluctant to commence those operations simultaneously. Accordingly, the number "1" representing the numbered entry for mobilization should be entered in the After column on the temporary road line of the Preliminary Schedule and Cost Control Summary Sheet. In other words, the entry indicates that item 2 (the temporary road) will occur immediately after completion of item 1 (mobilization). The Before and Concurrent With columns should be left blank at this time.

The third construction phase could include installation of the observation wells and relocation of the waterline once the contractor has access to the site via the temporary road. Although sheetpiling in the west shaft could be commenced simultaneously, it would seem wise to defer that operation until completion of the observation wells for two reasons: (1) data from the observation wells will be available during sheeting operations and (2) the complication of three, rather than two, simultaneous operations will be avoided. The number "2" should be entered in the After column for both observation wells and waterline relocation. In the Concurrent With column for waterline relocation, the contract administrator should write "6," which is the item number for the observation wells; conversely, he should enter the number "3" in the Concurrent With column of the observation well item line. The observation wells are scheduled to be completed in 2 days. The waterline relocation work should be well in progress in 2 days. Thus it seems reasonable to commence sheetpiling in the west shaft on the day after completion of the observation wells. Thus the number "6" should be entered in the After column for the sheetpiling, west shaft. Inasmuch as the waterline relocation will be continuing, the contract administrator should write "3" in the Concurrent With column for the sheetpiling, west shaft. The other column on that line should be left blank at present.

The excavation for the west shaft could begin as soon as the sheetpiling in the west shaft has been completed. Thus the contract administrator should enter "4" in the After column before excavation, west shaft, which is item 7. The other column should be left blank at present.

Commencement of the sheetpiling for the east shaft is constrained by completion of the waterline relocation. Also, it would seem reasonable that the contractor would prefer to move the crew from driving the sheetpiling in the west shaft to the east shaft rather than mobilize another crew for such a small item. Accordingly, the numbers "3" and "4" should be entered in the After column for item 5 (sheetpiling, east shaft).

Dewatering operations should commence at about the time of completion of the excavation of the east shaft. Thus the number "8" should be entered in the After column for item 9 (dewatering).

Excavation in the east shaft could begin as soon as the sheetpiling for the east shaft is complete. Thus the number "5" should be entered in the After column for item 8.

Tunneling would proceed, in all probability, from the east shaft only. This tunneling could begin as soon as the excavation of the east shaft was complete. Accordingly, the number "8" should be entered in the After column for item 10. We will assume the tunneling operation will take place on a basis of 24 hours per day, 5 days per week.

The 96-in. pipe would be installed immediately upon completion of the tunnel. Thus the number "10" should be entered in the After column for item 11.

Grouting would be commenced upon completion of the installation of the 96-in. pipe. Accordingly, the number "11" should be entered in the After column for item 12.

The dewatering would be halted upon the completion of the grouting. Hence the number "12" would be entered in the Before column for item 9 (dewatering).

Both shafts would be backfilled after the grouting; the number "12" should be entered in the After column for item 13.

Riprap could be installed after the west shaft is backfilled; the number "13" should be entered in the After column for item 14.

Cleanup and demobilization could occur after the placement of riprap on the west side. Thus the number "14" should be entered in the After column for item 15.

The contract administrator should then check his rationale in the completion of the After and Concurrent With columns by considering what the item he is considering is restricting from happening and then fill in the Before column.

This process will produce the completed Preliminary Schedule and Cost Control Summary Sheet as shown in Figure 4-1.

PRELIMINARY SCHEDULE SHEET

Having determined the duration and sequences of the various construction components, the contract administrator is now prepared to create the Preliminary Schedule Sheet, which takes the form of a bar chart. Inasmuch as the duration of this tunnel project is short in comparison with the usual construction project, it is suggested that the units of schedule measurement be stated by the week rather than the month. This bar chart—or any other type of schedule, for that matter—will be nothing more than a graphic representation of the data developed and presented verbally in the preceding pages. Each horizontal line will represent a construction activity, each vertical division 1 working day. Completion of the Preliminary Schedule Sheet contemplates merely a description of each construction component and creation of a "bar" to denote the beginning and end of that construction activity.

This task should not be unmanageable giving the contract administrator's now well-developed expertise with the contract and the project. A completed Preliminary Schedule Sheet for the project, as hypothesized by the contract administrator, is shown in Figure 4-2.

PRELIMINARY SCHEDULE AND COST CONTROL SUMMARY SHEET

Item No. (1)	Description (2)	Quantity (3)	Unit (4)	Estimating Guide Data — Unit (5)	Material Price (6)	Labor Price (7)	Total Price [(6)+(7)] (8)	Total Cost [(3)×(8)] (9)	Adjusted Total Cost [(9)×factor] (10)	Productivity Rate (11)	Productivity Unit (12)	Duration (Days) (13)	Before (14)	Concurrent With (15)	After (16)
1	Mobilization	L.S.	—	—	—	—	—	12,065	17,115	Allow		20	All,2	0	0
2	Haul Road	89.	yd²	yd²	1.25	0.22	1.47	131	186	1800	yd²/day	1	3,6	0	1
3	Waterline relocation												5	6	2
3a	Excavation	68.	yd³	yd³	0	1.30	1.30	88	125	20	yd³/day	4	5	6	2
3b	Pipe installation	105	lin ft	lin ft	15.75	3.00	18.75	1,969	2,793	120	lin ft/day	1 ⎱			
3c	Tie-in	L.S.	Allow	—	—	—	—	500	709	Allow	—	1 ⎰ 7			
3d	Backfill	55.8	yd³	yd³	—	3.55	3.55	198	281	20.6	yd³/day	3 ⎰			
4	Sheetpiling, west shaft	5269.1	ft²	ft²	6.85	1.50	8.35	43,998	62,415	1200	ft²/day	5	5,7	3	6
5	Sheetpiling, east shaft	6205.2	ft²	ft²	6.85	1.50	8.35	51,813	73,501	1200	ft²/day	6	8	7	3&4
6	Observation wells	60	lin ft	lin ft	5.50	5.50	11.00	660	936	40	lin ft/day	2	4	3	2
7	Excavation, west shaft	493.5	yd³	yd³	0.76	0.64	1.40	691	980	280	yd³/day	2	8	8	4
8	Excavation, east shaft	635.2	yd³	yd³	0.76	0.64	1.40	889	1,251	280	yd³/day	3	9,10	0	5
9	Dewatering	39	24-h day	24-h day	—	—	750.00	29,250	41,493	—	—	39	12	10,11,12	8
10	Tunnel														
10a	Cut & brace portals	4	Worker day	Worker day	37.50	800.00	837.50	3,350	4,752	Allow	—	4 ⎱			
10b	Excavation	404.1	yd³	yd³	—	24.25	24.25	9,799	13,901	Allow	—	23 ⎰			
10c	Mucking	404.1	yd³	yd³	—	12.55	12.55	5,071	7,194	Allow	—	17 ⎰ 26	12	9	8
10d	Muck removal	23	24-h day	24-h day	—	—	3000.00	69,000	97,882	Allow	—	23			
10e	Liner plate	126	lin ft	lin ft	109.09	131.95	241.04	30,371	43,084	Allow	—	23			
11	Install 96-in. pipe	227.67	lin ft	lin ft	110.00	38.00	148.00	33,695	47,800	20	lin ft/day	12			
12	Grouting	150	yd³	yd³	35.00	7.50	42.50	6,375	9,043	150	yd³/day	1			
13	Backfill shafts	1004.9	yd³	yd³	—	8.30	8.30	8,341	11,832	24	yd³/day	27			
14	Riprap	100	yd²	yd²	9.00	15.40	24.40	2,440	3,461	50	yd²/day	2			
15	Cleanup & Demobilization	L.S.	—	—	—	—	3000.00	3,000	4,256	Allow	—	5			

Total cost, excluding mobilization $301,629

Say 4% for mobilization = $301,629 × 0.04 = $12,065

Total estimated project cost = $301,629 + 12,065 = $313,694

Adjusted cost factor = bid price ÷ total estimated project cost = $\dfrac{\$445,000}{\$313,694} = 1.419$

FIGURE 4-1   Sample of completed Preliminary Schedule and Cost Control Summary Sheet.

Item No.	Description	Week 1 (1–5)	Week 2 (6–10)	Week 3 (11–15)	Week 4 (16–20)	Week 5 (21–25)	Week 6 (26–30)	Week 7 (31–35)	Week 8 (36–40)	Week 9 (41–45)	Week 10 (46–50)
1	Mobilization		$17,115								
2	Haul road					$186					
3	Waterline relocation					$3908					
4	Sheetpiling, west shaft					$62,415					
5	Sheetpiling, east shaft							$73,501			
6	Observation wells					$936					
7	Excavation, west shaft						$980				
8	Excavation, east shaft								$1261		
9	Dewatering									$41,493	
10	Tunnel									$166,812	
11	96-in. pipe										
12	Grouting										
13	Backfill shafts										
14	Riprap										
15	Cleanup and demobilization										

Week 11	Week 12	Week 13	Week 14	Week 15	Week 16	Week 17	Week 18	Week 19	Week 20	Week 21	Week 22
51 52 53 54 55	56 57 58 59 60	61 62 63 64 65	66 67 68 69 70	71 72 73 74 75	76 77 78 79 80	81 82 83 84 85	86 87 88 89 90	91 92 93 94 95	96 97 98 99 100	101 102 103 104 105	106 107 108 109 110

$41,493

$166,812

$47,800

$9,048

$11,832

$3461

$4256

FIGURE 4-2 Completed Preliminary Schedule Sheet.

CHAPTER 5

THE PRELIMINARY
CASH-FLOW CURVE

In Chapter 2, the contract administrator was encouraged to set down alternative theoretical construction sequences for the project in question. In Chapter 3, procedures were illustrated for developing a preliminary cost estimate through the theoretical pricing of the labor and material components of the project. In Chapter 4, a model preliminary schedule for the project was developed by abstraction from a cost estimating guide data concerning productivity rates and estimates of quantities required. Thus procedures explained in the three preceding chapters have permitted the contract administrator to *theorize* concerning the *sequence*, *cost*, and *timing* of construction.

During this process, two ties have been made between the theory developed by the contract administrator and the reality of the contract. First, the contract administrator's theoretical cost for each construction element was adjusted by multiplying that cost by a fraction, the numerator of which was the actual cost for the project (the contractor's bid price) and the denominator of which was the theoretical cost as estimated by the contract administrator. Second, the contract administrator's theoretical preliminary schedule was adjusted, if necessary, to meet the overall time constraints imposed by the contract. With the exception of these two adjustments, however, the results of the sequence, cost, and timing exercises remain *theoretical*. Considerations such as weather delays and delivery times for equipment and materials have not been taken into account; at this point, such matters are to be regarded as the concern of the contractor, not the contract administrator.

The theoretical exercises of the preceding chapters will be continued in this chapter toward the development of a preliminary cash-flow curve for the project. The contract administrator is cautioned to devote adequate time and concentration to these matters, for theory and reality will be joined in Chapter 6 when he meets the contractor to negotiate the lump-sum breakdown for the project.

The purpose of this chapter is to explain development of a theoretical preliminary cash-flow curve for a given project. This curve will be used by the contract administrator to:

1. Check the accuracy of his theoretical preliminary cost estimate and preliminary schedule

2. Provide a preliminary indication of expected rates of expenditure by the Owner

3. Provide a basis for analysis of the contractor's proposed lump-sum breakdown

4. Permit development of an *actual* cash-flow curve by which the contractor's performance may be gauged at any point in the project

Development of the actual cash-flow curve necessarily awaits submittal by the contractor of his project schedule and proposed lump-sum breakdown. Under most contracts, the project schedule is the sole responsibility of the contractor; the lump-sum breakdown, however, is a matter for negotiation usually between the contractor and the contract administrator. The preliminary cash-flow curve is a valuable tool to the contract administrator in these negotiations inasmuch as it provides a guide by which the time-materials-value relationships proposed by the contractor may be evaluated.

DEVELOPING THE PRELIMINARY CASH-FLOW CURVE

Statistical Considerations

Explanations set forth in this chapter will involve use of certain statistical concepts not previously addressed in this book. However, a comprehensive discussion of statistical techniques is both beyond the scope of this work and unnecessary for the purposes of this work: to master the procedures, systems, and techniques set forth herein, the contract administrator need understand only the most basic statistical concepts.

Ideally, the rate of expenditure by the owner for a given construction project would follow the "normal probability curve."

It is axiomatic that the larger the project, the more closely the actual curve would follow the theoretical curve. Hence the actual curve of a project valued at $100 million would be expected to resemble more closely the theoretical curve than would the actual curve of a project valued at $1 million. It is essential that the contract administrator keep the size of the project in mind when analyzing the preliminary cash-flow curve generated for a given project.

The preliminary cash-flow curve is nothing more than a graphic representation of proportionate project monies expended in relation to proportionate project time expired. The x coordinate, or abscissa (the horizontal axis of the graph), will be used to plot the period of time, in months, required to complete the project. The y coordinate, or ordinate (the vertical axis), will be used to indicate the percentage of the owner's accumulative total cost of the project. It follows that the contract administrator will be able to determine theoretical cumulative cost of the project at any time—once the cash-flow curve is generated—by plotting the appropriate project time on the abscissa, moving vertically from that point to intercept the cash-flow curve, and proceeding horizontally to determine the appropriate dollar amount indicated on the ordinate.

A graphic tabulation of proportionate project monies expended in relation to elapsed time is shown in Figure 5-1.

This theoretical curve supports several inferences. First, one may assume that the rate of expenditure for most construction projects will be very low at the beginning. Such an inference would seem consistent with experience, given the contractor's need to order materials, await deliveries, and mobilize his on-site forces among other things. Second, one might infer that in most projects the rate of expenditures from the point where the project is 25 percent complete (in terms of the project duration) through the point where the project is 75 percent complete

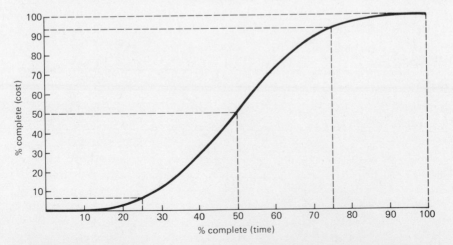

FIGURE 5-1 Probable percentage of total project cost expended at any time during the project as a percentage of the total project duration.

will be approximately uniform. This would also seem consistent with experience: this is the time in the project when work is seriously underway, minor preparatory work has been completed, short-term deliveries have been received, late deliveries have been offset by early deliveries of other items, and, in most cases, the contractor has been able to adjust his construction effort to meet such minor challenges without significantly affecting the projected incorporation of value into the project—and thus the projected rate of cash flow. Third, one may reasonably infer from the theoretical curve that the remaining quarter of the project time may be required to complete the last 6.7 percent of the total addition of value to, and corresponding cash-flow for, the project. By the time the project is 75 percent complete, it is likely that the large concrete pours will have been completed, the expensive equipment will have been installed, and the contractor will be engaged in such tasks as testing equipment and instrumentation, punch-list items, and general restoration. Such items, although time consuming, are relatively low-dollar-return construction items for the contractor.

As noted above, the smaller the project, the more likely that the theoretical and actual curves will vary. It should quickly be added, however, that in many cases, even a rough correspondence between the two will be sufficient. Analysis of a smaller project would begin with the presumption that approximately 7 percent of the owner's total cost would be expended by the time the project was 25 percent complete and that approximately 93 percent of the cost would be expended by the time the project was 75 percent complete. With that generalization in mind, the contract administrator could employ a straight edge to generate an approximate cash flow curve, as seen in Figure 5-2.

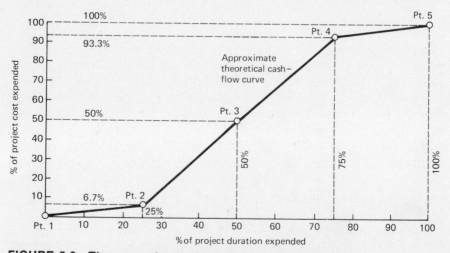

FIGURE 5-2 The approximate theoretical cash-flow curve.

Generation of the Curve

To generate an exact curve, it is necessary that the contract administrator redirect his attention to the preliminary schedule, the generation
of which was discussed at length in Chapter 4. The contract administrator will recall that each horizontal line on the Preliminary Schedule
Sheet (Figure 4-2) represents a construction component to be undertaken by the contractor over a period of time and that each vertical line
on the preliminary schedule represents 1 *working* day. He should also
recall that the dollar amount for a given item, adjusted to correspond to
the actual contract price, is stated for each item of construction within
the time block, or "bar," for that item. In order to make the necessary
conversion from "working days" in the preliminary schedule to
"month" in the preliminary cash-flow curve, the contract administrator
should divide working days by 22, the average number of working days
contained a calendar month. This division may be easily accomplished
by counting over 22 columns on the Preliminary Schedule Sheet, drawing a heavy vertical line, then repeating the process until the entire
preliminary schedule has been divided into "working-day months."

The next step is to add the dollar amount of each construction item
shown on the preliminary schedule for each such month. If a construction item involves more than 1 working-day month, the contract administrator should apportion the dollar amount for that item in accordance with the relative number of days involving work on the item
during each such month. Once the total dollar amount for each month
of construction has been determined for each item, the contract administrator should tabulate the *cumulative* total expenditures for *all*
items for each month. The contract administrator should then add the
total dollar amount of the first month to that of the second and, noting
the cumulative total under the second month, add that cumulative total
to the expenditure for the third month, noting the sum under the third
month, and continuing this process until the accumulative total for
each month has been determined. It is most important that the cumulative total for the last month equal the total contract price; if it does not,
the contract administrator should check his work first for mathematical,
then conceptual, errors.

The next step is to plot the cumulative total expenditures for each
month on graph paper, using an abscissa of construction months and
an ordinate of accumulative dollar amounts. Once this task has been
completed, the contract administrator should, using a pencil of another
color, superimpose the approximate theoretical curve on the page. He
should then compare the two graphs at length, attempting to account
for any pronounced variations between the theoretical curve and the
curve plotted from the preliminary cost estimate and preliminary

schedule. If he finds significant variations which are inexplicable, the contract administrator should review the preliminary schedule with a view toward resolving these variations by adjusting crew sizes—and hence the duration of the project. He may also wish to review those dollar amounts set forth in the preliminary cost estimate, in which he had the least confidence when generating that document, and make the necessary adjustments. He should make any and all adjustments—first to the preliminary schedule, then to the preliminary cost estimate—necessary to resolve major variations between the two curves which cannot be explained away. The contract administrator should then revise his plotted cash-flow curve to reflect any adjustment.

The phase of the project in which the need for such adjustments is most likely to appear is the last 25 percent of the project. Contract administrators often attempt to assign too many construction items to this period of time. It is worth noting that contractors are inclined to make the same mistake by deferring resolution of too many project problems to the last quarter.

SUMMARY

The preliminary cash-flow curve, generated and adjusted in accordance with the procedures set forth in this chapter, should equip the contract administrator with sufficient information to protect the owner's interest in negotiating the lump-sum breakdown with the contractor. In preparing the curve, the contract administrator has begun the mating of theory and reality in such a manner as best to prepare himself for the difficult task of administering interim payments both in furtherance of the project and in fairness to the participants.

COMPREHENSIVE ILLUSTRATION

The comprehensive illustration of this chapter follows the development of a preliminary cash-flow curve for the tunnel project. Due to the relatively short duration of the tunnel project, plotting of the cash-flow curve will be undertaken by the week rather than by the month.

The first step in construction of the preliminary cash-flow curve for the project is to determine the daily expenditure for each construction activity. This can be done by dividing the adjusted total cost for the construction activity, as it appears on the Preliminary Schedule and Cost Control Summary Sheet, by the duration for that construction activity as shown in Figure 5-3.

Item No.	Adjusted Total Cost	Duration (Days)	Daily Expenditure
1	$ 17,115	20	$ 856
2	186	1	186
3	3,908	7	558
4	62,415	5	12,483
5	73,501	6	12,250
6	936	2	468
7	980	2	490
8	1,261	3	420
9	41,493	39	1,064
10	166,813	26	6,416
11	47,800	12	3,983
12	9,043	1	9,043
13	11,832	27	438
14	3,461	2	1,730
15	4,256	5	851

FIGURE 5-3 The daily expenditure for each construction activity.

Using the above cost per day for each activity, the contract administrator should summarize the total cost per *week* for the project by referring to his Preliminary Schedule Sheet to determine which activities will occur each week of the project as shown in Figure 5-4.

The next step is to plot the cumulative weekly expenditure by the week in order to generate the preliminary cash-flow curve. After this plotting, the contract administrator should look at the general shape of the curve. In this case, it looks close to the cumulative plot of the theoretical probability curve, which is encouraging. Next, he should plot the approximation of the *theoretical* curve on the same graph: 6.7 percent of the project cost should be expended at the end of the first quarter of the project duration and 93.3 percent at the end of the third quarter of the project. Using a 22 week duration

$$22 \text{ weeks} \times \frac{1}{4} = \text{Week } 5\frac{1}{2}$$

$$6.7\% \times 445,000 = \$29,815$$

The point ($29,815, Week 5½) should be plotted, and a straight line should be drawn from the origin to it.

$$22 \text{ weeks} \times \frac{3}{4} = \text{Week } 16\frac{1}{2}$$

$$93.3\% \times 445,000 = \$415,185.$$

The point ($415,185, Week 16½) should be plotted, and a straight line should be drawn to the final project cost, $445,000 at Week 22.

Week No.	Con-struction Activities	Daily Cost	Days of Activity in Week	Total Weekly Cost	Cumulative Weekly Cost
1	1	856	5	$ 4,280	$ 4,280
2	1	856	5	4,280	8,560
3	1	856	5	4,280	12,840
4	1	856	5	4,280	17,120
5	2	186	1	186	
	3	558	4	2,232	
	4	12,483	2	24,966	
	6	468	2	936	
			Total	28,320	45,440
6	3	554	3	1,674	
	4	12,483	3	37,449	
	5	12,250	2	24,500	
	7	490	2	980	
			Total	64,603	110,043
7	5	12,250	4	49,000	
	8	420	1	420	
			Total	49,420	159,463
8	8	420	2	840	
	9	1,064	3	3,192	
	10	6,416	3	19,248	
			Total	23,280	182,748
9	9	1,064	5	5,320	
	10	6,416	5	32,080	
			Total	37,400	220,148
10	9	1,064	5	5,320	
	10	6,416	5	32,080	
			Total	37,400	257,548
11	9	1,064	5	5,320	
	10	6,416	5	32,080	
			Total	37,400	294,948
12	9	1,064	5	5,320	
	10	6,416	5	32,080	
			Total	37,400	332,348
13	9	1,064	5	5,320	
	10	6,416	3	19,248	
	11	3,983	2	7,966	
			Total	32,534	364,882
14	9	1,064	5	5,320	
	11	3,983	5	19,915	
			Total	25,235	390,117

Week No.	Con-struction Activities	Daily Cost	Days of Activity in Week	Total Weekly Cost	Cumulative Weekly Cost
15	9	1,064	5	5,320	
	11	3,983	5	19,915	
			Total	25,235	415,352
16	9	1,064	1	1,064	
	12	9,043	1	9,043	
	13	438	4	1,752	
			Total	11,859	407,211
17	13	438	5	2,190	429,401
18	13	438	5	2,190	431,591
19	13	438	5	2,190	433,780
20	13	438	5	2,190	435,971
21	13	438	3	1,314	
	14	1,730	2	3,460	
			Total	4,774	440,745
22	15	851	5	4,255	445,000

FIGURE 5-4 The cumulative weekly expenditure for all scheduled construction activities.

The contract administrator's next task is to sketch his preliminary cash-flow curve in such a way that it ties in at $445,000 to remove any discrepancies between the contractor's bid price and the contract administrator's earlier estimates. In Figure 5-5, the two curves match quite well. This is encouraging—especially since the project is relatively small.

A comparison of the two curves supports the inference either that mobilization will take about 6 weeks, not 4, or the estimate for the cost of item 4, sheetpiling, is too high; item 4 affects the slope of the curve the most. On the whole, the contract administrator could be quite satisfied that his estimated costs and sequence of construction activities are realistic. They may not be exact, but they are probable.

It is interesting to note that, since the contract administrator has allowed 4 weeks for mobilization, the entire curve appears to the left of the theoretical curve. This would not necessarily mean that an estimate of 4 weeks for mobilization is an error; perhaps that is all the time which would be required. It does mean, however, that the estimate is less probable than 6 weeks.

Based on the preliminary cash-flow curve, the contract administrator now has sufficient background and confidence in "costing" and scheduling the project to discuss the lump-sum breakdown with the contractor.

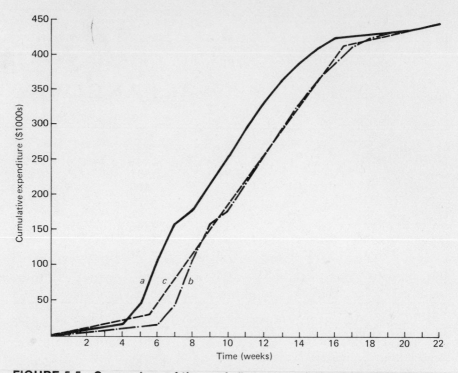

FIGURE 5-5 Comparison of the cash-flow curve derived from the Preliminary Schedule and Cost Control Summary Sheet for a (a) 4-week and a (b) 6-week mobilization to the (c) approximate theoretical cash-flow curve.

CHAPTER 6

THE LUMP-SUM BREAKDOWN

With the preliminary cash-flow curve in hand, the contract administrator now approaches his first negotiations with the contractor. Up to this point, the contract administrator's development of contract controls, undertaken virtually independent of the contractor, has had two goals: to become familiar with the contract and to prepare for the negotiations which are the subject of this chapter.

The "lump-sum breakdown" for the project is merely an allocation of the total contract price among the various components of the project as determined through negotiation between the contract administrator and the contractor. In the typical lump-sum contract, the contractor has committed himself by bid or proposal to construct the project in question for a given price. Most such projects are of sufficient duration that if the owner did not make any partial payments for work completed during the course of the project, the contractor would be required to finance temporarily all or most of the project and to factor the projected cost of this financing into his initial price. It may well be that the owner itself will be required to borrow in order to make interim payments to the contractor; however, it is probable that the owner will be able to do its borrowing, if any, on a far more favorable basis than the contractor. Since the costs of financing will, in any event, ultimately accrue to the owner, it is to the owner's advantage to minimize those costs by paying the contractor in proportion to the value added by the contractor to the project during its respective stages. Interim payments also have the important benefit to the owner of maintaining the contractor's attention to the need for steady progress and satisfactory workmanship. The formula by which these partial payments are to be determined is called the lump-sum breakdown.

It is critical to the success of the project that the contract administrator emerge from these negotiations with an analytically correct lump-sum breakdown which is equitable both to the owner and to the contractor. A lump-sum breakdown weighted too heavily in favor of the owner may place such burdens upon the contractor that he will be unable to complete the project; on the other hand, a lump-sum breakdown weighted too heavily in favor of the contractor may result in his receiving too much money too soon and a diminution of his interest in completing the project satisfactorily. It is *not* enough that the contract administrator strike this difficult balance at a *theoretical* level: he must establish "benchmarks" such that the contractor's completion of a project component will be readily determinable by *all* concerned participants.

The purposes of this chapter are to provide a method by which an acceptable lump-sum breakdown can be negotiated between the contract administrator and the contractor and to establish within that breakdown the divisions of work cutting across the various labor and material components of the project necessary to establish an effective cost control system.

DEVELOPING THE LUMP-SUM BREAKDOWN

The Preliminary Schedule and Cost Control Summary Sheet

The contract administrator should begin by reviewing his Preliminary Schedule and Cost Control Summary Sheets, noting the most expensive items. He should then attempt to envision methods by which the quantities of these major items could be effectively monitored during the course of the project. For example, concrete might be a major item. The task would then be to develop a means by which the quantity of concrete incorporated into the project at any given time might easily be determined. The contract administrator would, by reference to his preliminary cost estimate, know the approximate quantities of concrete to be incorporated into each component of the project. If he were to know how much concrete had been *poured in given structures* at any given time during the project, he could accurately estimate the quantity of concrete incorporated into the *entire project* at any given time and to recommend that the appropriate payment be made by the owner to the contractor. If, on the other hand, the concrete were being *supplied* to the contractor, these quantities could be determined by mere addition of delivery tickets, unless the contract administrator had reason to doubt their veracity. Thus whether the contractor in a given project is supplying the concrete directly or merely taking delivery from a supplier, the contract administrator will have a clear means of determining the amount of concrete added to the project at any given point.

Another example may be useful: If the cost of concrete is significant in the project, the cost of reinforcing steel may also be significant and therefore worthy of special consideration in the lump-sum breakdown. There are several methods by which the amount of reinforcing steel incorporated into the project at any given point may be monitored; the method chosen would probably be determined by the size of the project. First, as in the case of the concrete itself, it is possible to determine the quantity of reinforcing steel needed for each structure in the project or portion of each structure and to make interim payments for quantities actually installed during a given period. Second, it is possible to divide the total poundage of reinforcing steel required in the project by the total volume of concrete required in the project and to pay the contractor a pro rata payment for reinforcing steel based upon the units of concrete observed to be incorporated or computed from delivery tickets. Similarly, it is possible to make pro rata allowances for other items—such as form work, stripping forms, and finishing—directly related to the installation of concrete. Indeed, it is possible to come up with one cost per unit of concrete which encompasses all these items. If the quantity of concrete required in the project is relatively small, the contractor will probably agree to such an all-encompassing lump-sum breakdown item for concrete. However, where large amounts of concrete are required, this general approach might be unacceptable to the contractor because his scheme of work might be to install large amounts of reinforcing steel and form work well in advance of pouring of concrete; in that event, the all-encompassing approach would adversely affect the contractor, inasmuch as he could not expect payment for the reinforcing steel or form work until the concrete had, in fact, been poured.

The overriding point is that each item within the lump-sum breakdown must be considered on its own merits in the context of the project being reviewed. It follows, then, that the next task of the contract administrator is to decide what lump-sum breakdown items should be requested from the contractor and how their quantities can be monitored as they are incorporated into the work of the project. In performing this task, the following procedure is recommended.

Identification of Key Lump-Sum Items

The contract administrator should first examine the construction components of the preliminary cost estimate, compiling a list of those components which have costs equal to or exceeding 1 percent of the contract price. Smaller components should then be listed as subparts of the appropriate major components. This approach will result in a list of lump-sum breakdown items not exceeding 100 in any event and, in all probability, not exceeding 50, since many components (with minor components added as subparts) will have costs substantially in excess of 1 percent of the contract price.

Second, the contract administrator should request that the contractor submit *his* proposed lump-sum breakdown prices for those components he considers "significant" (as defined above) and assigning the costs of "insignificant" components to the appropriate significant components. He should also request that the contractor itemize the material cost and labor cost for each such significant component and state the quantities he has calculated for each such component.

Third, the contract administrator should request that the contractor submit his project schedule.

Fourth, upon receipt of the contractor's proposed lump-sum breakdown and project schedule, the contract administrator should plot the cash-flow curve from these two documents and compare this curve to both the contract administrator's preliminary cash-flow curve and the theoretical cash-flow curve previously generated for the project. For ease of comparison, the three curves may be plotted on the same sheet. If the contractor's cash-flow curve lies to the *left* of the preliminary cash-flow curve generated by the contract administrator, there is a possibility that the contractor is attempting to "front-end" the project. In other words, the contractor may be trying to maximize partial payment for work completed at the beginning of the project in order to reduce the amount of money he must invest or borrow. Put still another way, the contractor may be attempting to receive payments from the owner in excess of the value actually added to the project during its early stages.

It should be pointed out that front ending is not necessarily an evil to the owner. In some cases, it is actually to the owner's advantage to allow front ending. In a *negotiated* industrial contract, where the contractor must pay his lender for the time value of the money borrowed, the owner may *prefer* to make prepayments to the contractor in order to avoid the contractor's cost of money being passed on to the owner.

For the purposes of this book, however, it will be assumed that the contractor included in the price bid or quoted an amount sufficient to cover the time value of money obtained by him from lenders to sustain him until receipt of partial payment from the owner. Thus it will be assumed that the owner has, by agreement to the contractor's contract price, already agreed to reimburse the contractor's cost of money and should not be required to bear this cost twice by reason of the contractor's front ending. Given these assumptions, the objective inherent in this fourth step of the lump-sum breakdown procedure will be to eliminate front-ending.

Interpretation of Findings

There are two basic reasons for the contractor's cash-flow curve lying to the *left* of the contract administrator's cash-flow curve. The first is that the contractor has scheduled the work in question to be undertaken earlier than the time when it has been scheduled in the contract administrator's theoretical scheme. The second is that the contractor has assigned higher unit prices or more units than the contract administrator for items of work to be undertaken early in the project and, conversely, lower unit prices or fewer units than the contract administrator for items of work to be undertaken late in the project. In the first contingency—a mere difference in schedule—there is relatively little risk to the owner's interest. This is merely a case of difference of opinion remaining to be resolved by the actual progress of the project. If the contractor is correct in his belief that certain items of work will be undertaken prior to the time that the contract administrator believes they will be undertaken, he will be paid for the work as completed. If, on the other hand, the contract administrator is correct, and the work is not completed in accordance with the contractor's schedule, the interim payment to the contractor will be delayed until actual completion of the work. In either case, there will be no front ending. It has been our experience that most contractors are optimistic in their scheduling, but this optimism is reflected uniformly throughout the construction schedule, with the result that front ending is most often reduced or eliminated.

However, the sophistication of those contractors who *do* set out to front-end the costs of projects should not be lost upon the contract administrator. The usual method of front ending is to increase the lump-sum breakdown price proposal for items of work to be undertaken early in the project. In such event, reference to the preliminary cost estimate and comparison of it with the contractor's proposed lump-sum breakdown prices will readily provide to the contract administrator a list of searching questions to address to the contractor. Some contractors also attempt to misschedule items with higher-proposed lump-sum breakdown prices than normal in the later stages of the project, then perform those items at earlier dates. If the cost of these items relative to the other items in the project is inaccurate, front ending can occur. It follows that the contract administrator will be well advised to review all costs—even those which do not appear to affect the cash-flow curve with regard to front ending.

Negotiation of the Lump-Sum Breakdown

At the completion of this four-step procedure, the contract adminis-trator will have developed a list of matters to discuss with the contrac-tor concerning the contractor's proposed costs for lump-sum break-down items. Although the contract administrator lacks authority to change the contractor's project schedule, he retains the ability to ques-tion the contractor's lump-sum breakdown price proposal and enter into whatever negotiations are required to bring the prices into line with the schedule. The contract administrator should enter these negotiations with an open mind and mindful of his own fallibility, but should adopt a posture that it is the contractor's responsibility to point out the errors, if any, of the contract administrator.

Once the negotiations have been completed, any agreed-upon changes to the lump-sum breakdown prices proposed by the contractor should be charted on a revised cash-flow curve, and any significant variances between the revised cash-flow curve and the theoretical cash-flow curve should be explainable by reference to factors such as weather, delivery dates, etc., which have not been previously con-sidered.

Having completed the lump-sum breakdown negotiations with the contractor and generated a revised cash-flow curve, the contract ad-ministrator should have a thorough understanding of the schedule and cash-flow requirements of the project. All that remains in the estab-lishment of basic contract controls at this point is the incorporation of several controls into one document—called the Integrated Schedule Sheet—which is the subject of Chapter 7.

COMPREHENSIVE ILLUSTRATION

The contract administrator's first task in the negotiation of the lump-sum breakdown is to reach an agreement with the contractor as to what major construction components, or items, will be used. The number of these major components can be reduced by including only those with values in excess of a given percentage of the contract price. Using a 1 percent criterion, the contract administrator would derive fifteen such components in the tunnel example set forth in the preceding chapters. The monitoring of these fifteen should present no significant problems to the contract administrator, especially since no more than two are scheduled to occur on any given day.

Once agreement concerning these components has been reached, the contract administrator and the contractor must arrive at a joint decision as to the unit of measurement for each. The units stated in the prelimi-

TABLE 6-1 Proposed Payment Units

Item no.	Description	Unit
1	Mobilization	Lump sum
2	Haul road	Square yard
3	Waterline relocation	
	(a) Excavation	Cubic yard
	(b) Pipe installation	Linear foot
	(c) Tie-in	Lump sum
	(d) Backfill	Cubic yard
4	Sheetpiling, west shaft	Square foot
5	Sheetpiling, east shaft	Square foot
6	Observation wells	Vertical linear foot
7	Excavation, west shaft	Cubic yard
8	Excavation, east shaft	Cubic yard
9	Dewatering	Calendar day
10	Tunneling	
	(a) Cut and brace portals	Worker day
	(b) Excavation	Cubic yard
	(c) Mucking	Cubic yard
	(d) Muck removal	Cubic yard
	(e) Liner plate	Linear foot
11	Install 96-in. pipe	Linear foot
12	Grouting	Cubic yard
13	Backfill shafts	Cubic yard
14	Riprap	Square yard
15	Cleanup and demobilization	Lump sum

nary cost estimate (Chapter 3) should probably, although not necessarily, be employed. Table 6-1 is a listing of the construction items and their probable units of measurement (taken from the Preliminary Schedule and Cost Control Summary Sheet).

The appropriateness of these units of measurement for each item of construction in the lump-sum breakdown will now be considered.

1. MOBILIZATION—LUMP SUM

The purpose of having a lump-sum breakdown item for mobilization is to provide reimbursement to the contractor as soon as possible (without front ending) for initial administrative and physical costs. The preliminary cash-flow curve indicates that a lump-sum payment at the end of the first month after the signing of the contract would not constitute front ending. Therefore, the payment unit should remain the same as the estimating unit—lump sum, i.e., payable about 1 month after the signing of the contract.

2. HAUL ROAD—SQUARE YARD

When scheduling the time required to install the haul road, it was noted a bulldozer could level and compact the road in a half hour. It would be a waste of time to measure the number of square yards of surface area and pay for the road in this manner. Thus the estimating unit of square yards should be changed to a payment unit of lump sum. In other words, the contractor should be paid for the entire road once it is completed.

3. WATERLINE RELOCATION—4 ESTIMATING UNITS

The waterline relocation is composed of four separate estimate units. The cost of the relocation was estimated by adding (1) the cost of excavation per cubic yard of excavation, (2) the cost of the pipe and its installation per linear foot of pipe, and (3) the cost of backfilling the pipe trench per cubic yard of backfill required. The costs to tie the new pipe line into the old line were then added to that total. With the exception of the tie-in costs, these costs are directly related to the length and size of pipe being installed. Furthermore, all the reloca-tion work includes only one size of pipe. Thus the quantities of exca-vation and backfill, although calculated and estimated by the cubic yard, relate directly to the linear footage of pipe being installed. Linear footage is convenient to measure in the field as the work takes place. Therefore, the total of the four costs included in the cost esti-mate for the waterline relocation work should be added, and the total should be divided by the linear footage of pipe required to obtain a price per linear foot of pipe which encompasses all costs related to the work.

4. and 5. SHEETPILING—SQUARE FOOT

The next two items taken from the Preliminary Schedule and Cost Control Summary Sheets in the foregoing listing are the sheet-piling—one for the east shaft and one for the west shaft. The depths to which the sheetpiling is to be driven are the same for the east and west shafts: 52 ft.

It would be most convenient to monitor the progress of the sheetpil-ing installation by the horizontal linear foot of sheetpiling as mea-sured at the ground surface. Since all the sheetpiling is to be driven to a depth of 52 ft, it would be a simple matter to convert from square feet to linear feet. However, the problem with this approach is that it is sometimes impossible to drive the sheetpiling to predetermined depths due to subsurface interference. It is also possible that the contractor may not drive each section of sheetpiling to full depth prior to starting on the next section. Hence if this approach were used, sheets might not be fully driven when linear-footage measure-ments required full payment to the contractor for his progress.

On the other hand, it is possible that these two problems might not arise, in which case the linear-footage approach would work well.

We prefer to use the more conservative approach of square footage at uniform depth, and to convert from linear footage measured horizontally along the surface to square footage at a uniform depth of 52 ft is quick and simple.

6. OBSERVATION WELLS—VERTICAL LINEAR FOOT

This item is similar to the haul road item. A linear foot unit was employed in order to estimate the cost of the wells, but because of their relatively short depth, it will only take a day or so to install each. There is, therefore, no merit in recording linear footage of depth as a payment unit; rather, the contractor should be paid for each well upon its completion. Thus the payment unit will be "each."

7. and 8. EXCAVATION—CUBIC YARD

There is no advantage to changing this unit for payment purposes. The payment unit will also be the cubic yard.

9. DEWATERING—DAY

The price of the dewatering was estimated by the number of days dewatering would be required.

The same unit for payment purposes should be used since it is easy to monitor and there is no advantage to changing it. It should be recognized, however, that the number of days for which dewatering is paid cannot exceed the estimated number of days required.

10. TUNNELING—5 UNITS

The same method should be used in grouping all the estimating units used in estimating the price of the tunnel into one unit for payment purposes as was used in waterline relocation. The contract administrator should add the total estimated cost for the tunnel, divide that cost by the total length of the tunnel, and pay the contractor for the linear feet of tunnel completed on his Partial Payment Requests.

11. 96-in. PIPE—LINEAR FOOT

The estimating unit was linear foot of pipe in place. There is no advantage to changing the unit for payment purposes.

12. GROUTING—CUBIC YARD

The estimating unit was the cubic yard of grout complete and in place. The operation will take only 1 day; there is no merit in keeping track of the cubic yards of grout used for payment purposes. Thus the payment unit should be changed to lump sum, meaning, of course, that the contractor will be paid for all the grouting at one time once it is complete.

13. BACKFILL SHAFTS—CUBIC YARD

Backfilling the shafts will take enough time to warrant keeping track of the backfill utilized by the cubic yard.

14. RIPRAP—SQUARE YARD

The contract administrator estimated the cost of riprap by the square yard. It will take 2 days to install all the riprap. The estimating unit of square yard should be changed to lump sum for payment purposes.

15. CLEANUP AND DEMOBILIZE—LUMP SUM

The lump-sum approach was employed to estimate the cost of this time. The same unit—lump sum—should be used to pay for it.

The revised payment units are presented in Table 6-2.

Once these breakdown items and payment units for these items have been decided, the next step is to request the contractor's proposed lump-sum breakdown composed of the same items and units. The contract documents usually require the contractor to submit his schedule within a certain period of time after the contract is signed. It is usually

TABLE 6-2   Revised Payment Units

Item no.	Description	Cost estimating unit	Payment or cost control unit
1	Mobilization	Lump sum	Lump sum
2	Haul road	Square yard	Lump sum
3	Waterline relocation	Cubic yard / Linear foot / Lump sum	Linear foot
4	Sheetpiling, west shaft	Square foot	Square foot
5	Sheetpiling, east shaft	Square foot	Square foot
6	Observation wells	Vertical linear foot	each
7	Excavation, west shaft	Cubic yard	Cubic yard
8	Excavation, east shaft	Cubic yard	Cubic yard
9	Dewatering	Calendar day	Calendar day
10	Tunneling	Worker day / Cubic yard / Linear foot	Linear foot
11	96-in. pipe	Linear foot	Linear foot
12	Grouting	Cubic yard	Lump sum
13	Backfill	Cubic yard	Cubic yard
14	Riprap	Square yard	Lump sum
15	Cleanup and demobilization	Lump sum	Lump sum

up to the *contract administrator* to advise the contractor what the lump-sum breakdown items will be and how they will be measured, but the benefits of *mutually* accepted items and units in establishing a cooperative working relationship are obvious.

Upon receipt of the contractor's schedule and lump-sum breakdown, the contract administrator should plot the cash-flow curve derived from these two documents, which for the purposes of this illustration, will be assumed to have been submitted by the contractor.

The contract administrator's first step, in the analysis of the contractor's proposed lump-sum breakdown prices, in Table 6-3, would be to compare them to the previously developed adjusted total price per item from the preliminary cost estimate. While doing this, the contract administrator will also note when in the contractor's schedule, in Table 6-4, each item of work is to take place.

This schedule may be plotted as shown in Figure 6-1.

It appears that the contract administrator has either underestimated the cost of most items of work to take place before the midpoint of the schedule and overestimated most items of work after the midpoint in the schedule or that the contractor has shifted costs for items after the midpoint in the schedule to those items which occur prior to midschedule. This would not have a great impact in lowering the amount of interest paid on borrowed operating costs required by the contractor in the example because of the short duration of the project— the contractor says 16 weeks. On projects of 3- and 4-year duration, the impact would be significantly greater.

Indeed, at some point in a long-term project, the contractor could draw *all* his anticipated profit prior to the completion of the work if blatant front ending were allowed. The dollar impact on *this* project of the contractor's apparent attempt to front-end the project will be disregarded; the focus will be placed upon the procedure by which this attempt may be overcome.

Most contractors scoff at the contract administrator's ability to estimate prices—in many cases rightly so. After all, estimating is literally the contractor's bread and butter. The contract administrator is not as experienced and lacks knowledge of construction details, generally, when compared to the contractor.

The cash-flow curve helps the contract administrator overcome this initial disadvantage. The curve is not an all-powerful tool; it does, however, increase the contract administrator's confidence as to what actual costs can be expected. He may need this confidence when negotiating the final lump-sum breakdown prices for the project.

The contract administrator should plot the cash-flow curve that would result if he accepted the contractor's proposed lump-sum *break-*

TABLE 6-3 Proposed Lump-Sum Breakdown of Contractor

Item no.	Description	Quantity	Unit	Unit material	Unit labor	Unit total	Total cost
1	Mobilization	—	L.S.	—	—	—	40,000
2	Haul road	—	L.S.	—	—	—	1,000
3	Waterline	110	lin ft	40.00	20.00	60.00	6,600
4	Sheetpiling, west shaft	5500	ft^2	13.00	2.00	15.00	82,500
5	Sheetpiling, east shaft	6500	ft^2	13.00	2.00	15.00	97,500
6	Observation wells	2	each	1.00	—	500.00	1,000
7	Excavation, west shaft	500	yd^3	1.00	1.00	2.00	1,000
8	Excavation, east shaft	650	yd^3	1.00	1.00	2.00	1,300
9	Dewatering	35	day	—	—	1630.00	57,050
10	Tunnel	126	lin ft	400.00	600.00	1000.00	126,000
11	96-in. pipe	126	lin ft	100.00	20.00	120.00	17,120
12	Grouting	—	L.S.	—	—	—	5,000
13	Backfill shafts	1150	yd^3	3.00	2.00	5.00	5,750
14	Riprap	—	L.S.	—	—	—	1,000
15	Cleanup and demobilization	—	L.S.	—	—	—	2,180
							445,000

TABLE 6-4 Comparison of Prices

Item no.	Description	Contractor proposed price	Estimate price	Differ- ence (approxi- mate)	Week of contractor's schedule
1	Mobilization	40,000	17,115	(+) 23,000	1 & 2
2	Haul road	1,000	186	(+) 1,000	3
3	Waterline	6,600	3,908	(+) 3,000	3 & 4
4	Sheetpiling, west shaft	82,500	62,415	(+) 20,000	3 & 4
5	Sheetpiling, east shaft	97,500	73,501	(+) 24,000	4, 5, & 6
6	Observation wells	1,000	936	—	3
7	Excavation, west shaft	1,000	980	—	4
8	Excavation, east shaft	1,300	1,261	—	6
9	Dewatering	57,050	41,493	(+) 16,000	7–12
10	Tunnel	126,000	166,813	(−) 40,000	7–12
11	96-in Pipe	17,120	47,800	(−) 30,000	13
12	Grouting	5,000	9,043	(−) 4,000	14
13	Backfill shafts	5,750	11,832	(−) 6,000	14 & 15
14	Riprap	1,000	3,461	(−) 2,000	15 & 16
15	Cleanup & demobilization	2,180	4,256	(−) 2,000	16

down. He has no recourse, of course, but to accept the contractor's *schedule.* Legally, the contractor has the sole right to schedule work as he sees fit. Should the contract administrator alter the schedule, he would incur the risk of developing a nondefensible claim and extra compensation to the contractor, with an ultimate claim by the owner against the contract administrator himself a likely prospect.

In order to draw the *contractor's* proposed cash-flow curve, the contract administrator must tabulate the cost of construction per week that the proposal would produce, as in Table 6-5.

After tabulation, he should plot the cumulative dollar amount against the *end* of the week that dollar amount is accumulated. He should then, for the purposes of comparison, plot the approximate theoretical cash-flow curve on the same graph (Figure 6-2). When plotting, he should next assume that 6.7 percent of the total project price will be expended at the first quarter of the project's duration and that 93.3 percent will be expended at the third quarter.

$$\$445,000 \times 0.067 = \$29,815, \text{ or } \$30,000$$

At the (93.3 percent, 12 weeks) point the cumulative dollar amount would be

$$\$445,000 - \$30,000 = \$415,000$$

Description	Item No.	Week 1	Week 2	Week 3	Week 4	Week 5	Week 6	Week 7	Week 8	Week 9	Week 10	Week 11	Week 12	Week 13	Week 14	Week 15	Week 16
Mobilize	1	XXXXX	XXXXX														
Haul Road	2			XX													
Waterline	3			XXXXXX													
Sheetpiling, west	4			XXXXXXXX													
Sheetpiling, east	5				XXXXXXXX												
Observation wells	6			XX													
Excavation, west	7				XX												
Excavation, east	8						XXX										
Dewatering	9							XXXXXXXXXXXXXXXXXXXXXXXXXXXXXXX									
Tunnel	10							XXXXXXXXXXXXXXXXXXXXXXXXXXXX									
96-in. pipe	11													XXXXX			
Grouting	12														X		
Backfill shafts	13														XXXXXXXXXX		
Riprap	14															XX	
Cleanup and Demobilization	15																XXXX

FIGURE 6-1 The contractor's schedule.

TABLE 6-5 Cost of Construction per Week Based on Contractor's Proposals

Week no.	Item of work underway	Dollar amount of work items	Cumulative dollar amount
1	$1/2$ mobilization	20,000	20,000
2	$1/2$ mobilization	20,000	40,000
3	haul road	1,000	
	$1/2$ waterline	3,300	
	$5/8$ sheetpiling, west shaft	51,560	
	Observation wells	1,000	
	Total	56,860	96,860
4	$1/2$ waterline	3,300	
	$3/8$ sheetpiling, west shaft	30,940	
	$2/9$ sheetpiling, east shaft	21,666	
	Excavation, west shaft	1,000	
	Total	56,906	153,766
5	$5/9$ sheetpiling, west shaft	54,165	207,931
6	$2/9$ sheetpiling, east shaft	21,669	
	Excavation, east shaft	1,300	
	Total	22,969	230,900
7	$1/7$ dewatering	8,150	
	$1/6$ tunnel	21,000	
	Total	29,150	260,050
8	$1/7$ dewatering	8,150	
	$1/6$ tunnel	21,000	
	Total	29,500	289,200
9	$1/7$ dewatering	8,150	
	$1/6$ tunnel	21,000	
	Total	29,500	318,350
10	$1/7$ dewatering	8,150	
	$1/6$ tunnel	21,000	
	Total	29,500	347,500
11	$1/7$ dewatering	8,150	
	$1/6$ tunnel	21,000	
	Total	29,500	376,650
12	$1/7$ dewatering	8,150	
	$1/6$ tunnel	21,000	
	Total	29,500	405,800
13	$1/7$ dewatering	8,150	
	96-in pipe	17,120	
	Total	25,270	431,070
14	Grout	5,000	
	$4/10$ backfill shafts	2,300	
	Total	7,300	438,370

TABLE 6-5 (Continued)

Week no.	Item of work underway	Dollar amount of work items	Cumulative dollar amount
15	⁵/₁₀ backfill shafts	2,875	
	¹/₂ Riprap	500	
	Total	3,375	441,745
16	¹/₁₀ backfill shaft	575	
	¹/₂ Riprap	500	
	Cleanup and Demobilization	2,180	
	Total	3,255	445,000

After plotting the contractor's proposed cash-flow curve, the contract administrator should begin analysis, noting the following:

1. The contractor anticipates completion of the project in 16 weeks, not 20 weeks as the contract administrator's preliminary schedule indicated.

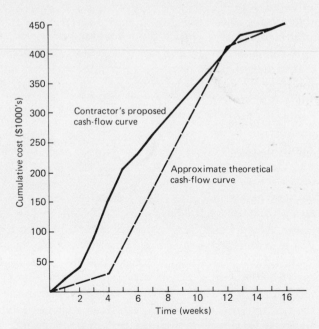

FIGURE 6-2 Comparison of the contractor's proposed cash-flow curve to the approximate theoretical cash-flow curve.

2. The configuration of the contractor's proposed cash-flow curve does not follow the theoretical cash-flow curve (for 16 weeks) as closely as the contract administrator's preliminary cash-flow curve followed the approximate theoretical cash-flow curve (for 20 weeks).

3. The contractor's proposed cash-flow curve has a steeper slope over the first 5 weeks than the approximate theoretical curve, then has a less steep slope from Week 5 to the end of the 16-week project.

4. The contractor has anticipated the completion of the mobilization phase of the project in 2 weeks, not 4 weeks as assumed or as indicated by the approximate theoretical curve.

The observations merit further consideration. The contract administrator might have been encouraged by the probable accuracy of his preliminary cost estimate adjusted to the contract price and his preliminary schedule by its relatively close fit to the theoretical cash-flow curve. This did not mean our cost estimate and schedule were necessarily correct. It did mean, however, that there was a good probability that it was correct.

The first item scheduled for payment is mobilization. He estimated that mobilization would cost between 2 and 12 percent of the project cost. The adjusted total cost for mobilization was $17,115 for the $445,000 project price, or a little less than 4 percent. The contractor's proposed mobilization price is $40,000. If one were to allow the contractor $40,000 rather than $17,115, it would seem to be much to the contractor's advantage, but 9 percent is within the 2 to 12 percent range for mobilization, and this is a relatively small project. If it took the contractor 4 weeks to mobilize rather than the 2 weeks he anticipates, the contractor would be right on the approximate theoretical cash-flow curve if he were to allow about $30,000 for mobilization: $30,000 is about 6.7 percent of the project price. The median of the estimate range of 2 to 12 percent is 7 percent—quite close to 6.7 percent. This does not mean that it should be assumed that the first quarter of any project will be taken up by mobilization exclusively. On larger projects, the mobilization will be a lower percentage of the overall project cost. For the purposes of this project, $30,000 should be set as the target for the mobilization price in the negotiations with the contractor. If he can prove that his actual mobilization costs are $40,000, not the targeted $30,000, $40,000 can be accepted, but for now it will be assumed that his proposed $40,000 figure will ultimately be reduced to $30,000. If the contractor is wrong and mobilization takes 4, rather than 2, weeks, the first 4 weeks on the contractor's proposed cash flow will be almost an exact duplication of the approximate theoretical cash-flow curve. The contractor may have front-ended, but, based on the mobilization percentage range in the contract administrator's estimate, not too badly. If the contractor does mobilize in 2, rather than 4, weeks, he has done a good job and earned his mobilization price sooner than was considered probable.

The slope of the contractor's proposed cash-flow curve is steeper than the approximate theoretical curve during Weeks 3, 4, and 5. This means the contractor's curve calls for a faster rate of expenditure than would be normally expected during those 3 weeks. Reference to the "takeoff sheet" from which the contractor proposed cash-flow curve was generated indicates that the following construction items are scheduled to be undertaken in this time period:

• Haul road

• Waterline relocation

• Sheetpiling

• Excavation

The contract administrator should compare his preliminary estimates for these items to the contractor's proposed lump-sum breakdown.

2. HAUL ROAD

The adjusted total cost from the estimate is $186. The contractor's lump-sum breakdown proposal is $1000. This is over 500 percent of the adjusted total cost. It is a relatively small dollar amount, but it is probable the contractor should not be allowed his proposed $1000. It is possible that the contractor will have to pay for an operator and bulldozer for the entire day to do less than an hour's work (even though he claims in the schedule it will take 2 days) due to union rules and rental agreements, if this was the only bulldozer work he had.

Giving him the benefit of the doubt for now, the price for the road could be targeted and negotiated as follows:

Material $1.25/yd^2 × 89 yd^2	$111.25
Full-day bulldozer rental (from the cost Estimating guide)	325.00
Full-day operator (from the cost estimating guide)	95.00
	$531.25

Times the 1.41 factor between our total
estimated cost and the bid price

$$\times\ 1.41$$
$$\$749.06, \text{ or } \$750$$

If the contractor can prove that he must, in fact, pay for an operator
and a bulldozer for an entire day for the haul road and has no other
use for either that day, the contract administrator would accept
$750.

3. WATERLINE RELOCATION

The total adjusted cost for the waterline relocation work was:

Excavation	$ 125
Pipe installation	2793
Tie-in	709
Backfill	281
Total	$3908

In this estimate, the contract administrator neglected the cost to
remove the old pipe; the rest of his estimate was quite detailed. He
cannot analyze the contractor's proposed lump-sum breakdown
price because he has included five separate operations in one catch-
all price. The only discrepancy he could find is that the contractor
anticipates 110 lin ft of pipe rather than 105 lin ft measured. This
might be attributable to the length in which the contractor must
purchase the pipe or to a measurement error on the part of either
party. It is insignificant in either case. Setting a targeted price of
$4500 for negotiations will account for the difference in pipe length
and allow a contingency for cost of removal of the old pipe. The
contractor should be advised to bring in detailed data from which he
derived his $6,600 price.

4. and 5. SHEETPILING

This item has the largest dollar difference from the estimate and,
hence, requires detailed inspection to determine whether the contractor's price should be accepted. The contractor proposes $15 per
ft^2 for 5500 ft^2, or $82,500 for the west shaft sheetpiling. The contract
administrator estimated 5269 ft^2 at $8.35 $\times$ 1.419 (the adjusted cost
ratio), or at $11.85 per ft^2, = $62,415. He used the price for the
heaviest sheetpiling in the cost estimating guide due to the depth of
the shaft. The wales and bracing were part of the price from the cost
estimating guide. He used average figures, not a takeoff from a design. It is possible the contractor has designed the sheeting, wales,
and struts and is absolutely fair in his price; it is also possible he
is not.

The contract administrator is not in a position to design the shaft and make a quantity takeoff. Hence he should request that the contractor submit his design for review during negotiations. For now, the contract administrator should assume front ending and his own figure of $62,415 as a target for west shaft sheeting and $73,501 for east shaft sheeting.

7. and 8. EXCAVATION

The contractor has proposed $2300 for the excavation of both shafts; the contract administrator's estimate is $1916. It appears that the contractor has randomly selected unit prices; they do not correlate with the data from the cost estimating guide. The contract administrator should keep $1916 as his target for negotiations!

The contract administrator should now add his negotiation target amounts for items contributing to cost during Weeks 3, 4, and 5 (Table 6-6). He should then compare his targeted negotiation prices to the approximate theoretical cash-flow curve for Weeks 1, 2, 3, 4, and 5 (Table 6-7) to see whether it is closer than the contractor's proposal (Figures 6-3 and 6-4).

From the three curves plotted, it is apparent that the target, negotiation prices will result in a slope slightly less steep than the approximate theoretical cash-flow curve, whereas the contractor's proposed cash-flow curve will be steeper. The contract administrator probably can afford to negotiate a bit higher than his targeted negotiation prices. This will undoubtedly occur anyway to achieve compromise with the contractor.

Once again, there is no right answer; there is no wrong answer; there are only different answers when comparing data to the theoretical curve. The closer the contract administrator gets to the theoretical curve the more *probable* he is correct, however. It should be noted that with a slight relaxation of the targeted, negotiation prices and an actual 4-week mobilization period, the targeted price curve would duplicate *exactly* the approximate theoretical curve.

TABLE 6-6   Targeted vs. Proposed Prices

Item	Target price	Contractor's proposal
Haul road	$ 750	$ 1,000
Waterline relocation	4,500	6,600
Sheetpiling	62,145	82,500
Excavation	1,916	2,300
	$69,581	$92,400

TABLE 6-7   Targeted Prices vs. Theoretical Cash-Flow Curve

Week no.	Item of work underway	Target price of work item	Cumulative cost
1	1/2 mobilization	$15,000	$ 15,000
2	1/2 mobilization	15,000	30,000
3	haul road	750	
	1/2 waterline	2,250	
	5/8 sheetpiling, west	39,009	
	Observation wells	1,000	
	Total	$43,009	73,009
4	1/2 waterline	2,250	
	3/8 sheetpiling, west	23,406	
	2/9 sheetpiling, east	16,334	
	Excavation, west	980	
	Total	$42,970	115,999
5	5/9 sheetpiling, east	40,834	
	Excavation, east	0	
	Total	$40,834	$156,833

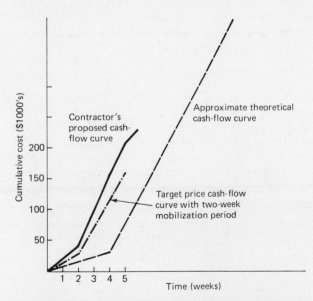

FIGURE 6-3 Comparison of the contractor's proposed cash-flow curve and the target price cash-flow curve to the approximate theoretical cash-flow curve for the first 5 weeks of the project.

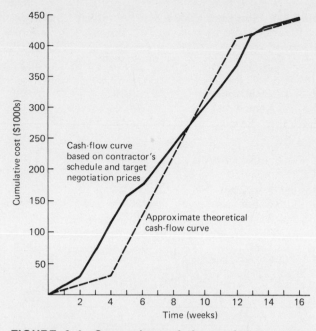

FIGURE 6-4 Comparison of the cash-flow curve derived from the contractor's schedule and the target negotiation prices to the approximate theoretical cash-flow curve.

As the contract administrator proceeds through the contractor's proposed lump-sum breakdown prices and schedule, he should be comforted by the fit between the negotiated price curve and the theoretical curve. Reassurance is the sole product of the comparative exercise, for the similarity of the two, per se, proves nothing.

If the contractor has inflated the prices for his work at the *beginning* of the project, his stated costs at the end of the schedule will necessarily be unduly low. If one or more underpriced items appear at the *end* of the schedule to compensate for the apparently overpriced items at the beginning, the contract administrator will have increased confidence in his suspicion that the sheetpiling price is inflated.

Turning to the remaining construction components, the contract administrator will note that the contractor's proposed price for observation wells of $1000 is quite close to the contract administrator's estimate of $936. He should accept the $1000 price.

Dewatering is priced by the contractor at $1630 per day for a period of 35 days, for a total price of $57,050. The contract administrator's estimate was $41,493. With that disparity in mind, the contract ad-

ministrator should refer to the contractor's proposed lump-sum breakdown price for the tunnel, which is 126 lin ft at $1000 per ft, or
$126,000. If one adds the tunnel estimate to the dewatering, it totals
$183,056 ÷ 126 lin ft, or approximately $1453 per lin ft. The contract
administrator's 96-in. pipe estimate is $47,800, or slightly more than
$210 per lin ft; the contractor's proposed price is only $120 per lin ft. In
addition, the contractor has only assumed 126 lin ft of 96-in. pipe. If
one multiplies the material price for the pipe (as taken from the cost
estimating guide) of $110 per lin ft by the 1.419 factor (to adjust the
material price to the ratio of the contractor's bid to the contract administrator's total estimate), he finds the material price for the pipe is
about $170 per lin ft, which is more than the contractor has requested
for material and labor. Thus it appears that the tunnel and the pipe are
the components in which the inflated costs assigned to the sheetpiling
have been "buried" to the greatest extent. In addition, the contractor's
"error" in the length of 96-in. pipe may cause him to claim he has made
a takeoff error and should be considered for additional compensation.

To summarize this seeming shifting of costs: The dewatering (to be
paid for by the day) has been assigned a price by the contractor doubl-
ing the contract administrator's estimate. The contractor's proposed
price for tunneling was less than the contract administrator's estimate:

Component	Contractor	Contract administrator	Difference
Dewatering	$1,630/day	$\dfrac{\$41,493}{39 \text{ days}}$ = $1064/day	(+) $566/day
Tunneling	$1000/lin ft	$\dfrac{\$166,813}{126 \text{ lin ft}}$ = $1324/lin ft	(−)$324/lin ft

In dollars this would amount to:

Dewatering:
Contractor	$57,050
Contract administrator	41,493
	(+)$15,557

Tunneling:
Contract administrator	$166,813
Contractor	126,000
	(−)$ 40,813

TABLE 6-8   Summary of Component Prices

Item no.	Description	Contractor	Contract administrator estimate	Target
1	Mobilization	$40,000	$17,115	$30,000
2	Haul road	1,000	186	750
3	Waterline relocation	6,600	3,908	4,500
4	Sheetpiling, west shaft	82,500	62,415	62,415
5	Sheetpiling, east shaft	97,500	73,501	73,501

Thus it appears that the contractor has shifted some funds from the tunnel item, to be reimbursed through productive effort (payable by the linear foot), to the dewatering item, to be reimbursed by the calendar day regardless of productivity. It also seems that he has "low-balled" the tunnel price to compensate for other front ending as well.

With the foregoing discussion in mind, the contract administrator should continue targeting construction component prices. A summary of components addressed previously is in Table 6-8. The items in Table 6-9 are close enough to the contract administrator's estimate to permit acceptance of the contractor's proposed prices:

TABLE 6-9   Acceptable Proposed Prices

Item no.	Description	Contractor	Contract administrator estimate	Target
6	Observation wells	$1000	$ 936	$1000
7	Excavation, west shaft	1000	980	1000
8	Excavation, east shaft	1300	1261	1300

Reference to the contractor's proposed cash-flow curve indicates a rate of expenditure less than would be expected from the theoretical curve. It appears the tunnel price is too low, dewatering too high. Both will occur at the same time but are reimbursed using different units. The safe course would be to attempt to adjust the contractor's proposed costs for these items to their actual costs. It will be assumed that the contractor has attempted to front-end his proposed lump-sum break-down prices. Furthermore, in order to compensate for front ending and to hold any unknowns at the midpoint in the schedule, it will be assumed that the contract administrator's estimated prices for items 11 through 15 are correct: these items total $76,392. Targeted prices for work items 1 through 8 total $174,466.

Project Price $445,000
less items 11 through 15 (−) 76,392
$368,608
less Item 1 through 8 (−) 174,466
Leaves $194,142

Having $194,142 for dewatering and tunneling, consider the following proposals of the contractor:

Dewatering $ 57,050
Tunneling 126,000
$183,050

The contract administrator has estimated:

Dewatering $ 41,493
Tunneling 166,813
$208,306

The contract administrator should subtract from his $194,142 "remainder" his estimated prices for dewatering and tunneling ($194,142 − $41,493, or $152,649).

Next, he should plot a cash-flow curve based upon the contractor's 16-week schedule and the contract administrator's targeted lump-sum breakdown prices in Table 6-10.

TABLE 6-10 Contractor's Schedule vs. Targeted Lump-Sum Breakdown

Week no.	Item of work underway	Dollar amount of work items	Cumulative dollar amount
1	1/2 mobilization	$15,000	$ 15,000
2	1/2 mobilization	15,000	30,000
3	Haul road	750	
	1/2 waterline	2,250	
	5/8 sheetpiling, west shaft	39,009	
	Observation wells	1,000	
	Total	43,009	73,009
4	1/2 waterline	2,250	
	3/8 sheetpiling, west shaft	23,406	
	2/9 sheetpiling, east shaft	16,334	
	Excavation, west shaft	1,000	
	Total	42,990	115,999
5	5/9 sheetpiling, east shaft	40,833	156,832

TABLE 6-10 (Continued)

Week no.	Item of work underway	Dollar amount of work items	Cumulative dollar amount
6	2/9 sheetpiling, east shaft	16,334	
	Excavation, east shaft	1,300	
	Total	17,634	174,466
7	1/7 dewatering	5,928	
	1/6 tunnel	25,441	
	Total	31,369	205,835
8	1/7 dewatering	5,927	
	1/6 tunnel	25,440	
	Total	31,367	237,202
9	1/7 dewatering	5,928	
	1/6 tunnel	25,441	
	Total	31,369	268,571
10	1/7 dewatering	5,927	
	1/6 tunnel	25,440	
	Total	31,367	299,938
11	1/7 dewatering	5,928	
	1/6 tunnel	25,441	
	Total	31,369	331,307
12	1/7 dewatering	5,927	
	1/6 tunnel	25,440	
	Total	31,367	362,674
13	1/7 dewatering	5,928	
	96-in. pipe	47,800	
	Total	53,728	416,402
14	Grout	9,043	
	4/10 backfill shafts	4,733	
	Total	13,776	430,178
15	5/10 backfill shafts	5,916	
	1/2 riprap	1,730	
	Total	7,646	437,824
16	1/10 backfill shaft	1,191	
	1/2 riprap	1,730	
	Cleanup and demobilization	4,256	
	Total	7,176	445,000

The cash-flow curve based on the contractor's schedule and the contract administrator's target prices for lump-sum negotiation appears to be acceptable: it does not follow the approximate theoretical curve closely, but it is balanced quite well to the theoretical curve. The center point at Week 8 and $222,500 does not witness an ideal crossing of the curves, but they do cross only 1 week away (at Week 9); in other words, the curve is only ½ week away from crossing the theoretical curve at the ideal $222,500 point.

The contract administrator is now prepared to negotiate his "target" prices with the contractor. Unlike the case of the schedule (which lies within the exclusive province of the contractor), the contract administrator has both the right and the duty to attempt to negotiate final lump-sum breakdown prices which are fair to all parties of the contract. By this point, the contract administrator has a good deal of experience in examining the prices for each item and, guided by the cash-flow curves, should have a feeling as to how far he will bend. In this illustration, he also has a fairly clear impression that the contractor has weighted his proposed lump-sum breakdown prices to his cash-flow advantage, i.e., that these weighted prices are not actually the prices he used to bid the project.

The contract administrator's attitude during the actual negotiations should be polite, attentive, and open-minded, but he should yield on important points only in the face of clear and credible documentation supporting the contractor's position. With this attitude, he should be able to negotiate prices fair to both the owner and the contractor.

CHAPTER 7

THE INTEGRATED
SCHEDULE

Once the scope of a given project has been determined and formalized in a construction contract, the components of the project are subject to adjustment with regard to three basic elements: time, cost, and quality. One such adjustment would be to shorten the amount of time required to construct the project by increasing its cost (to provide for overtime or employment of larger, but less productive, work crews) or by reducing its quality (i.e., by permitting more rapid but less careful work). Another adjustment would be to reduce the cost of the project by reducing the quality of the materials and workmanship. Still another adjustment would be to extend the time, but increase quality, or decrease cost, thereby permitting the project to be extended in order that smaller, but more efficient, crews might be employed. Finally, the quality of the project may be increased, usually with consequent increases in cost and the amount of time required to complete it.

An important task of the contract administrator is to establish contract controls—such as the ones explained and illustrated in Part 1—to permit both the control and the adjustment of the time, cost, and quality dimensions of the project. The contract administrator's ultimate function in the construction process is to increase the probability that the construction contract will be performed, i.e., that the project will be constructed, at the level of the quality contemplated by the owner and at the contract price within the amount of time provided in the contract. However, recognizing that the art of construction is subject to innumerable variables, the contract administrator must establish his contract controls such that the three dimensions may be adjusted to reflect the realities of the project.

In the previous six chapters of Part 1, the necessary mechanisms for controlling the time, cost, and quality of a construction project have been explained in series with emphasis upon the relationships between the consecutive control techniques. However, the task of combining all the control mechanisms discussed to this point remains.

The purpose of this chapter is to explain and illustrate the development of a single, integrated device for *general* control of a construction project. This document will be called the "Integrated Schedule Sheet." It should be noted that *detailed* control may require reference to the data from which the integrated schedule was derived.

DEVELOPING THE INTEGRATED SCHEDULE SHEET

The integrated schedule sheet is a derivative document; it is a transposition of summary data, the generation of which was explained in the preceding chapters. The point of beginning is the approved project schedule. The project schedule should be copied onto a piece of paper with vertical divisions (representing working days) and horizontal lines (representing lump-sum breakdown components of the project in bar chart form). The dollar amount of each lump-sum breakdown component should be noted in *each month* the construction activity, or activities, for that component is scheduled to take place. As in the case of the preliminary cash-flow curve, the vertical lines—representing working days—should be combined into working months, using as an average 22 working days per month. Also, as before, the dollar amounts for all construction activities scheduled for each working month should be added vertically for that month, noted at the bottom of the sheet, then totaled horizontally at the bottom as a check against the contract price. The contract administrator should next add to the left-hand side of this sheet a scale representing the division of the total cost of the project, then plot the cumulative dollar amount for each month, to create a superimposed project cash-flow curve directly over the project schedule.

The numerical entries on the sheet having been completed, the contract administrator should redirect his attention to the Control Responsibility Summary Sheets described in Chapter 1. He should note all control responsibilities required to be discharged during a particular work month on a vertical line at the top of the sheet on an extension of the vertical line representing the beginning of that work month. Although completion of these entries may require some thought, this task should not be unmanageable given the contract administrator's now well-developed expertise with the contract and the project.

The foregoing completed entries comprise the Integrated Schedule Sheet, a single reference by which the time, cost, and quality of the project may be controlled at a general level. This document, together with its underlying data, will provide the foundation for effectively systematizing and monitoring these contract controls, the subjects of Parts 2 and 3.

COMPREHENSIVE ILLUSTRATION

The comprehensive illustration contemplates a mere *transfer* of the data derived from these separate controls to one control sheet—called the Integrated Schedule Sheet.

Naturally, in large or complex projects, this transfer of data will be more time-consuming than for small or simple projects. For projects which do not require, or permit, computerized critical-path-method (CPM) schedules, the integrated schedule should be of significant benefit to the contract administrator.

TRANSFERRING THE CONTRACTOR'S SCHEDULE

The first step in the process is to transfer the contractor's schedule onto a piece of paper long enough to allow each day contemplated by the schedule plus 50 additional days to be represented by a separate vertical division. Reference is made to the contractor's schedule (Figure 6-1) used in the example in Chapter 6.

The contractor's schedule has a 16-week duration: allowance should be made for an additional 20 days' contingent time on the integrated schedule to provide for the possibility that the contractor will not complete the project on schedule. Therefore, the contract administrator should divide the paper into 20 weeks, each week having sufficient space to have 5 days each.

At the left-hand side of the sheet, descriptions of the items being scheduled should be listed vertically. The contractor's schedule contains fifteen construction components. Each component will require two horizontal lines; one line will be used to represent the time which the contractor's schedule allows for completion of the item; the other will be used to record the number of days actually required. On the first line of each of the scheduled items, going downward, the contract administrator should write the description of the item. Then referring to the contractor's schedule, he should draw a bar on the top line for each item to represent the days during which the contractor intends to work on that item. This technique will produce a basic bar chart schedule for the project which will provide the contract administrator's *time* control device.

Inside each bar, the contract administrator should write the dollar amount for the described item of work as negotiated with the contractor to pay for that item in the lump-sum breakdown. For the purposes of this illustration, it will be assumed that all "targeted" lump-sum breakdown prices were agreed to in the negotiations. The totals for each week and cumulative totals for each week should be noted below each scheduled week.

SUPERIMPOSING THE CASH-FLOW CURVE

The next step in construction of the integrated schedule will be to superimpose the cash-flow curve for the project onto the bar chart. These are horizontal lines on the sheet. The dollar amount of the bid is $445,000. Dividing $450,000 by 30, each line will represent $15,000 when the cash-flow curve is superimposed. This will be easy enough to tabulate; however, had the numbers not worked out as well as they did, the contract administrator could merely have reduced the height of the cash-flow curve to obtain an easily plotted number. For example, he could have used twenty-three vertical spaces at $20,000. In this case, since the vertical lines of the bar chart are already in weekly increments, all that need be done to enter the dollar amounts for the cash-flow curve is to note them at any convenient location on the integrated schedule. The best place would appear to be immediately to the right of the last scheduled week for the bar graph; the contract administrator should start at the bottom of the sheet and note cumulative $15,000 increments going upward until he reached $450,000. Then starting at the beginning of Week 1, he should plot the anticipated cash-flow curve for the project—superimposed over the bar chart schedule. The contract administrator may wish to use a different color to allow the superimposed cash-flow curve to stand out from the bar chart. As progress payments are made to the contractor, the contract administrator should also plot the *actual* cash flow allowed the contract, in another color also superimposed on the integrated schedule.

Just as the plotting of both the contractor's preconstruction schedule and his actual performance on the bar chart established a device for *schedule* control, the plotting of both the anticipated cash-flow curve and actual cash flow will provide a device for *cost* control. The best uses of these two devices will be explained in detail in Part 3.

ITEMS FROM THE CONTROL RESPONSIBILITY SUMMARY SHEETS

The contract administrator should next address creation of a device for *quality* control. He should refer to items defined in his Control Responsibility Summary Sheets and begin transferring them to the integrated schedule.

Section G-1.01   The first item on the Control Responsibility Summary Sheet, generated in Chapter 1, was section G-1.01, requiring the contractor to advise the contract administrator 5 days in advance of his intended entry onto the site. The start of actual work on the site is haul road construction and sheetpiling for the west shaft. Both these items are scheduled to begin on Day 11. If the Contractor meets his schedule, he must advise us of his intent to enter the site 5 days in advance, or Day 6.

The contract administrator should note that the required advance notice is stated in calendar, rather than working, days. Therefore, he must allow 2 days for the weekend, and the contractor must notify him by Day 7. Thus the contract administrator should write on the integrated schedule near Day 7, the contract citation and "Contractor to advise he will enter site" with an arrow pointing to the end of Day 7.

Section G-1.02   The next item on the Contract Responsibility Summary Sheet refers to G-1.02 which requires the contractor to submit his proposed schedule within 10 days following his execution of the contract. In this illustration, it was earlier assumed that the contractor acted well within this period, i.e., that the project commenced when the contract was executed. This means that by Day 8 (assuming Day 1 is a Monday), the contractor should have submitted his schedule. The contractor should note the contract citation—G-1.02—and "Contractor to submit schedule" near Day 8 with an arrow pointing to the end of Day 8.

The same section of the contract documents requires the contractor to submit a "schedule update" every 3 months. Three months is 13 weeks. Therefore, near the third day of Week 15 the contract administrator should write, i.e., 13 weeks after submission of the Schedule, "G-1.02, Contractor's revised schedule to be submitted" with an arrow pointing to the end of Day 73.

Section G-2.01   The next item on the Contract Responsibility Control Sheet refers to section G-2.01, notification of claim. This item cannot, of course, be predetermined on the integrated schedule. Accordingly, the contract administrator should make no entry.

Section G-3.01 The next item refers to G-3.01 and requires the contractor to submit his lump-sum breakdown proposal and detailed schedule 10 days prior to submission of his first monthly progress payment request. Most owners will make payments on a particular day each month; furthermore, time for the processing of progress payment requests is required by both the owner and the contract administrator prior to the owner making payment. This sequence usually requires an agreed-upon cutoff date each month for the contract administrator to calculate and agree with the contractor as to the amount of payment he is due. It will be assumed for the purposes of this illustration that the first cutoff date will be Day 24, that there are 31 calendar days in Month 1, 30 calendar days in Month 2, 31 calendar days in Month 3, 31 calendar days in Month 4, and 30 calendar days in Month 5. With this information in hand, the contract administrator can determine the remaining cutoff dates as follows:

Day 24: First cutoff date	*Cumulative total*
Day 25 (1 day) + weekend (2 days) = 3 days	3
Week 6 (5 days) + weekend (2 days) = 7 days	10
Week 7 (5 days) + weekend (2 days) = 7 days	17
Week 8 (5 days) + weekend (2 days) = 7 days	24
Week 9 (5 days) + weekend (2 days) = 7 days	31

The second cutoff date is therefore a Sunday. The contract administrator should note submittal by the contractor is due the preceding Friday—Day 45. The contract administrator should then proceed in the same manner to determine the third cutoff date:

Day 45: Second cutoff date	*Cumulative total*
Week 10 (5 days) + weekend (2 days) = 7 days	7
Week 11 (5 days) + weekend (2 days) = 7 days	14
Week 12 (5 days) + weekend (2 days) = 7 days	21
Week 13 (5 days) + weekend (2 days) = 7 days	28
Week 14 (2 days)	30

Therefore, Day 67 is the third cutoff date.

Day 67: Third cutoff date	Cumulative total
Week 14 (3 days) + weekend (2 days) = 5 days	5
Week 15 (5 days) + weekend (2 days) = 7 days	12
Week 16 (5 days) + weekend (2 days) = 7 days	19
Week 17 (5 days) + weekend (2 days) = 7 days	26
Week 18 (5 days) + weekend (2 days) = 7 days	31

If the contractor fails to meet his schedule, the fourth cutoff date will be Day 90; otherwise, final payment will be upon completion of the project prior to Day 90.

Section G-3.02   The contract administrator should write the following on his integrated schedule: "G-3.02: Payment cutoff date" with arrows pointing to Days 24, 45, 67, and 90.

Section G-3.04   The next item recorded on the Contract Responsibility Summary Sheet refers to contract provision G-3.04, which provides the basis for reimbursement to the contractor for materials and equipment inventoried at the site which have yet to be incorporated into the work of the project. Although these control responsibilities will receive separate treatment in Part 2, notation is not required on the integrated schedule since inventoried materials will be included in the same payments previously noted on the integrated schedule for G-3.02.

Section G-3.05   The next item on the Control Responsibility Summary Sheet is G-3.05, owner's payments, which calls for payment to the contractor, if appropriate, within 30 days of presentation of the payment request. This means that the first payment could be due as early as the first cutoff day plus 10 days (see G-3.02) plus 30 days, i.e., 40 days after the cutoff date.

Day 24: First cutoff date	Cumulative total
Day 25 (1 day) + weekend (2 days) = 3 days	3
Week 6 (5 days) + weekend (2 days) = 7 days	10
Week 7 (5 days) + weekend (2 days) = 7 days	17
Week 8 (5 days) + weekend (2 days) = 7 days	24
Week 9 (5 days) + weekend (2 days) = 7 days	31
Week 10 (5 days) + weekend (2 days) = 7 days	38
Week 11 (2 days)	53

Item No.	Description	Week 1					Week 2					Week 3					Week 4					Week 5					Week 6					Week 7					Week 8				
		1	2	3	4	5	6	7	8	9	10	11	12	13	14	15	16	17	18	19	20	21	22	23	24	25	26	27	28	29	30	31	32	33	34	35	36	37	38	39	40
1	Mobilization, scheduled / actual				30,000																																				
2	Haul road, scheduled / actual								750																																
3	Waterline, scheduled / actual													4500																											
4	Sheetpiling, west shaft, scheduled / actual											62,415																													
5	Sheetpiling, east shaft, scheduled / actual																	73,501																							
6	Observation wells, scheduled / actual												1000																												
7	Excavation, west shaft, scheduled / actual																		1000																						
8	Excavation, east shaft, scheduled / actual																															1300									
9	Dewatering, scheduled / actual																																					41,493			
10	Tunnel, scheduled / actual																																				152,649				
11	96-in. pipe, scheduled / actual																																								
12	Grouting, scheduled / actual																																								
13	Backfill shafts, scheduled / actual																																								
14	Riprap, scheduled / actual																																								
15	Cleanup and demobilization, scheduled / actual																																								
	Weekly estimated expenditure	15,000					15,000					43,009					42,990					40,833					17,634					31,369					31,367				
	Cumulative weekly estimated expenditure	15,000					30,000					73,009					115,999					156,832					174,466					205,835					237,202				

Anticipated cash-flow curve

Engineer's list of sheet drawings to go to contractor

Engineer's review of sheet pile sheet drawings to be completed

G-1.01: Contractor to advise he will enter site

G-1.02: contractor to submit schedule

Sheetpiling to be delivered

Engineer to receive shop drawings for liner plate

Engineer's review of liner plate to be completed

G.3.02: Payment cutoff date

Liner plate to be delivered

FIGURE 7-1 Completed Integrated Schedule Sheet.

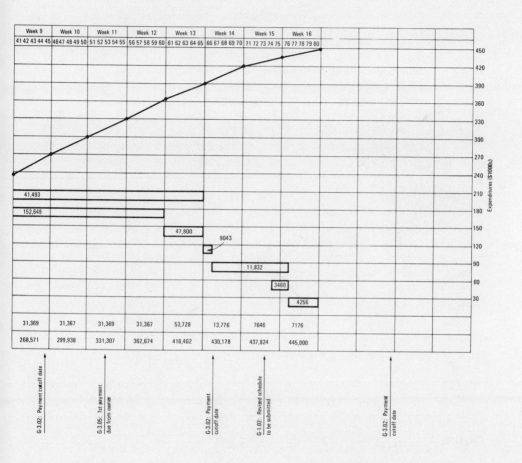

The contract administrator should enter the following note on the integrated schedule: "G-3.05: First payment due from owner" and an arrow going to Day 53.

The second payment cut off date was Day 67:

Day 67: Second cutoff date	Cumulative total
Week 14 (3 days) + weekend (2 days) = 5 days	5
Week 15 (5 days) + weekend (2 days) = 7 days	12
Week 16 (5 days) + weekend (2 days) = 7 days	19
Week 17 (5 days) + weekend (2 days) = 7 days	26
Week 18 (5 days) + weekend (2 days) = 7 days	33
Week 19 (5 days) + weekend (2 days) = 7 days	40

Therefore, on the first day of Week 20, the second payment will be due from the owner to the contractor, but since the project should be completed by then, the contract administrator should make no entry.

Section G-4.02   The next item is G-4.02, subcontract, which requires that the contractor submit a statement, at least 30 days in advance of the date he intends to utilize the subcontractor, disclosing the proposed subcontractor's name and planned project activity. No entry can be made for this item, because the contract administrator does not know what, if any, parts of the project the contractor intends to subcontract. If the contractor *had* advised the contract administrator he intended to subcontract installation of the 96-in. pipe, the contract administrator would merely have counted back 30 days from the starting date scheduled for the 96-in. pipe and have noted that the named subcontractor submittal was required on that day.

Section G-5.01   The next item G-5.01 (2 and 3) relate to changes. These cannot be scheduled in advance, because it is not known what they might be or when they might occur.

Section G-6.01   Item G-6.01 requires that the engineer transmit to the contractor a listing of all items for which the contractor will be required to submit shop drawings. The sequence of events will be:

1. The engineer transmits the list to the contractor.

2. The contractor submits the shop drawings.

3. The engineer reviews the shop drawings.

4. The contractor orders the necessary materials and equipment.

5. The materials and equipment are delivered.

6. The materials and equipment are installed.

The engineer usually submits the listing of required shop drawings as soon as possible to reduce the period between ordering and receiving the materials and equipment.

On a project of short duration such as that chosen for this illustration, the expediting of all items in the six-part chain is especially important. It will be assumed that shop drawings will be required by the engineer for sheetpiling design (for both the east and west shafts) and for the liner plates to be used in the tunnel. (This may be an oversimplification of actual practice, but it will suffice for the purposes of this illustration.) It will also be necessary to assume the time required between ordering of materials and delivery. The contract administrator should work backward on the schedule to determine dates on the integrated schedule when given materials must be ready for incorporation into the project. The integrated schedule indicates that tunneling will start on Day 31. Hence delivery of liner plate shall occur on Day 30. Assuming 2 week's delivery time between ordering and receiving of the liner plate, the liner plate must be ordered by Day 20. The contractor would be imprudent to order the plate prior to the completion of the engineer's review; thus the engineer's review of the shop drawing submittal should be completed on or before Day 20, depending upon the length of time required to advise the contractor that the review has been completed. It will be assumed that they are working in the same city and that only 1 day will be required. Hence Day 19 is the day the engineer's review should be complete.

The engineer may require as much as 2 weeks to review the shop drawing submittal; it will be assumed that 1 week will be required. Thus the contractor must submit the shop drawings not later than Day 14, less 1 day for transmittal, or Day 13. Assuming that preparation of the shop drawings will require 1 week, the contractor must begin preparation on Day 8. An allowance of 1 day for the list of required shop drawings to be transmitted to the contractor by the engineer means that the engineer must complete and transmit the list (so far as the liner plate is concerned) not later than Day 7.

The contract administrator should note these key dates on the integrated schedule—with the exception of the day the list has to be sent to the contractor, because the *other* item (shop drawings for the shaft sheetpiling) may be more critical. The notes might be as follows:

Day number	Description
7	Engineer's list of shop drawing requirements sent to contractor (hold)
14	Engineer to receive shop drawing submittal for liner plate
19	Engineer's review of liner plate shop drawings to be complete
30	Liner plate to be delivered

The timing of the other item, the sheetpiling, may be more difficult to plot. The sheetpiling must be delivered by Day 10 to allow driving to start on Day 11. Allowing 1 week for delivery, the engineer's approval of the shop drawing must be completed by Day 5 and telephoned to the contractor. Assuming that the engineer will require 1 week to review the shop drawing, it will be necessary for the contractor to submit the shop drawing to the engineer on Day 0—the day he executes the contract. The inherent problem is that this early submittal may *precede* the engineer's list of required submittals. The contract administrator can only enter the required data on his integrated schedule. The contractor indicated he could mobilize within 2 weeks; this must mean either that he understood the sequential dilemma and is prepared or that he will not meet the schedule.

Day number	Description
1	Engineer's list of shop drawings to go to contractor
5	Engineer review of sheet-pile shop drawings to be complete
10	Sheetpiling to be delivered

A complete Integrated Schedule Sheet is shown in Figure 7-1.

PART TWO

SYSTEMATIZATION

Chapter 1 set forth the method by which the Control Responsibility Summary Sheet could be generated. "Control responsibilities" were defined as responsibilities imposed by the contract documents which would either:

1. Require positive action by one of the participants engaged on the project

2. Require interaction of two or more participants

3. Require extensive record keeping

Control responsibilities which require interaction between two or more of the participants are candidates for systematization. The interaction of these participants must be recorded in order that each has a clear understanding of "whose move is next." Furthermore, the action required to keep a given process moving will require standardized letters to the various participants. Thus the systematization process will involve the generation of status sheets to keep track of whose move is next and a number of standard letters to save the contract administrator's time in generating and transmitting repetitious correspondence.

The control responsibilities which should be systematized can be determined from review of the Control Responsibility Summary Sheet for the contract being administered. Part 2 will discuss establishment of the systems for these interactive processes. Other complementary systems—such as those dealing with clarifications and unit-price items—will also be illustrated. Timely development and diligent application of the systems described in Part 2 will afford the contract administrator both the satisfaction of thorough, timely administration of routine matters and the freedom to devote additional time to the more difficult aspects of the project.

CHAPTER 8

CLARIFICATIONS

The clear meaning of contract provisions cannot always be determined by mere reading, however diligent. Provisions may be incomplete, contradictory, or otherwise confused. Some of these contract provisions may merely be ambiguous, i.e., they have two distinct but plausible possible meanings, and the reader cannot determine which should apply; others are vague, i.e., their meanings are utterly unclear, and no plausible alternative meanings are evident to the reader. Given the tremendous dollar consequences which can attend misinterpretations of the contract, it is essential to develop an efficient mechanism by which ambiguity and vagueness in the contract can be effectively resolved. The task of developing this mechanism usually falls to the contract administrator.

A clarification is an interpretation of the meaning of the contract. It usually takes the form of written communication from the contract administrator to the contractor, the party responsible for construction of the project. Inasmuch as the contract administrator will encounter innumerable requests for clarification during his career—and possibly during a single major project—he will be well advised to develop a routine procedure, i.e., a *system*, to promote comprehensive treatment of each clarification and to permit routine functions to be handled at a clerical level, freeing the contract administrator to attend to matters which require expertise.

THE CLARIFICATION SYSTEM

The clarification process may be initiated by a request, either oral or written, from the contractor or the contract administrator or by the design engineer's unilateral decision to provide further detail for the contract or to cure existing ambiguity or vagueness in the contract. The contract administrator is, in most cases, not the participant who generates the contract documents. Therefore, in processing clarifications, it is necessary that the contract administrator consult with the party who did generate the contract, usually the design engineer. Upon receipt of either the design engineer's reply to a request for clarification or material submitted unilaterally by the design engineer, the contract administrator should evaluate the submittal in light of his knowledge of the contract documents. It is important that the material submitted be in the form of a directive which will occasion no change in cost to the owner rather than one which will lead to a modification ultimately affecting the contract price. It should be noted that this consideration by the contract administrator is not a final determination of whether or not the clarification will occasion additional expense to the owner; the contractor always has the option to claim additional compensation (see Chapter 9). Rather, the reasons for the contract administrator's consideration at this point are twofold: first, if the clarification will occasion a change in the contract price, addressing the matter at this point may reduce or eliminate processing expenses which attend claims; second, a feeling of mutual trust between the contractor and contract administrator is promoted when the contractor recognizes that the contract administrator is attempting to treat him fairly.

In the event the contract administrator determines that the clarification should not occasion a change in the contract price, he must advise the contractor of the details of the clarification. In his transmittal document, the contract administrator should also note that, should the contractor disagree with the contract administrator's position that no additional compensation is warranted, the contractor should so advise the contract administrator immediately and in writing. In Part 1, it was pointed out that many contracts require that the contractor give notice of claim within certain time periods: these deadlines would preclude reimbursement to the contractor for clarification which occasions additional expense unless the contractor raised that matter within the time periods set forth in the claim provisions of the contract. Methods by which valid additional costs incurred by the contractor are to be reimbursed will be considered in Chapter 9. The foregoing discussion provides the likely scenario for generation of clarifications to the contract.

The reader will recall the suggestion in Chapter 1 that any provisions of the contract which were unclear to the contract administrator during his review of the contract documents be noted and discussed with the design engineer with regard to issuance of clarification to the contract. It is likely that the contract administrator's clarification file would receive its first entries during this early review by the contract administrator himself. As the project progresses, most additional clarifications will be issued in reply to questions raised by the contractor.

The need for tabulation of clarifications, the strict time provisions of the claim provisions of the contract, and the probable recurrence of clarifications during each major project make it advisable for the contract administrator to establish a system for efficient and effective handling of clarifications. It is important that each clarification during a given project remain distinct. The suggested method to distinguish clarifications is to number them sequentially.

The Clarification Status Sheet

The sequence of possible events for each clarification may be presented in outline form:

1. Who initiated the clarification?

    a. The contract administrator

    b. The contractor

    c. The design engineer

2. Did the contract administrator request written clarification for the meaning of the contract from the design engineer except for those clarifications initiated by the design engineer?

3. Did the contract administrator receive a response to his inquiry from the design engineer?

4. If the contract administrator found the clarification did not change the cost to the owner, did he transmit the written clarification to the contractor?

5. Did the clarification system terminate for a given clarification by reason of the contractor's failure to reply within the time period established in the contract for filing a claim (see Chapter 9)?

6. If the contractor made a timely reply containing the position that, in his opinion, additional cost would be occasioned, was the reply recorded by the contract administrator as a bona fide claim?

This outline should be carried forward into a Clarification Status Sheet in order that the status of a given clarification may be determined at any given point and that the contract administrator's personnel can refer to a single checklist for comprehensive treatment of the clarification. Since many clarifications may be in process simultaneously in a large construction project, it is important that the sheet contain a heading which provides ready distinction among clarifications and be attached to the left-hand side of a separate file folder created for each clarification. Following the heading on the sheet, a space should be provided for a brief description of the clarification. The next information required is identification of the participant initiating the clarification and the date of initiation. A letter or note which initiated the clarification process should be filed as the first entry on the right-hand side of the file folder. The contract administrator should provide space to record the fact and date of notice to the design engineer and receipt of his response. The sheet should next allow for indication of the fact and date of advice to the contractor. If the contract administrator and the design engineer concur that there should be no increase to the contract price in consequence of the clarification, the contract administrator should write to the contractor to provide the clarification and to indicate that no change in the contract price is contemplated. If the contractor fails to provide a response, no further entries are required on the sheet; however, if the contractor makes an *untimely* response, the contract administrator should send to the contractor a letter confirming his failure to meet the deadline and should note on the sheet "Claim Rejected" and the date of rejection. On the other hand, a timely exception by the contractor would constitute a claim, and space to record the transformation of the clarification into a claim and acknowledgment of this new claim should be provided on the Clarification Status Sheet. Figure 8-1 is a copy of a sample Clarification Status Sheet.

As each letter is transmitted or received, a copy should be affixed to the right-hand side of the clarification file folder, an "x" inserted in the appropriate box on the Clarification Status Sheet, and the date noted in the space provided.

Standard Letters for the Clarification System

Having devised his Clarification Status Sheet, the contract administrator's next task is to develop the standard letters necessary to complete the system. The first such standard letter would be a form for request for clarification to be sent to the design engineer. Figure 8-2 is a sample standard letter for this purpose.

It is suggested that in major projects an original, preaddressed letter be typed in advance and that numerous copies be put into a general file to permit rapid communication as required: the various components of the letter could be completed as the need for clarification arose.

The next standard letter (Figure 8-3) required for the clarification

CLARIFICATION STATUS SHEET

Project _____

Contractor _____

Owner _____

Contract No. _____

Clarification No. _____

Description _____

_____

☐ Clarification Initiated by:

    ☐ The Contractor   Date: _____

    ☐ The Contract Administrator   Date: _____

    ☐ The Design Engineer   Date: _____

☐ Design Engineer Advised   Date: _____

☐ Design Engineer Reply Received   Date: _____

☐ Contractor Advised   Date: _____

☐ Contractor's Claim Received   Date: _____

    ☐ Claim Rejected   Date: _____

    ☐ Claim Acknowledged   Date: _____

         Transferred to Claim No.   _____

FIGURE 8-1 Clarification Status Sheet.

(Date) _____

(Design Firm) _____
(Address) _____
(City, State) _____

Attn: (Design Engineer) _____

Re: (Project Title) _____

Subject: Clarification (No.) _____

File: (File No.) _____

Gentlemen:

Please advise me of your interpretation of the meaning of the Contract Documents for the above referenced project related to the

☐ attached written request for clarification from the Contractor
_____

☐ the following: _____
_____
_____

This request for Clarification was initiated by ☐ this office
☐ the Contractor
☐ other.

Very truly yours,

(Contract Administrator) _____

cc: Clarification File

FIGURE 8-2 Request for clarification.

(Date)

(Contractor)
(Address)
(City, State)

Attn: (Contractor Rep.)

Re: (Project Title)

Subject: Clarification (No.)

File: (File No.)

Gentlemen:

We have been advised by Mr. (Design Engineer) of (Design Firm) of the following Clarification to your Contract on the above referenced project:

It is our opinion that the foregoing Clarification should result in no additional cost to the Owner. Should your opinion differ, so advise this office immediately and in writing.

Very truly yours,

(Contract Administrator)

cc: (Design Engineer)
     Clarification File

FIGURE 8-3 Advice of clarification.

system is the notice of clarification to be sent to the contractor. As in the case of the first standard letter, partly completed copies can be prepared in advance to facilitate immediate processing.

Close adherence to this straightforward system for processing clarifications will allow the contract administrator to reduce the time which he previously had to spend in discharging this relatively mundane responsibility of his position. The system reduces clarification activity to a near-clerical function. The need for rethinking the handling of each request for clarification and reorigination of correspondence for each clarification is eliminated. With these processing requirements reduced to a routine, the contract administrator is left with sufficient time to consider the *problem* which underlies the clarification, with the result that the quality of his effort will be improved to his own satisfaction and the owner's benefit.

CHAPTER 9

CLAIMS

During the course of a construction project, a contractor may conclude that compensation beyond that provided for in the contract documents is due. If the contractor so notifies the owner in accordance with procedures set forth in the contract documents, the contractor will be deemed to have made a "claim."

In Part 1, it was pointed out that a contract provision which defines claims and which sets forth claim procedures constitutes a "responsibility requiring interaction between two or more participants in the construction arrangement," i.e., a control responsibility. The purpose of this chapter is to explain and illustrate the systematization of the claim "responsibility" so as to permit monitoring (the subject of Part 3) in the most efficient and effective manner. The method of illustration will be analysis of sample claim provisions. Naturally, variations between these sample provisions, on the one hand, and those actually encountered by the reader, on the other, will occasion some differences in his or her systematization of the latter provisions; however, the technique for systematization will remain unchanged.

SAMPLE CONTRACT CLAIM PROVISIONS

CLAIMS

If the Contractor claims (1) that any work he has been ordered to do is extra work or (2) that he has performed or is going to perform extra work or (3) that any action or omission of the Owner or the Engineer is contrary to the terms and provisions of the Contract, he shall:

a. Promptly comply with such order;

b. File with the Owner and the Engineer within fourteen working days after being ordered to perform the work claimed by him to be Extra Work or within fourteen working days after commencing performance of the Extra Work, whichever date shall be the earlier, or within fourteen working days after the said action or omission on the part of the Owner or the Engineer occurred, a written notice of the basis of his claim and request a determination thereof;

c. File with the Owner and the Engineer, within thirty calendar days after said alleged extra work was required to be performed or said alleged extra work was commenced, whichever date shall be earlier, or said alleged action or omission by the Owner or the Engineer occurred, a verified detailed statement, with documentary evidence, or the items and basis of his claim;

d. Produce for the Owner's examination, upon notice from the Owner, all his books of account, bills, invoices, payrolls, subcontracts, time books, progress records, daily reports, bank deposit books, bank statements, checkbooks, and canceled checks, showing all of his actions and transactions in connection with or relating to or arising by reason of his claim, and submit himself and persons in his employment and in his subcontractor's employment for examination under oath by any person designated by the Owner to investigate any claims made against the Owner under the Contract, such examination to be made at the offices of the Owner or the Owner's agent;

e. Proceed diligently, pending and subsequent to the determination of the Owner with respect to any such disputed matter, with the performance of the Contract and in accordance with all instructions of the Owner and the Engineer.

The Contractor's failure to comply with any or all of the foregoing provisions of this Section shall be deemed to be: (1) a conclusive and binding determination on his part that said order, work, action, or omission does not involve Extra Work and is not contrary to the terms and provisions of the Contract; and (2) a waiver by the Contractor of all claims for additional compensation or damages as a result of said order, work, action, or omission.

No person has power to waive or modify any of the foregoing provisions and in any action against the Owner to recover any sum in excess of the sum certified by the Owner to be due under or by reason of the Contract, the Contractor must allege in his complaint and prove at the trial compliance with the provisions of this Section.

Nothing in this Section shall in any way affect the Owner's right to obtain an examination before or a discovery and inspection in any action that might be instituted by or against the Owner or the Contractor.

THE SYSTEM FOR CLAIMS

Briefly, the systematization technique to be employed consists of (1) defining the interaction required of participants in the claim provisions of the contract documents and generating a "status sheet" to afford the contract administrator ready access to information concerning the progress of interaction for a given claim at any given point in the construction process and (2) generation of "standard letters" to permit effective processing of claims at the most efficient level.

The Status Sheet for Claims

The reader will note that the sample claim provisions describe three situations in which a claim may be filed:

1. Where the contractor has concluded that he has been ordered to do work which is at variance with the provisions of the contract

2. Where the contractor has concluded that he has performed, or is about to perform, extra work

3. Where the contractor has concluded that an act or omission of either the owner or its agents, at variance with terms and conditions of the contract, has been, or will be, committed

The sample provisions then delineate the contractor's responsibilities in any such circumstances:

- To comply with any such work order, notwithstanding the contractor's opinion that the order is at variance with the terms and conditions of the contract

- To deliver to the owner and its engineer (contract administrator) within 14 days of the receipt of such an order a written statement of the basis of his claim in connection with that order

- To deliver to the owner and its engineer (contract administrator) within 30 days of receipt of the order a detailed, verified statement with documentary evidence of the items and basis of the claim

The sample provisions go on to state that the contractor's failure to discharge any of these responsibilities will result in a waiver of the claim; in other words, no compensation will be due the contractor in connection with the circumstance which gave rise to the contractor's claim.

In developing the Claim Status Sheet, the contract administrator should closely follow the sense and sequence of the contract claim provisions. For example, the sample provisions establish three circumstances in which a claim may be asserted and place a premium upon time in that assertion. Hence the first general heading on the Claim Status Sheet should deal with the type of circumstance giving rise to the generation of the claim and the date of generation. This may be accomplished by merely outlining the sample provisions as follows:

1. Claim generation

   a. Date alleged work was ordered   __/__/__

         or

   b. Date contractor states he
   (has performed, will perform)
   alleged extra work   __/__/__

         or

   c. Date contractor alleges
   (act, omission) of the
   (owner, engineer, contract
   administrator) occurred   __/__/__

(The inapplicable items within parentheses should be deleted by the person completing the sheet for a given claim.)

Standard Letters in the Claim System

In addition to the mere recording of dates on the Claim Status Sheet, the contract administrator will be well advised to provide certain notices to the contractor who has made a claim in order to increase the probability that the claim provisions will be upheld in the event the matter ultimately proceeds to arbitration or litigation. In projects of substantial size and in multiple projects where identical claim provisions are employed, these notices will be most effectively and efficiently accomplished by the use of standard letters. These letters serve two purposes: first, they remind the contractor of the terms and conditions of the contract in a timely manner; second, they create valuable evidence of dates and sequences in complex and protracted matters.

Date _____

(Contractor) _____

(Address) _____

_____

Attention: (Contractor Representative)

Re: (Project Title)

_____

Contract (No.)

Subj: Order to Proceed

(No.) _____

File: _____

Gentlemen:

The purpose of this letter is to order (Contractor) to proceed immediately, pursuant to the abovementioned Contract, to perform the following work:

_____

_____

_____

Should it be (Contractor) opinion that the work detailed above is extra work and not a Contractual obligation, file with the Owner and the Engineer, within fourteen (14) days from the date of this letter, written notification of the basis of your Firm's Claim and request determination of it in strict accordance with the General Provisions Section _____, CLAIMS, of the Contract Documents.

Very truly yours,

(Contract Administrator)

cc: Proceed Order File

FIGURE 9-1 Order to proceed.

Date _____

(Contractor)_____

(Address)_____

_____

Attention: (Contractor Representative)

Re: (Project Title)____

(Letter Dated)____

Contract (No.)____

Subj: Claim No. _____

File: _____

Gentlemen:

The purpose of this letter is to acknowledge receipt of said letter, dated _____, (copy attached), and to advise that said letter will be documented as Claim No. _____ in the above mentioned Contract.

Proceed in strict accordance with General Provisions Section _____, CLAIMS, of the Contract Documents.

Very truly yours,

(Contract Administrator)

cc: Owner
     Engineer
     Claim File

FIGURE 9-2   Acknowledgment of claim letter.

Date _____

(Contractor) _____

(Address) _____

Attention: (Contractor Representative)

Re: (Project Title) _____

_____

Contract (No.) _____

Subj: (Claim No.)_____

_____

File: _____

Gentlemen:

It is the (Owner's, Engineer's) understanding that it is (Contractor's) opinion, that the alleged (action, omission) by the (Owner, Engineer) described below is contrary to the terms and provisions of the above-mentioned Contract:

_____

_____

_____

_____

Should this understanding of your Firm's opinion be correct, file with the Owner and the Engineer, within fourteen (14) working days from the date that (action, omission) occurred (date), written notification of the basis of your Claim and request determination of it in strict accordance with General Provisions Section _____, CLAIMS, of the Contract Document for the above referenced project.

Very truly yours,

(Contract Administrator)

cc: Owner
    Engineer
    Claim File

FIGURE 9-3 Acknowledgment of contrary opinion.

The first such standard letter is that which orders the contractor to proceed with given items of work in the first instance. This letter should contain standard language insofar as reference to the contract itself is concerned but should allow for case-by-case entries concerning specific items of work. Figure 9-1 is a sample work order letter.

The second circumstance in which a claim may be initiated by a contractor is that in which the contractor has concluded that he has been, or will be, required to perform work beyond the scope of the contract, i.e., extra work. In such a circumstance, it is incumbent upon the contractor to provide timely notice to the owner and the engineer (contract administrator). Accordingly, a second standard letter which contains standard language acknowledging receipt of such a claim should be prepared in advance by the contract administrator. The over-riding purpose of this letter is to create an *independent* record of the date on which the contract administrator received the contractor's notice of claim; this dating can be most valuable in refuting the validity of an untimely—but backdated—claim letter from the contractor. Figure 9-2 is a sample claim acknowledgment letter.

The third and final circumstance in which the contractor may generate a claim arises when the contractor has concluded that some alleged act or omission of the owner or the engineer (contract administrator) entitles the contractor to additional compensation. This conclusion may follow the contractor's issuance of a proceed order letter which, in the contractor's judgment, calls for work beyond the scope of the contract or in substantial modification of the scope contemplated in the contract. On the other hand, the contractor may believe that the owner or an agent of the owner—including the contract administrator—has done something at variance with the contract or has failed to do something required by the contract, with resulting expense to the contractor. Among the most common types of such acts and omissions are failures to furnish the site on a timely basis after issuance of the "notice to proceed," hindrance of the contractor's activities, and delays in commenting upon submittals by the contractor. Whatever the alleged act or omission giving rise to the contractor's conclusion, it is incumbent upon the contract administrator to create an independent record of the first assertion of the claim. Figure 9-3 contains a sample acknowledgment in the form of an action or omission letter.

The possible responses of the contract administrator to the three types of claims which might be asserted under the sample claim provisions can now easily be reflected on the Claim Status Sheet by revising the sheet to indicate the use or nonuse of the foregoing standard letters. The revised sheet should include the following items:

1. Claim generation

   a. Date alleged work was ordered   __/__/__

       Date standard letter Figure 9-1 transmitted   __/__/__

          or

   b. Date contractor states he
   (has performed, will perform)
   alleged extra work   __/__/__

       Date standard letter Figure 9-2 transmitted   __/__/__

          or

   c. Date contractor alleges
   (action, omission) by the
   (owner, agent) occurred   __/__/__

       Date standard letter Figure 9-3 transmitted   __/__/__

The systematization of claims has to this point been concerned exclusively with the *type* of claim the contractor is permitted to assert and appropriate standard responses to such assertions. The next requirement of the sample claim provisions concerns the timeliness and completeness of the contractor's initial *explanation* of the claim. Under the terms of the sample, the contractor must not only provide notice of the event giving rise to the claim but also provide notice of the contractual *basis* of the claim within 14 working days of the occurrence of the event. If the contractor fails to meet this obligation, the claim will be deemed to have been waived, i.e., no compensation will be due the contractor for work in connection with the claim.

The possibility that a claim may be waived through the mere passage of time occasions development of a fourth standard letter, the 14-day waiver letter, in Figure 9-4.

The issuance of the 14-day waiver letter ends the contract administrator's claim procedure for that claim inasmuch as the contractor failed to meet an absolute deadline in its assertion. Further disputes in such matters are best deferred, by agreement, to the end of the project for additional examination or, failing such agreement, referred to the *owner's* legal counsel. The first priority, from the contract administrator's perspective, is to keep the project moving; referring the dispute to a third party—owner's counsel—promotes that goal by making *him* the adverse party in the contractor's eyes and by acquainting the owner's legal experts with the facts at the earliest practical time.

Assuming, however, that the contractor *does* comply within the 14-day provision (i.e., that the 14-day waiver letter is not required to be used), the contractor must then meet another strict requirement of time

Date _____

(Contractor) _____

(Address) _____

_____

Attention: _____

Re: (Project Title) _____

_____

Contract _____

Subj: Claim No. _____

File: _____

Gentlemen:

The purpose of this letter is to confirm that Claim No. _____ in the above mentioned Contract is deemed to be waived, in accordance with General Provisions _____, CLAIMS, of the Contract Documents, due to your Firm's failure to file with the Owner and the Engineer a written notice of the basis of its claim within fourteen (14) working days from the date documented by (our letter of _____, your letter of _____, whichever is earlier).

Very truly yours,

(Contract Administrator)

cc: Owner
    Engineer
    Claim File

FIGURE 9-4   Notice of waiver of claim (14 days).

and substance under the sample claim provisions. Within 30 calendar days of the occurrence of the event giving rise to the claim, the contractor must deliver to the owner and the engineer (contract administrator) a verified, detailed statement of the items of the claim and their bases. If such a statement is received by the contract administrator, he should immediately note the date of *actual* receipt on the Claim Status Sheet: he can then determine whether the submittal was timely and adequate. Should the submittal be found to be untimely or inadequate, or should the contract administrator determine during monitoring (see Part 3) that no submittal was made during the 30-day period, a written communication similar to the 30-day waiver letter shown in Figure 9-5 should be sent immediately to the Contractor.

This communication will have the same effect in terminating the contract administrator's claim procedure as that accomplished by the 14-day waiver letter; further disputes concerning the claim should be deferred by agreement or referred to the owner's legal counsel.

Assuming that the procedural requirements placed by the contract with the contractor have been met (i.e., assuming that the contractor's claim fell into one of the three categories, that notice was provided in adequate form to the proper participants within 14 days, and that adequate substantiation in proper form was provided to the proper participants within 30 days), it will be necessary under the sample claim provisions for the owner to resolve the claim on its merits within a reasonable time. There are three possible resolutions of a claim on its merits:

1. Issuance of a modification by the owner to pay ultimately to the contractor an agreed-upon sum in satisfaction of the claim

2. Receipt by the owner or the contract administrator of written communication from the contractor withdrawing the claim

3. Negotiation, arbitration, or litigation of the claim (and perhaps others) at the conclusion of the project

In order to achieve resolution of the claim by any of these media, a number of meetings may be required. The Claim Status Sheet should specify the dates of all such meetings; the contract administrator's detailed minutes of such meetings should be filed with the sheet. If the claim was resolved by issuance of a modification to pay ultimately an agreed-upon sum, the number and date of the modification should be recorded on the sheet. Similarly, the date of receipt of any withdrawal letter from the contractor should also be noted. The record of any negotiation, arbitration, or litigation at the end of the project would transcend the sheet.

Date _____

(Contractor) _____

(Address) _____

_____

Attention: _____

                    Re: (Project Title) _____

                         _____

                         Contract _____

          Subj: Claim No. _____

          File: _____

Gentlemen:

The purpose of this letter is to confirm that Claim No. _____ in the above mentioned Contract is deemed to be waived, in accordance with General Provisions _____, CLAIMS, of the Contract Documents, due to your Firm's failure to file with the Owner and the Engineer a verified detailed statement with documentary evidence of the items and basis of your claim within thirty (30) days of the date documented by your Firm's letter of _____.

Very truly yours,

(Contract Administrator)

cc: Owner
      Engineer
      Claim File

FIGURE 9-5   **Failure of timely submittal (30 days).**

The method by which the systems established in Part 2 can best be employed to prosecute the project and protect the interests of the owner and the contract administrator will be discussed at length in Part 3.

The Claim Status Sheet can now be expanded to address the full range of eventualities contemplated by the sample claim provisions. Also, uniform sheet headings can be developed for use where the contract administrator becomes involved with more than one project at one time. Finally, multiple claims in any one project should be numbered consecutively to facilitate record keeping and to avoid redundant payments. Figure 9-6 is a complete Claim Status Sheet for the sample claim provisions.

Once the sheet *form* has been determined, the final step in the systematization is preparation of a file folder for each claim pursuant to each contract. The sheet should be stapled to the left inner side of a manila folder; all claim correspondence and meeting minutes should be bound onto the other side. Additional folders should be used to accommodate volume, and in such cases cross-references to key documents in succeeding folders should be marked on the sheet.

SUMMARY

In Part 1, contractual responsibilities requiring interaction of two or more participants were defined as control responsibilities and were tabulated in a Control Responsibility Summary Sheet. It was pointed out that such interactive responsibilities often required systematization for efficient and effective administration. The typical claim features of contracts were noted to constitute such interactive control responsibilities.

In Part 2 sample claim provisions have been dissected to distill quasi-clerical tasks by which the contract administrator might easily discharge *his* responsibilities for administration of claims. The development of standard letters and a Claim Status Sheet has been the principal means to this end. (Further standardization through computerization is possible but beyond the scope of this book.)

In Part 3, the claim system will be employed to achieve expeditious processing without disturbing the project.

Again, the reader is cautioned that variations between the sample claim provisions presented here and those actually encountered will necessarily occasion adjustments to the development of standard letters and the Claim Status Sheet. The entries in the letters and the sheet will vary according to the contract, but the technique for creating them will stand.

PROJECT _____   FILE NO. _____
OWNER _____
CONTRACTOR _____   CONTRACT NO. _____

CLAIM NO. _____

CLAIM GENERATION	DATES	CROSS-REFERENCE TO OTHER FOLDERS
Date alleged extra work was ordered	_/_/_	
Date (Figure 9-1) transmitted	_/_/_	
or		
Date Contractor states he (has or will) perform alleged extra work	_/_/_	
Date (Figure 9-2) transmitted	_/_/_	
or		
Date Contractor alleges (action or omission) of the (Owner or Engineer occurred	_/_/_	
Date (Figure 9-3) transmitted	_/_/_	
Date (Figure 9-4) transmitted	_/_/_	
or		
Date of written notice of basis Claim received from the Contractor	_/_/_	
Date (Figure 9-5) transmitted to Contractor	_/_/_	
Date letter containing detail statement or items and basis of Claim	_/_/_	
Date of Meeting No. 1	_/_/_	
Date of Meeting No. 2	_/_/_	
Date of Meeting No. 3	_/_/_	
Resolution Obtained in Meeting No. __	_____	
Date Order No. ____ Issued	_/_/_	
Date Withdrawal Letter Received	_/_/_ "	

FIGURE 9-6   Claim Status Sheet.

CHAPTER 10

MODIFICATIONS

Section G-5.01 of the sample contract provisions, in Chapter 1, provides for modifications to the contract documents. It was noted in Chapter 1 that section G-5.01 is comprised of certain control responsibilities and that it requires interaction of two or more of the participants in the construction process. Since modifications are somewhat complex, and since many modifications may be necessary in a large construction project, it is useful for the contract administrator to have at his disposal a routine procedure, i.e., a *system*, for processing modifications.

A "modification" is merely a mechanism by which an alteration to the contract may be approved in concept by the owner, detailed by the design engineer, and priced by the contractor, then confirmed by the contract administrator as to its necessity and desirability for the project and as to the appropriateness of the price. Once a modification has undergone these processes, it is documented by issuance of a change order (the subject of the next chapter).

A modification may increase, decrease, or leave unchanged the contract price. It may be initiated by the owner, the contractor, the design engineer, or the contract administrator; or it may evolve from a validated claim.

THE MODIFICATION SYSTEM

It is important to the contract administrator to have a clear understanding of the routes usually traveled by modifications as determined by the respective participant who initiates them. Where the modification is initiated by the owner, the owner usually advises either the contract administrator or the design engineer of the owner's desire to change either the contract specifications or the contract drawings. A commonly desired change is the manufacture of certain equipment or repartitioning of a building to change room sizes. Assuming that the owner contacted the contract administrator, the contract administrator then advises the design engineer of the desired change. The design engineer would review the proposed change to ascertain whether it falls within the design parameters of the project and whether it necessitates other changes not envisioned by the owner. If he finds the proposed change to be compatible with the overall design, he generates the necessary revisions to the project to incorporate the change and develops a cost estimate for the change, all of which he transmits to the contract administrator. The contract administrator then issues the revised drawings or specifications to the contractor and requests that the contractor propose a price or credit, if any, for incorporating the change into the project. Upon receipt of the proposed price, the contract administrator reviews it for conformance with the contract (see sample contract provision G-5.02 in Chapter 1) and compares the proposed price to the design engineer's estimate. If the disparity between the two cost estimates seems unreasonable, the contract administrator would schedule a meeting of concerned participants to resolve the matter. If the contractor's price proposal meets both the terms of the contract and the design engineer's estimate, the contract administrator prepares the paperwork necessary to obtain the owner's approval and transmits it to the owner. Upon receipt of an approved document, the contract administrator transmits the document to the contractor; in the event of the owner's disapproval, the contract administrator so advises the contractor in writing. In the event of the owner's approval, the contract administrator subsequently incorporates the approved modification into a "change order," the subject of Chapter 11.

Modifications initiated by the design engineer follow a somewhat different path. The design engineer would provide notice of the change, the reason for the change, and a cost estimate to the contract administrator. Reasons for such a request might include the availability of better equipment than that originally specified, design omissions, or changed legal requirements for the project. The contract administrator would then request the owner's approval to proceed with the desired change. Upon receipt of the owner's advice that the proposed change is accepted, accepted with conditions, or rejected, the contract administrator would so advise the design engineer. Assuming that the proposal was accepted by the owner, the design engineer would transmit the necessary revised drawings or specifications to the contract administrator. These materials would be forwarded to the contractor, whereupon the modification procedure would become identical to that employed where the owner initiated the changes.

The procedure for modifications initiated by the contractor and the contract administrator, respectively, are virtually identical. If the contractor desired a change, he would so advise the contract administrator. Typical reasons for such a request include projected delays for certain types or brands of equipment, value engineering considerations, and special construction difficulties occasioned by the design. Whether the change is initiated by the contractor or by the contract administrator himself, the contract administrator would then request the owner's approval and the design engineer's preliminary clearance to initiate the modification and his cost estimate. The owner would furnish notice that it had approved initiation of the modification, approved it with conditions, or rejected it. Assuming approval, the contract administrator would advise the design engineer of the desired change in detail. The design engineer would then review the proposed change for conformance to the overall project design, and so forth.

The Modification Status Sheet

Given the several routes which modifications can take, the contract administrator's first task in systematizing this sector of his activity is to develop a single "Modification Status Sheet" in order to know the status of a given modification at any given point and for use in developing the standard letters described subsequently in this chapter. The conceptual sequence of the sheet, in outline form, is as follows:

1. Who initiated the modification?

   a. Owner

   b. Design engineer

   c. Contractor

   d. Contract administrator

2. What was owner's response to the request for modification?

   a. Approval

   b. Approval with conditions

   c. Rejection

3. What was input of design engineer?

   a. Concurrence with the proposed change

   b. Revised drawings and/or specifications

   c. Detailed cost estimate

4. What was disposition of contractor's price proposal:

   a. Requested

   b. Reviewed

   c. Accepted

   d. Discussed, changed, and/or accepted

5. What materials were furnished to Owner?

   a. Letter of intent

   b. Summary of the modification

   c. Contractor's price proposal

   d. Design engineer's estimate of cost

6. Was contractor advised of owner's decision?

7. Is change order to be issued?

A sample Modification Status Sheet based on the foregoing conceptual sequence is seen in Figure 10-1.

Standard Modification Letters

It is essential that all but the most trivial deviations from the contract be documented through the modification process irrespective of whether they affect the contract price. The contract administrator must always bear in mind that it is the owner—and not he—who is the ultimate beneficiary of the work of the contract and that all departures from the contract are to be approved by the owner and recorded by the contract administrator.

It is readily apparent that employment of the modification procedures can result in heavy administrative effort on the part of the contract administrator. The amount of effort required and the repetitive nature of the modification process make the use of standard letters especially advantageous. Also, the use of standard letters permits development of standard verbiage among modifications and among

MODIFICATION STATUS SHEET

Project _____ Mod. No. _____

Owner _____

Contractor _____

Initiated by: □ Owner □ Engineer □ Contractor
□ Contract Administrator

□ Claim No. _____

I		□ Date Modification Initiated	(Date)_____
II		□ Date Owner's Permission to Proceed Requested	(Date)_____
III	A	□ Date of Owner's Rejection	(Date)_____
		or	
III	B	□ Date of Owner's Permission to Proceed	(Date)_____
IV		□ Date Engineer's Concurrence Requested	(Date)_____
V		□ Date Engineer's Concurrence Received	(Date)_____
VI	A	□ Date Engineer's Estimate of Cost Received	(Date)_____
VI	B	□ Date Revised Dwgs/Verbal Description Rec'd	(Date)_____
VII	A	□ Date Contractor's Price Proposal Requested	(Date)_____
VIII	A	□ Date Contractor's Price Proposal Received	(Date)_____
IX	A	□ Date Contractor's Price Proposal Reviewed	(Date)_____
VII	B	□ Date Contractor's Revised Price Proposal Requested	(Date)_____
VIII	B	□ Date Contractor's Revised Price Proposal Received	(Date)_____
IX	B	□ Date Contractor's Revised Price Proposal Reviewed	(Date)_____
X		□ Date Owner's Acceptance of Mod. Requested	(Date)_____
XI		□ Date Owner's Acceptance of Mod. Received	(Date)_____
XII		□ Date Letter of Intent Sent to Contractor	(Date)_____
XIII		□ Incorporated into Change Order No. _____	
		on	(Date)_____

FIGURE 10-1   Modification Status Sheet.

documents in the same modification. It is important that the description of the scope of work employed by the design engineer be identical to that upon which the contractor bases his price, to which the owner agrees, and which ultimately appears in a change order. Any substantial differences in these descriptions could lead to disputes which might result in legal action. Finally, the use of standard letters and standard verbiage permits employment of sophisticated processing techniques, such as computerization, which are beyond the scope of this book.

The starting point in generating the necessary standard letters for modifications is the Modification Status Sheet. The reader will recall that multiple modifications for a single contractor should be numbered consecutively to facilitate distinction among them. The sequence of events described in the Modification Status Sheet is variable until line VII(A) is reached: the reason for the variability is that, to this point, a modification can follow any of the numerous routes described earlier in this chapter. For example, if a modification were to result from a claim by the contractor, the procedure outlined in the sheet would be followed step by step. The same would be true if either the contractor or the contract administrator initiated an ordinary modification. If, however, the owner were to request the modification, the written request would be filed in the right-hand side of the file folder for documentation of steps I, II, and III(B); the remainder of the sheet would then be followed in order. If the design engineer were to request a modification, the request would be followed in the right-hand side of the file folder for documentation of steps I, IV, and V. The contract administrator would then return to step II, skip the already-completed steps IV and V, and complete the sheet. Notwithstanding this variety of possible sequences, in generating standard letters the contract administrator should proceed sequentially through the entire Modification Status Sheet.

The title block of the sheet and line I are self-explanatory. Step II requires the permission of the owner to proceed with the modification process. In order to render an informed decision, the owner must be advised of the reason for the modification, the scope of work contemplated, an estimate of additional construction cost (if any), an estimate of additional design cost, and the identity of the participant requesting the modification. To provide this information, the contract administrator should generate a standard letter, such as Figure 10-2. The owner's return of one copy of this standard letter, with the owner's decision noted, will enable the contract administrator to complete line III(A) or III(B).

It is possible that, at this stage, the contractor would have no knowl-

(Date) _____

(Owner) _____

_____

Attn: _____

Re: Project Title

Subject: Modification No. _____

File: _____

Gentlemen:

The purpose of this letter is to request your permission to proceed with the Modification Process for the subject modification on the above referenced project.

This modification was initiated by:

☐ the Contractor
☐ the Design Engineer
☐ the Contract Administrator
☐ Claim No. _____

Reason for the Modification

_____
_____
_____

Scope of Work of the Modification

Modification No. ___ provides for _____
_____
_____
_____

Conceptual Estimate of Construction Price/Credit

☐ price
The construction ☐ credit resultant from the subject modification is conceptually estimated to be $_____.

Conceptual Estimate of Engineer Price

The engineering price for the subject modification is conceptually estimated to be $_____.

Please return one copy of this letter noting your decision below.

Very truly yours,

_____
Contract Administrator

cc: Engineer
Mod. File

Response:

☐ Proceed with the Modification
☐ Void the Modification

_____   _____
Owner   Date

FIGURE 10-2 Request for permission to proceed with modification.

edge of the request for modification. Nevertheless, even if the owner rejected the request for modification, the contractor must be advised that the modification has been rejected in order to maintain the proper numerical sequence for subsequent modifications involving the contractor in question. Also, it will be prudent for the contract administrator to provide notice of the owner's grant or denial of permission to proceed with the modification to all concerned participants and to retain documentation of that notice in his file. The standard letter seen in Figure 10-3 would be useful in informing the contractor of the owner's decision to deny permission to proceed with the modification.

The second entity from which permission to proceed with the modification must be obtained is the design engineer. This permission would most likely be granted in conversation between the contract administrator and the design engineer, but it should be documented. The design engineer's concurrence could be obtained at the same time as, or prior to, solicitation of the owner's permission. Of course, if the contract administrator and design engineer are parts of the same firm, prior concurrence would be more likely. If a design engineer were the participant who initiated the request for the modification, his concurrence would already be on record; on the other hand, if that concurrence is not already in hand, transmission of the standard letter shown in Figure 10-4, together with a copy of the standard letter soliciting the owner's concurrence, should suffice. Should the design engineer's permission be denied, a meeting would be required to determine alternative courses of action. If the design engineer's concurrence were obtained in conjunction with the owner's approval, it would be necessary for the contract administrator to generate a standard letter to the contractor requesting his price proposal for the modification.

However, in order to request the price proposal of the contractor, the contract administrator must have in hand the design engineer's revised specifications for the modification and/or the design engineer's revised drawings indicating the scope of the modification. These materials should be requested at the time the design engineer's permission to proceed with the modification is sought, and the responsive transmittal memo should be filed, together with a copy of the materials forwarded, upon receipt.

The contract administrator's standard letter to solicit the contractor's price proposal should describe the modification with the language "Modification no. __ provides for . . . " in order to keep the same descriptive verbiage throughout the modification process. A suggested standard letter is shown in Figure 10-5.

Upon receipt of the contractor's price or credit proposal and transmittal of copies of that proposal to the owner and design engineer, the

(Date) _____

(Contractor) _____
_____
_____

Attn: _____

                              Re: (Project Title)

                         Subject: Modification No. _____

                            File: _____

Gentlemen:

The purpose of this letter is to inform you that this office has been advised by the Owner to void the subject modification on the above referenced project.

Very truly yours,

_____
Contract Administrator

cc: Owner
    Engineer
    Modification File

FIGURE 10-3 Voiding of modification.

(Date) _____
Design Engineer _____

_____

_____

Attn: _____

                                            Re: (Project Title)

                                     Subject: Modification No. ____

                                        File: _____

Gentlemen:

Please advise me, by return of a copy of this letter, as to your
concurrence with the processing of the subject modification as detailed on
the attached letter to the Owner.

Upon receipt of the Owner's permission to proceed with the subject
Modification, please transmit a detailed scope of work and cost estimate
for the subject Modification.

Very truly yours,

_____
Contract Administrator

cc: Modification File

Response:

☐ Agreed
☐ Not Agreed

_____   _____
Design Engineer   Date

FIGURE 10-4   Request for design engineer's concurrence.

(Date) _____

Contractor _____
_____
_____

Attn: _____

Re: (Project Title)
Subject: Modification No. ____

File: _____

Gentlemen:

It is the purpose of this letter to request your

☐ Price Proposal
☐ Credit Proposal for the subject modification.

Modification No. ____ provides for _____
_____
_____
_____

Very truly yours,

_____
Contract Administrator

cc: Owner
     Engineer
     Modification File

FIGURE 10-5   Request for price or credit proposal.

contract administrator would either accept the proposal or negotiate an acceptable price or credit with the contractor in one or more meetings, ultimately obtaining from the contractor a revised price or credit proposal. Upon receipt of an acceptable quotation, the owner's concurrence to proceed with the *scope of work* of the modification would be required. A standard letter should be developed to solicit this concurrence. The letter should describe the scope of work of the modification in exactly the same language employed in the standard letter requesting the contractor's price or credit quotation. Figure 10-6 shows a sample standard letter for this purpose. This letter is the core of the modification process, for it authorizes a change to the contract, the document upon which all project relationships between the owner and the contractor are based. Given the importance of this letter, the contract administrator would be well advised to transmit it under a cover letter, such as the one in Figure 10-7, emphasizing its importance and the need for thorough review and providing detailed instructions to the owner.

Once the contract administrator has received the owner's written authorization for the contractor to proceed with the work of the modification, a copy should be forwarded to the contractor under the standard letter shown in Figure 10-8.

SUMMARY

The Modification Status Sheet and the seven standard letters proposed in this chapter provide a workable method to systematize the modification procedure for incorporating changes in the project. Although the details of the system as applied to a given project may vary due to the provisions of the contract itself, in-house procedures of the owner, the design engineer, or outside funding agencies, the general features of the modification system will remain. The system should be devised to describe the interaction required by the participants, compile an outline of those interactions, generate a Modification Status Sheet to note the steps in the process which have been discharged at any given point, and provide for standard letters to expedite the modification process and to reduce the mundane activities to a clerical level. This systematization will leave the contract administrator with the time necessary for consideration of project matters which require his expertise.

The best applications of the modification system will be examined in detail in Part 3, when monitoring of construction contracts will be considered.

(Date) _____

Contractor _____
_____
_____

Attn: _____

                    Re: (Project Title)

                Subject: Modification No. ____

                   File: _____
Gentlemen:

We have been advised by (Owner's Representative's Name), acting for (Owner's Name) to direct you to proceed with the work of Modification No. ____ to your Contract on the above referenced project.

Modification No. ____ provides for _____
_____
_____
_____

It is mutually agreed that a lump sum

☐ Price
☐ Credit of $_____ will be

☐ Added to
☐ Subtracted from the Contract price for this modification.

All work is to be completed in accordance with applicable articles of the Contract Documents.

A formal Change Order will be issued in the near future.

Very truly yours,

_____
Contract Administrator

cc: Engineer
     Modification File

Authorized by:

OWNER

By: _____
Date: _____

FIGURE 10-6 Order to proceed.

(Date) _____

Owner _____
_____
_____

Attn: _____

Re: (Project Title)

Subject: Modification No. ____

File: _____

Gentlemen:

Attached, please find a letter authorizing the Contractor to proceed with the work of the subject Modification.

Please review this letter in detail, and, if it be found acceptable, sign and return it to this office for further processing.

Thank you.

Very truly yours,

_____
Contract Administrator

cc: Modification File

FIGURE 10-7   Request for approval of order to proceed.

(Date) _____

Contractor _____
_____
_____

Attn: _____

                         Re: (Project Title)

                 Subject: Modification No. ____

                      File: _____

Gentlemen:

Attached is a copy of the letter from the Owner authorizing you to proceed with the work of the subject Modification.

Very truly yours,

_____
Contract Administrator

cc: Owner
     Engineer
     Modification File

FIGURE 10-8   Transmittal of approval to proceed.

CHAPTER 11

CHANGE ORDERS

A change order is a legal document which changes the scope—and usually the price—of a contract by mutual consent of the parties to the contract. The systematization required of the contract administrator to facilitate the change order process is usually quite simple: the change order merely formalizes the changes to the contract (and adjusts the price) in accordance with the agreement reached by the parties to the contract in the modification process described in the preceding chapter. The contract administrator's principal concern in developing the system for change orders is to ensure that the change order is actually issued and that issuance occurs within a reasonable time after the modification in order to allow the contractor the appropriate cash flow for that modification.

THE CHANGE ORDER SYSTEM

Change orders should be issued periodically—perhaps once a month—to incorporate all agreed-upon modifications into the contract. In the event of a relatively high-priced modification, a change order should be issued immediately to afford the contractor the necessary cash flow as soon as practicable after the owner authorizes the modification. The usual order of events for change orders will be the following:

1. The contract administrator gathers all letters authorizing the contractor to proceed with modifications negotiated during a given month.

2. The contract administrator generates a change order incorporating specific wording previously determined by the owner and the design engineer.

3. The contract administrator transmits the change order to the contractor for execution.

4. Upon receipt of the executed change order from the contractor, the contract administrator transmits the change order to the design engineer to obtain the design engineer's recommendation that the change order be executed on behalf of the owner.

5. Upon receipt of the change order and recommendation from the design engineer, the contract administrator forwards the change order to the owner for execution.

6. Upon receipt of the fully executed change order from the owner, the contract administrator transmits copies to the owner, design engineer, and contractor and files the original.

7. A copy of the change order is then transferred to the contract administrator's *internal* files to permit payment for the modifications incorporated into the change order as the work on those modifications progresses.

The Change Order Form

In composing a change order, such as the one in Figure 11-1, the contract administrator should begin with a heading which includes the owner's name, the project title, and the contract number. The change order should be dated and addressed to the contractor in letter form. The first paragraph should note the section of the contract which establishes authority for changes to the contract. The modifications to be included in the change order should then be listed and described, with additions or deductions to the contract price noted for each modification. The net total of all modifications incorporated into the change order should be stated at the end of the modifications. In the second paragraph, the stipulations underlying the change order should be set forth in detail exactly as worded by the owner and/or its delegate, the design engineer. These stipulations usually include the following statements:

1. That the amounts listed are acceptable to both the owner and the contractor

2. That indirect as well as direct costs are included in the stated prices

Owner's Name
Project Name
Contract Number
Change Order No. ___

(Date)

Contractor ____
Address ____
City & State ____

Gentlemen:

Pursuant to Section G-5.01 of the Contract Documents for the above referenced project, you are hereby authorized to proceed with:

Modification No. ____

Modification No. ____ provides for _____
_____
_____

ADD TO THE CONTRACT PRICE $_____

Modification No. ____

Modification No. ____ provides for _____
_____
_____

DEDUCT FROM THE CONTRACT PRICE $_____

Modification No. ____

Modification No. ___ provides for _____
_____
_____

NO CHANGE TO THE CONTRACT PRICE $_____

TOTAL AMOUNT OF CHANGE ORDER NO. ___ _ ADD $_____
                                     _ DEDUCT

In executing this Change Order, it is mutually agreed that the amount provided for herein will be accepted by the Contractor as full compensation for all costs associated with these changes in work, including all direct and indirect costs and any and all costs associated with delays or additional time, if any, which may be required as a result of said changes.

Unless otherwise specifically provided for herein, this Change Order does not change the time of completion of this Contract or the Contract Completion Date currently in effect.

It is mutually agreed that the lump sum price or prices listed above will be accepted by the Contractor as the sole basis for payment for all work as indicated, or as credits to the Contract Amount if deletions of work are included.

All work included in this Change Order is subject to all applicable terms and conditions of the captioned Contract Documents.

Accepted by: Recommended by:

CONTRACTOR'S NAME   ENGINEER'S NAME   OWNER'S NAME

By _____   By _____   By _____

Title _____   Title _____   Title _____

Date _____   Date _____   Date _____

FIGURE 11-1   Change order.

3. That the cost of any delays to the contractor arising out of the modifications included in the change order are included in the price of the modification

4. That, unless otherwise expressly provided, the completion time of the contract has not been amended by the change order

5. That no payments beyond those set forth in the change order will be made for the modification

6. That the terms of the contract apply to the work identified in the modifications

Appropriate blanks should be provided at the end of the change order for countersignature by the contractor, recommendation by the engineer, and approval by the owner. All signatures should be dated.

Standard Letters and Change Order Status Sheet

Once the change order has been prepared, it should be transmitted to the contractor for execution by a standard letter such as the one in Figure 11-2. When the contract administrator receives the executed change order from the contractor, he should send it to the design engineer for recommendation and return to the contract administrator. The contract administrator can easily develop a second standard letter of transmittal to the design engineer by merely changing the addressee on his first standard letter. Similarly, the third standard letter can easily be developed for transmittal to the owner.

One copy of each transmittal letter should be filed in a change order file to be opened for each change order. This separate file will permit the contract administrator to determine the status of a given change order at any time. If the contract administrator is charged with a number of projects or if the project in question is large, he may wish to generate a Change Order Status Sheet (Figure 11-3) for attachment to the left-hand side of the change order file.

When the contract administrator receives the fully executed change order from the owner, he should send *copies* to the owner, design engineer, and contractor. He should retain the original change order in his own change order file. Figure 11-4 shows a standard letter for transmission of copies of the fully executed document.

(Date)

Contractor
Address
City & State

                    Re: Project Title

             Subject: Change Order No. ___

                File: _____

Gentlemen:

Attached is the subject Change Order to your Contract on the above referenced project.

Review this Change Order in detail and, if acceptable, sign it and return it to this office for further processing.

Very truly yours,

_____
Contract Administrator

cc: Change Order File

FIGURE 11-2 Transmittal of change order to contractor.

CHANGE ORDER STATUS SHEET

Project Title

Owner

Engineer   Change Order # _____

Contractor

☐ C.O. sent to Contractor   ____(date)____

☐ C.O. received from Contractor   ____(date)____

☐ C.O. sent to Engineer   ____(date)____

☐ C.O. received from Engineer   ____(date)____

☐ C.O. sent to Owner   ____(date)____

☐ C.O. received from Owner   ____(date)____

☐ Executed Copies of C.O. sent to
  Owner, Engineer & Contractor   ____(date)____

FIGURE 11-3 Change Order Status Sheet.

(Date)

Owner, Engineer or Contractor (1 letter for each)

_____

_____

                                    Re: Project Title

                              Subject: Change Order # _____

                                  File: _____

Gentlemen:

Attached, for your records, please find one copy of the subject Change Order, fully executed.

Very truly yours,

_____
Contract Administrator

cc: Change Order File

FIGURE 11-4 Transmittal of executed change order (reference copies).

CHAPTER 12

THE SYSTEM FOR CONTROL OF SUBCONTRACTORS

During a major construction project, it may be in the interest of the owner to permit the contractor to delegate from time to time certain responsibilities allocated to him under the contract. The process by which this delegation occurs in most projects requires the interaction of several project participants. Section G-4.01 of the sample contract provisions presented in Chapter 1 provided for delegation by subcontract and contemplated the interaction of the owner, design engineer, contract administrator, and contractor; accordingly, this interaction was found in Chapter 1 to denote a control responsibility to be tabulated on the Control Responsibility Summary Sheet.

The several control responsibilities to be derived from section G-4.01 are:

- The owner's approval of any subcontractor to be used by the contractor

- The contractor's submittal to the design engineer of a statement which defines the nature of the work to be subcontracted, indicates the amount of the work to be subcontracted, names the person or entity to whom the subcontract is proposed, and, if requested, sets forth a statement of the subcontractor's experience, financial responsibility, and such other qualifications as the design engineer may reasonably require

- The subcontractor's submittal of acceptable evidence of insurance to the owner prior to commencement of work

In the absence of contractual provisions to the contrary, it is customary for the contract administrator to be the "clearing house" for transactions between the contractor and the engineer with regard to site-related items. Thus correspondence to and from the contractor would be routed through the contract administrator. Adherence to this custom will be assumed later in this chapter in establishing the system for subcontractor control.

A typical chronology for proposal and acceptance of subcontractors follows:

1. The contractor submits to the contract administrator a description of work to be subcontracted, the projected dollar value of that work, and the name of a subcontractor.

2. The contract administrator forwards this material to the design engineer.

3. The design engineer may request that the contract administrator obtain from the contractor additional information regarding the subcontractor's experience, financial responsibility, and other qualifications.

4. The contract administrator forwards this request, if made by the design engineer, to the contractor.

5. The contractor supplies the appropriate information to the contract administrator.

6. The contract administrator forwards the responsive material to the design engineer.

7. The design engineer obtains the owner's approval or disapproval of the proposed subcontractor and forwards confirmation to the contract administrator.

8. The contract administrator furnishes written approval or disapproval to the contractor.

9. In the event of approval, the subcontractor submits evidence of insurance (usually through the contractor) to the contract administrator.

10. The contract administrator forwards the evidence of insurance to the owner.

11. Once the evidence of insurance has been determined to be acceptable, the subcontractor is permitted to enter the site and begin work.

Although this chronology is quite typical, the system developed by the practicing contract administrator should be adapted to fit the stipulations of his or her particular contract.

Inasmuch as numerous requests to subcontract work could occur in any major project and each such request would be similar to, but independent of, all others, it is advisable that a routine procedure, i.e., a *system*, be developed to process these requests effectively at the lowest possible level of the contract administrator's personnel.

THE SYSTEM FOR CONTROL OF SUBCONTRACTORS

The Subcontractor Status Sheet

The foregoing chronology permits development of a "Subcontractor Status Sheet," as shown in Figure 12-1, by which the contract administrator and subordinates may track the progress of a given request to any given point. In developing the status sheet, the contract administrator should provide headings sufficient to distinguish each particular request on each particular project, as well as the names of the owner, design engineer, contractor, and proposed subcontractor. The remainder of this sheet would then be a mere checklist paralleling the foregoing chronology.

Each Roman numeral notes a separate task to be performed. Roman numerals III, IV, V, and VI are indented to indicate they will not be required unless the design engineer requests additional data.

Roman numeral VII has either an "A" or a "B" after it to indicate it is an either-or situation.

In addition, line XI bears special mention. The date on which the subcontractor entered the site could be derived from other records, but by including it in the status sheet, the contract administrator creates a check against premature entry by the subcontractor which could create a liability without recourse for the owner should the subcontractor be uninsured or underinsured for the risk created.

As in the case for other systems developed in this book from the sample contract provisions, the box immediately after the Roman numeral designation is meant to be marked when data is received or transmitted, and the date of that receipt or transmittal should be noted on the line following the description of the activity. These entries give the contract administrator or his designate a method by which the status can be determined at a glance.

The Subcontractor Status Sheet should also be affixed to the left-hand side of a file folder and copies of data received and transmitted affixed to the right-hand side of the same file folder in a manner similar to that employed for systems discussed earlier in this book.

SUBCONTRACTOR STATUS SHEET

Project _____

Owner _____

Design Engineer _____

Contractor _____

Proposed Subcontractor _____

I   ☐ Subcontractor approval requested by Contractor   _(Date)_

II   ☐ Contractor's request forwarded to Design Engineer   _(Date)_

    III   ☐ Design Engineer requested additional data   _(Date)_

    IV   ☐ Design Engineer request forwarded to Contractor   _(Date)_

    V   ☐ Additional data received from Contractor   _(Date)_

    VI   ☐ Additional data forwarded to Design Engineer   _(Date)_

VIIA ☐ Subcontractor disapproved   _(Date)_

VIIB ☐ Subcontractor approved   _(Date)_

VIII ☐ Contractor advised   _(Date)_

IX   ☐ Evidence of insurance received   _(Date)_

X   ☐ Evidence of insurance forwarded to Owner   _(Date)_

XI   ☐ Subcontractor entered the site   _(Date)_

FIGURE 12-1   **Subcontractor Status Sheet.**

Standard Subcontractor Control Letters

Having created an effective monitoring device, the contract administrator can proceed to the second phase of his subcontractor control system: the development of standard letters to conserve the contract administrator's time and to expedite the subcontractor control process itself.

Although subcontractual requirements are usually reviewed by the contractor and contract administrator prior to commencement of construction activity, experience teaches that clarification during the project is usually required. Accordingly, the prudent contract administrator, immediately following execution of the contract, will call to the attention of the contractor the provisions of the contract concerned with subcontracting. The letter by which this task may be accomplished is merely a reiteration of the contract provisions such as the letter shown in Figure 12-2.

The second standard letter (Figure 12-3) required pursuant to the Subcontractor Status Sheet is the one which would forward to the design engineer the contractor's request for the subcontracting of certain work.

The third standard letter is provisional in that its issuance depends upon receipt of a request from the design engineer for additional information. In the event such a request is received from the design engineer, a standard letter such as the one in Figure 12-4 should be transmitted to the contractor.

Upon receipt of the additional information from the contractor, forwarding to the design engineer would be hastened by use of the transmittal letter shown in Figure 12-5.

The next standard letter, indicated by the Subcontractor Status Sheet, would advise the contractor that his proposed subcontractual arrangement has been disapproved by the owner. It is doubtful that a significant time savings could be realized by having a standard letter for this purpose prepared in advance. Rather, should such a letter be required, it should merely contain a statement to the effect that "The purpose of this letter is to advise you that your request to use (Subcontractor's name) as a Subcontractor, on the above-referenced project, has been disapproved by the project Owner."

On the other hand, the contract administrator would be well advised to prepare in advance a standard letter for *approval* of subcontractors. The model letter shown in Figure 12-6 accomplishes this purpose.

The final standard letter (Figure 12-7) contemplated by the status sheet is one which forwards the appropriate evidence and insurance to the owner.

(Date) _____

(Contractor) _____
(Address) _____
_____
_____

Attn: _____

                                    Re: (Project Title) _____
                                         _____
                                         _____

                                    Subj: Subcontracts _____
                                           _____

                                    File: _____

Gentlemen:

Your attention is directed to General Provisions Section G-4.01, SUBCONTRACTS, of the Contract Documents for the above referenced project.

General Provisions Section G-4.01 requires, should you desire to subcontract any part of the work included in your contract, that you submit a statement to the Engineer, showing the character and amount of the work to be subcontracted and the party to whom it is proposed to subcontract this work, at least thirty (30) days prior to the performance of any work by that Subcontractor.

The same section of the Contract Documents further requires that you obtain the approval of the Owner prior to his performance of any work on the site.

Should it be your desire to subcontract any part of the work included in your contract, on the above referenced project, proceed in strict accordance with General Provisions Section G-4.01, SUBCONTRACTS. Transmit all correspondence related to General Provisions Section G-4.01 through this office.

Very truly yours,

Contract Administrator

cc: Engineer
     Owner

FIGURE 12-2 Reminder to contractor of subcontracts approval requirements.

(Date) _____

(Engineer) _____
_____
_____

Attn: _____

                  Re: Project Title

           Subject: Proposed Subcontractor

              File: _____

Gentlemen:

Attached herewith is the Contractor's request to utilize the following firm(s) as Subcontractors on the above referenced project:

        _____

        _____

        _____

You are respectfully requested to review this request and obtain the Owner's acceptance or rejection related to the Subcontractors proposed.

Advise this office, in writing, as to the Owner's decision; should you require further data prior to this decision being made, so advise this office in writing.

Very truly yours,

Contract Administrator

cc: Owner
      Subcontractor File

FIGURE 12-3 **Transmittal of contractor's request to subcontract.**

(Date) _____

Contractor _____

Address _____

Attn: _____

Re: Project Title

Subject: Proposed Subcontractor Name

File: _____

Gentlemen:

The purpose of this letter is to request you to submit the following additional data related to the subject, Proposed Subcontractor:

    ☐ Experience

    ☐ Financial Ability

    ☐ Other _____

Very truly yours,

Contract Administrator

cc: Owner
    Engineer
    Subcontractor File

FIGURE 12-4 Request for additional data.

(Date) _____

(Engineer) _____
(Address) _____
_____
_____

Attn: _____

                        Re: (Project Title)

               Subject: (Proposed Subcontractor)

                  File: _____

Gentlemen:

Attached is the additional data, as received from the Contractor, which you requested related to the subject Proposed Subcontractor.

You are respectfully requested to review this additional data and obtain the Owner's acceptance or rejection related to the Subcontractor proposed.

Advise this office, in writing, as to the Owner's decision.

Very truly yours,

_____
Contract Administrator

Attachment

cc: Owner
     Subcontractor File

FIGURE 12-5 **Transmittal of additional data.**

(Date) _____

(Contractor) _____
(Address) _____

_____

Attn: _____

                                 Re: (Project Title) _____

                                                 _____

                                   Subj: Subcontractors _____

                                               _____

                                   File: _____

Gentlemen:

The purpose of this letter is to advise you, in response to your letter dated _____, the Subcontractor(s) listed below have been approved, (for the above referenced project), for the character and amount of work indicated:

Subcontractor	Character of Work	Amount of Work
_____	_____	_____
_____	_____	_____
_____	_____	_____

You are reminded that evidence of insurance for the Subcontractors noted above is required _prior_ to their entering the site.

Very truly yours,

Contract Administrator

cc: Owner
      Engineer
      Subcontractor File

FIGURE 12-6 Notice of approval of subcontractors.

(Date) _____

(Owner) _____

(Address) _____

Attn: _____

Re: (Project Title) ____

Subject: (Subcontractor's Name)

File: _____

Gentlemen:

Transmitted herewith is evidence of insurance as received from the subject Subcontractor.

Advise this office immediately should you have any concern related to this evidence of insurance.

Very truly yours,

Contract Administrator

cc: Engineer
     Subcontractor File

FIGURE 12-7 Transmittal of evidence of insurance.

SUMMARY

As with the other systems described in Part 2, the system for control of subcontractors will require adjustment to accommodate unique provisions of given construction contracts. However, the contract administrator's *systematization technique* will remain unchanged. Whatever the contract provisions, the contract administrator who seeks to conserve time while improving administrative effort will use the following approach to systematize his activities:

1. Search the Control Responsibility Summary Sheets to find candidates for systematization—primarily those control responsibilities which require interaction of two or more parties involved in the contract.

2. Review the control responsibilities previously highlighted to define what must be done.

3. Interject the role of the contract administrator to assure that what should happen does happen.

4. Place the control responsibilities and the contract administrator's required action in probable chronological sequence.

5. Generate a status sheet.

6. Generate standard letters.

7. File in a separate folder:

   a. Item 5 on the left-hand side.

   b. All letters (standard or otherwise) on the right-hand side.

Thoughtful use of the system to control the use of subcontractors in the project will both improve the contract administrator's performance in subcontractor-related matters and free him or her from the drudgery of routine paperwork to consider those aspects of the project more deserving of his or her expertise.

CHAPTER 13

THE SYSTEM FOR CONTROL OF MANUFACTURERS AND VENDORS

In Chapter 1, it was pointed out that the acceptance of manufacturers and vendors constitutes a control responsibility, because it requires the interaction of participants in the construction process. The sample contract provisions of that chapter provided, in section G-6.02, that the contractor must submit to the design engineer the name of each proposed manufacturer or vendor for approval by the owner (or its delegate) prior to the contractor's placement of any orders with that manufacturer or vendor. It follows that the contract administrator must receive timely information from the design engineer of approvals of manufacturers and vendors in order that the contract administrator may know which materials and equipment are appropriate for incorporation into the project. Since the flow of information would occur many times during a major project, it is advisable that the contract administrator develop a system—a routine set of procedures—to promote occurrence of the necessary activity in an effective and efficient manner.

Often the design engineer and the contract administrator are complementary parts of the same firm. However, in order to portray the system in its classic form, it will be assumed that the design engineer and the contract administrator are separate entities. In either case, development of a system is the prudent course.

CONTROLLING MANUFACTURERS AND VENDORS

The contract between the owner and engineer usually includes a detailed list of materials and equipment for which approvals of manufacturers or vendors are required. Several alternative approval routes could then be followed: First, with the concurrence of the design en-

201

gineer, the contractor could submit his request for approval to the design engineer through the contract administrator. Second, an alternative would be direct submittal to the design engineer with an information copy to the contract administrator, who could maintain periodic contact with the design engineer to verify the status of such requests. Third, the design engineer could forward copies of all requests to the contract administrator. For the purpose of this illustration, however, it will be assumed that the following procedure would be employed:

1. The contractor would request the design engineer's approval of a given manufacturer or vendor and would send a copy of that request to the contract administrator.

2. The design engineer would obtain the owner's assent to use of that manufacturer or vendor, then confirm that assent by letter to the owner, with a copy to the contract administrator.

3. Upon receipt of the letter, the contract administrator would transmit to the contractor a letter of approval of the manufacturer or vendor in question, with a copy to the design engineer.

The Manufacturer/Vendor Approval Status Sheet

The contract administrator should file all correspondence related to a given manufacturer or vendor in a separate folder. To the left-hand side of the file folder should be attached a status sheet. Figure 13-1 is a sample of a Manufacturer/Vendor Approval Status Sheet. The reader will note that the sheet has the usual heading, i.e., spaces for identification of the project, contractor, and owner. The next line facilitates characterization of the supplying entity as either a manufacturer or a vendor and provides space for naming the entity. Lines I through III provide a dated checklist of required items in the previously described sequence. The sheet next provides space for notation of the pertinent sections of the contract and corresponding equipment or material furnished. The final line on the sheet provides a "checkoff" to be marked by the contract administrator once equipment and materials noted on the sheet have been transferred to the "inventory control system" (to be described in detail later in this part). This checkoff aids the contract administrator in precluding payments for inventory materials unless the manufacturer or vendor has been approved to supply those materials.

MANUFACTURER/VENDOR APPROVAL STATUS SHEET

Project _____

Contractor _____

Owner _____

Design
 Engineer _____

Proposed ☐ Vendor
         ☐ Manufacturer _____
                              (Name)

I   ☐ Contractor Requested Approval _____
                                          (Date)
II   ☐ Owner's Concurrence Documented _____
                                          (Date)
III ☐ Contractor Advised of Approval _____
                                          (Date)
     ☐ Design Engineer Advised of
       Approval by Copy _____
                             (Date)

     ☐ Equipment and/or Material approved to be supplied:

       Contract Citation   Equipment/Material

       _____   _____

       _____   _____

       _____   _____

       _____   _____

     ☐ Data Transferred to Inventory Control System

FIGURE 13-1   Manufacturer/Vendor Approval Status Sheet.

(Date) _____

(Contractor) _____

_____

_____

Re: Project Title

Subject: Manufacturer/Vendor
Approval

File: _____

Gentlemen:

We have been advised by (Design Engineer) of (Design Firm) that your request of _____ (Date) _____ for the approval of (Vendor or Manufacturer Firm Name) to supply the equipment and/or materials listed below for the referenced Project has been approved:

Contract Citation	Equipment and/or Material
_____	_____
_____	_____
_____	_____

Very truly yours,

_____
Contract Administrator

cc: Design Engineer
    Owner
    Manufacturer/Vendor
     Approval File

FIGURE 13-2 Approval of manufacturers or vendors.

Standard Letters

Thus the only standard letter (Figure 13-2) required of the contract administrator in his system for control of manufacturers or vendors is the one he sends to the contractor to advise the contractor of the owner's approval of the manufacturer or vendor.

CHAPTER 14

THE SYSTEM FOR INVENTORY CONTROL

During the course of most major construction projects, the contract administrator will be faced with the arrival of a steady stream of equipment and nonperishable materials proposed by the contractor for ultimate incorporation into the project. The Control Responsibility Summary Sheet, developed in Chapter 1, identifies a control responsibility in section G-3.04 ("Payments for Materials Delivered to the Site") of the sample contract provisions set forth in that chapter. This control responsibility arises out of the interaction of participants required to deal with these items of equipment and material.

The reader may abstract from section G-3.04 the following eight elements:

1. The contractor may, subject to the approval of the owner or as required by law, include in his current monthly estimates the delivered cost of equipment and nonperishable material which have been:

   a. Tested for adequacy

   b. Delivered to the site or placed in owner-approved storage facilities

   c. Adequately protected from fire, theft, vandalism, weather, and other potential causes of damage

2. The contractor must furnish to the contract administrator invoices establishing the value of said materials and equipment.

3. The contract administrator must inspect the materials and equipment.

4. The contractor must provide to the owner fire insurance policies covering the materials and equipment.

5. The contractor must furnish to the contract administrator evidence that he has paid the vendors of the equipment or materials in full within 60 days of the submission of the monthly estimate to the owner or within 30 days of the owner's monthly payment to the contractor.

6. In the event the contractor fails to meet the time limits set forth in 5, the contract administrator should recommend to the owner that the payments for the equipment and materials in question previously made to the contractor be deducted from the next monthly payment.

For the purposes of this chapter, it will be assumed that the owner is willing to pay the contractor for inventoried equipment and materials, that these items will all be stored at the site, that the site storage area is adequately protected from the previously identified risks, and that all necessary testing has been conducted with satisfactory results confirmed by the design engineer.

Although the nature of the equipment and materials may vary from project to project—indeed, from delivery to delivery—the activity required of the contract administrator and the other construction participants will be repetitive. Accordingly, it seems logical that routine procedures, i.e., *systems*, be developed to promote efficient monitoring of discharge of the respective responsibilities of the participants and to free the contract administrator from mundane detail in order to dedicate time to matters more worthy of close attention.

CONTROLLING INVENTORY

As in the cases of other systems developed in Part 2 the foundation of the system for inventory materials will be a status sheet, the "Inventory Control Sheet." However, unlike the previously developed systems, the system for inventoried materials will employ a ledger-type status sheet rather than the checkoff type. The reason for this deviation is the necessity that numerous items of equipment and material be traced each month from submitted invoices, paid invoices, and canceled checks and the corresponding need to minimize the number of file folders employed in the system. Figure 14-1 is an example of the Inventory Control Sheet.

In creating a system for control of inventoried materials, the contract administrator must first understand the means by which discharge of the control responsibilities abstracted from paragraph G-3.04 of the sample contract provisions can be confirmed by the contract administrator. As previously noted, the very need for the inventory control system arises out of the owner's agreement or necessity to make periodic payments for equipment and materials which meet certain conditions. In the instant case, the owner has agreed to make full payment (less retainages) for all suitable materials which are delivered to the site and adequately protected. It is usually the responsibility of the design engineer to ascertain the acceptability of equipment arriving on site and proposed for incorporation into the project and to determine the need for testing to establish acceptability. Should a test for adequacy be required, it is customary for the design engineer to so indicate in the materials and performance section of the contract documents. In such a case, the contractor could submit to the design engineer test reports indicating that the equipment or materials met the required levels of performance or the design engineer could witness the tests. The design engineer would then be in a position to either reject the item tested as nonconforming or "pass" it and so advise the contract administrator. For the purposes of this chapter, it will be assumed that all equipment and material has been found adequate by the design engineer and that the contract administrator has been so advised. The ledger sheet will include a column in which these facts may be indicated by checkoff.

Another control responsibility indicated in the introduction to this chapter was the requirement that the equipment or material be delivered to the site or to approved storage quarters. As previously noted, it will be assumed that all materials were to be delivered to the site. The most direct method by which the contract administrator can verify delivery is to require that the contractor provide copies of delivery tickets. The numbers and dates of all delivery tickets, the supplier's name, and a description of the item being delivered should be noted by the contract administrator on the ledger sheet.

The next control responsibility is proper storage of equipment or materials delivered to the site. In most major construction projects, there will probably be at least one inside storage area and one outside storage area, since some equipment to be stored will require a heated, ventilated area, but most common materials can be stored outside with proper precaution. The numbers of such areas, of course, will vary with the size and nature of the project. The contract administrator may wish to designate multiple storage areas by use of numbers or letters or combinations of both. The ledger sheet will provide a column for storage area designation.

The next control responsibility requires adequate protection of stored equipment and materials. Here, adequate protection has been assumed.

INVENTORY CONTROL SHEET								
Delivery Ticket		Vendor's Name	Approved	Description of Material/Equipment Inventoried	Storage Area	Inspected	Fire Insurance	
Number	Date						Policy Number	Amount

FIGURE 14-1 Inventory Control Sheet.

SHEET___OF___

Lump-Sum Breakdown Price	Invoice			Date Con-tractor Paid	Date Vendor Paid	Date Removed from Inventory	Dollar Amount Removed from Inventory	Location to Be Installed
	Amount	No.	Date					

The next control responsibility of section G-3.04 of the sample contract provisions requires the contractor to furnish to the contract administrator invoices from vendors or suppliers to establish the value of the equipment or materials being transferred to "reimbursable inventory" by adequacy, delivery, and protection as outlined above. It will be necessary for the contract administrator to record the invoice amount, number, and date on the ledger sheet.

The next control responsibility requires that the contract administrator inspect the inventoried equipment and materials. The purpose of this inspection is to provide reasonable assurance to the owner that the materials or equipment were approved by the design engineer for incorporation into the work of the project and that the materials or equipment are in acceptable condition at the time they are placed in storage. In Chapter 13, it was noted that certain data required on the Manufacturer/Vendor Approval Status Sheet would need to be transferred to the inventory control system; it is at this point that the transfer will occur. The contract administrator would confirm that the invoice forwarded by the contractor was originated by a manufacturer or vendor approved for the items listed on the invoice, then mark the appropriate box on the line entitled "Data Transferred to Inventory Control System" on the Manufacturer/Vendor Approval Status Sheet and in the space provided for that purpose on the Inventory Control Sheet. If, in his inspection, the contract administrator determines that the equipment and materials have been damaged, he will so advise the contractor and exclude the damaged items from "reimbursable inventory." If, on the other hand, the equipment and materials appear to be acceptable, the contract administrator will make the appropriate notation on the ledger sheet.

Section G-3.04 also requires that the contractor provide the owner with a fire insurance policy covering the equipment or materials placed in reimbursable inventory. Space should be provided on the Inventory Control Sheet to record both the policy number and the dollar amount of the coverage provided.

The next control responsibility requires that the contractor provide proof to the contract administrator that the contractor has made full payment to the vendor or supplier within the stipulated time limits. Thus it will be necessary for the contract administrator to record the date on which the contractor was reimbursed for the inventoried material and the date on which the vendor or supplier confirmed receipt of payment from the contractor. The ledger sheet should provide spaces for recording these data.

The final control responsibility of section G-3.04 rests with the contract administrator. In the event the contractor fails to meet the time limits set forth above with respect to proof of payment to vendors or suppliers, the contract administrator must move expeditiously to effect a deduction in the appropriate amount from the next monthly payment to the contractor. This control responsibility does not require that a space be provided on the ledger sheet, but it does require that the cost control system—to be discussed later in this book—include any such deductions.

The foregoing discussion of control responsibilities as they relate to the development of the Inventory Control Sheet has yet to touch upon the accounting mechanisms required to accommodate transfers from "reimbursable inventory" into the work of the project itself. As these transfers occur, i.e., as inventory equipment or materials are incorporated into the work of the project, they will be paid for by the owner in accordance with the lump-sum breakdown dollar amounts previously negotiated with the contractor. Thus it will be necessary to remove periodically certain items of equipment or material from the Inventory Control Sheet and to subtract the value of those items from the total dollar amount of all inventoried materials and equipment, then enter corresponding increases in the value of the work completed by the contractor and reflect those increases in monthly payments. Exact values of the invoiced equipment and materials probably will not correspond exactly to the values established in the lump-sum breakdown. Therefore, the inventoried equipment and material system and the cost control system must remain separate, and some judgment must be exercised by the contract administrator both as the systems function separately and as they interact. For example, if the lump-sum breakdown contemplated a higher cost for the equipment or materials to be inventoried than the amount actually invoiced by the vendor or supplier, the excess could be released to the contractor when the equipment or materials are removed from inventory. Additional payment for labor to install the equipment or materials (as provided in the lump-sum breakdown) would subsequently be paid to the contractor as the equipment or materials were incorporated into the work of the project. On the other hand, if the invoiced cost of the equipment or materials is *greater* than the value established in the lump-sum breakdown, the lump-sum breakdown should take precedence over the invoiced value. The contractor administrator would be well advised to reach agreement with the contractor as to procedures in the event of substantial disparities between the lump-sum breakdown and the invoiced amounts. In the absence of such an agreement, the contract administrator exposes himself to the prospect of an invoice greater than the lump-sum breakdown prices for *both* the equipment or materials and their installation. In that situation, the contract administrator would suffer the embarrassment and confusion of insufficient funds for installation of the items. The problems can be avoided by reserving space on the Inventory Control Sheet to note the dollar amount for the equipment or materials as established in the lump-sum breakdown negotiations, then reimbursing to the contractor the lower of the lump-sum breakdown or invoiced figures.

The exact location where the inventoried material will be ultimately incorporated into the work of the project should be noted on the Inventory Control Sheet to facilitate keeping track of which materials and equipment should be removed from inventory and paid for during the month.

Any remaining space on the ledger sheet should be reserved to note *partial* deductions from reimbursable inventory on a regular basis.

SUMMARY

In summation, the contract administrator would utilize the Inventory Control Sheet as follows:

1. Upon delivery of the materials or equipment, he would fill in the delivery ticket number and date and the vendor's name; check the Vendor/Manufacturer Approval Status Sheet to confirm the vendor has been approved and, if approved, put a checkmark under the Approved column; write a description of the materials or equipment under the Description column; note the storage area the material or equipment is stored in (e.g., area A, area B, etc.); note the inspector's initials under the Inspected column; and then go to the last column on the sheet to note the location where the inventoried materials will ultimately be incorporated into the work of the project.

2. Upon receipt of the fire insurance policy applicable to the materials or equipment, the contract administrator would note the policy number and the policy amount under those headings on the Inventory Control Sheet and would then also check the dollar amount agreed upon in the lump-sum breakdown and note it in that column, at the same time checking that the insurance policy amount is adequate to cover the amount of the lump-sum breakdown.

3. Upon receipt of the vendor's invoice from the contractor, the contract administrator would note the invoice amount, the invoice number, and the invoice date in the appropriate columns. If (a) all columns to the left are complete and (b) the dollar amount of the invoice is equal to, or less than, the lump-sum breakdown price and

the fire insurance policy amount which had previously been checked in relation to the lump-sum breakdown price, the contract administrator may include the dollar amount of the invoice into the contractor's next partial payment, noting the date of that payment under the Date Contractor Paid column.

4. Within 60 days of the date in the Date Contractor Paid column, the contractor should submit to the contract administrator proof that he has paid the vendor for the equipment or materials. If this is not done, the contract administrator must deduct the amount given the contractor previously for the materials or equipment from his next partial payment. If proof of payment is received, the contract administrator notes the date of such payment in the Date Vendor Paid column.

5. When the contractor removes the inventoried materials or equipment from storage and installs it, the contract administrator should note the date under the Date Removed from Inventory column and, in the contractor's next partial payment, the contract administrator should deduct the dollar amount of the equipment or materials from reimbursable inventory with a corresponding payment for the equipment or materials, plus the labor to install it, in the same partial payment to the contractor. The contract administrator should note the dollar amount of the equipment and materials being transferred from inventory in the Dollar Amount Removed from Inventory column.

CHAPTER 15

THE SYSTEM FOR CONTROL OF UNIT-PRICE ITEMS

The reader will recall that, in Chapter 3, the type of construction contract chosen for illustrative purposes was a lump-sum contract with unit prices. There are two purposes of this chapter: (1) to explain the development of routine procedures, i.e., systems, to control the incorporation of unit-price items into the project and (2) to develop unit-price controls which can be integrated into the overall cost control system to be discussed in Chapter 16.

A brief explanation of the purpose of unit prices seems in order. In certain construction projects, it is known that a given type of labor or a given type of component is necessary, but the quantity of such labor or components is indeterminate. A typical example might be linear footage of piles. The design engineer may be able to estimate with reasonable certainty the aggregate length of all required piles based upon his general knowledge of the soils into which the piles are to be driven as well as the loads which each pile must support; however, variations in subsurface conditions may preclude an estimate sufficiently accurate for contractual purposes. In such a case, use of a lump-sum price for all piles required would probably produce a windfall to one party to the construction contract and a corresponding loss to the other. The inequities inherent in the lump-sum alternative can be avoided by providing for payment to the contractor for the exact amount of piling actually installed at a predetermined price per unit of length.

It is possible to pay for all labor and material components of the project on a unit-price basis; indeed, some construction projects are written on precisely that basis. However, the readily determinable quantities of most project components and the additional contract administration cost attending lump-sum items (to be discussed later in

217

this chapter) would seem to render this approach unduly cumbersome and expensive.

The best alternative in many construction projects appears to be complementary use of the lump-sum and unit-price payment mechanisms. The lump-sum portion provides for one fixed-amount payment to the contractor for the work contemplated which can be quantified with sufficient accuracy. This mechanism requires that the contractor accept all risks inherent in that part of the project, and the prudent contractor would include in his lump-sum price adequate provision for contingencies. The unit-price part of this hybrid construction project would, on the other hand, provide for the addition of predetermined prices to the lump-sum part of the contract for those parts of the work for which quantities could not be predetermined. Thus this combination of payment mechanisms appears to place properly the risk of the relatively determinate parts of the project with the contractor and the relatively indeterminate parts of the project with the owner, who will derive ultimate benefit from the completed project.

CONTROLLING UNIT-PRICE ITEMS

Inasmuch as the payment to the contractor for a given unit-price item will be based upon the exact quantity of work incorporated into the project for that item, it follows that the contract administrator must equip himself with a mechanism by which the exact quantities of that unit-price item may be readily determined and documented. The repetitive nature of this task makes advisable the development of routinized procedures, i.e., *systems*, to promote adequate discharge of the contract administrator's duties and to conserve his time and energies for matters more deserving of them. In most cases, the contract administrator (through his subordinates) will be required to verify that certain quantities of unit-price items (1) have been installed and (2) are in accordance with the provisions of the contract documents. Verifications for some unit-price items, e.g., piles, may require completion of a separate report for each item installed; others may require only that a continuous tabulation of quantities installed and their locations be maintained.

In Chapter 6, a lump-sum breakdown for a tunnel project was examined in detail. The reader will recall that no mention was made in that example of items of work of indeterminate quantity. It may now be instructive to return to that example to note items of indeterminate quantity whose inclusion as unit-price items during preparation of bid documents would have been advantageous to all participants. Among the items included in the lump-sum breakdown was "waterline relocation." Although the quantity of waterline and *normal* depth of excavation were predetermined, it is possible that once the contractor had reached the predetermined depth of excavation, the contract administrator would become concerned that the soils of that depth would not properly support the waterline. In order to anticipate adequately such a situation, the design engineer could have provided two unit-price items: one for "additional excavation" to permit compensation to the contractor for such additional excavation as might be required and another for "special bedding" to provide a suitable base material of adequate bearing capabilities for the waterline due to the overexcavation. The contractor would then have bid a price per unit for each. Thus upon encountering the subsoil situation in the field, the contract administrator (through his inspector) could have directed that the contractor "overexcavate" the trench bottom and fill the overexcavated space with special bedding to the quantities required to obtain suitable bearing capacity for the waterline. The contractor would then be paid for these additional quantities of labor and materials in accordance with the price established in his bid.

In creating his system to document the incorporation of unit-price items into the project, the contract administrator must refer to the contract to determine (1) the permitted unit-price items, (2) the unit of measurement for each such item upon which payment is to be based, and (3) the method by which the contract administrator may best measure the incorporation of each such item. He should then prepare a separate file folder for each unit-price item established in the contract. He should affix to the right-hand side of the file folder all data recorded concerning the quantities and locations of the unit-price item incorporated into the work of the project by means of the forms in Figures 15-1 and 15-2 that are discussed below. To the left-hand side of the folder, he should affix a tabulation form to summarize entries on the right-hand side. Finally, he should provide for transfer of data from the left-hand side of the file folder to the contractor's partial payment request for reimbursement.

We will now return to the example of possible overexcavation and subsequent installation of additional pipe-bedding materials in the explanation for the use of the unit-price item forms, but will envision a project where the installation of the pipe will be over a substantial distance and require a period of months to complete. During the course of installing a sewer line, the contract administrator or the inspector might be required one or more times to direct the contractor to overexcavate and to install additional pipe bedding in order to achieve proper support for the pipe due to poor subsurface soil conditions. Each time this would occur, the contract administrator or the inspector would

UNIT–PRICE ITEM _____ (Title) _____

CONTRACTOR _____

PROJECT _____

Date	Location	Quantity*	Unit	Unit Price	Price	Inspector
____	_____	_____	____	_____	____	_____
____	_____	_____	____	_____	____	_____
____	_____	_____	____	_____	____	_____
____	_____	_____	____	_____	____	_____
____	_____	_____	____	_____	____	_____
____	_____	_____	____	_____	____	_____
____	_____	_____	____	_____	____	_____
____	_____	_____	____	_____	____	_____
____	_____	_____	____	_____	____	_____
____	_____	_____	____	_____	____	_____
____	_____	_____	____	_____	____	_____
____	_____	_____	____	_____	____	_____
____	_____	_____	____	_____	____	_____

Total _____   Total _____

*Calculations Appended

FIGURE 15-1 Daily tabulation sheet for a unit-price item.

UNIT–PRICE ITEM

UNIT–PRICE TOTALS

From	To	Total Quantity	Total Price	Partial Payment Made	Date of Payment
(Date)	(Date)			(Payment #)	
		Project Total	Project Total		

FIGURE 15-2 Cumulative monthly summary sheet for a unit-price item.

note in the field diary the depth of overexcavation required and the horizontal location and limits of the overexcavation. Upon return to the office at the end of the day, the contract administrator or the inspector would calculate the quantities of such overexcavation and additional pipe bedding authorized during the day, noting the location and depths on the sheet of calculations. The calculations would be affixed to the right-hand side of the unit-price folder for that unit-price item and summarized on a form such as that shown in Figure 15-1.

This procedure would be followed each day for the predetermined time interval between monthly partial payments to the contractor. When the last day of the month for partial payments within that month was reached (the cutoff date), the contract administrator would total (1) the quantity of the unit-price item expended during that month and (2) the price due the contractor for that month for that unit-price item. Figure 15-1 would remain in the right-hand side of the file folder on top of all calculations summarized below it. It would provide a convenient tabbed sheet on that side of the folder to divide the calculations within 1-month time periods.

The contract administrator would then transfer the totals for the month from the bottom of Figure 15-1 to a line item on Figure 15-2, which would be affixed to the left-hand side of the file folder, as follows: In the From column would be entered the date which begins the monthly pay period for the contractor. In the To column would be entered the date which ends the monthly pay period for the contractor. The Total Quantity column entry would be taken from Figure 15-1 for the period between the From and To columns. The Total Price column would also be taken from Figure 15-1. The number of the partial payment to the contractor would be entered under the Partial Payment Made column and the date of that payment would be entered under the Date of Payment column.

Upon completion of the project, the Total Quantity and Total Price columns would be added to determine the total project cost for that particular unit-price item.

On larger projects, the cost of the unit-price item to any particular time could also be found, of course, by totaling the Total Price column.

CHAPTER 16

THE SYSTEM FOR
COST CONTROL

A key responsibility of the contract administrator in most projects is approval of partial payments to the contractor for value added to the project during contruction. In order to discharge this responsibility, the contract administrator must determine the amount of work performed by the contractor during a given time period (usually 1 month), advise the owner of the quantity of work performed, and recommend payment to the contractor in an amount based upon (1) the lump-sum breakdown; (2) unit-price items in the contract, if any; (3) reimbursable inventory; and (4) changes to the contract, if any.

Given this important responsibility, it is essential that the contract administrator devise procedures to quantify the work of the contractor with accuracy sufficient to assure all participants that the proper payments are being made. If the contract administrator's estimates of the amount of work by the contractor are too low, the resulting payment deficiency will be unfair to the contractor in that his burden of "financing the project" will be extended and his borrowing costs increased. If, on the other hand, the estimates of work are too high, the resulting premature payment will deprive the owner of the time value of the money paid. Thus inaccurate estimates may subject the contract administrator to criticism from both the contractor and the owner.

In addition to the need for accuracy, it is important that the estimating procedures be developed so as to minimize the contract administrator's direct involvement. Freeing the contract administrator from daily involvement in the important, but relatively mundane, process of interim payment estimating will permit him or her to devote more time to those aspects of the project which truly merit direct handling.

Most major construction projects contemplate the making and filing of daily inspection reports by the contract administrator's staff. The most direct method by which the data required for partial payment can be collected is to expand the daily inspection report to permit daily quantification of the amount of work incorporated into the project and its value based upon the lump-sum breakdown, unit prices, reimbursable inventory, and change orders. This expanded reporting will permit the inspector responsible for monitoring the *quality* of the work to measure simultaneously the *quantity* and *value* of the work within his area of responsibility. Upon receipt of the reports, the contract administrator (or, more likely, a member of his clerical staff) can tabulate the quantities and values of work reported by the inspection staff, confirm these quantities with the contractor, and approve reimbursement.

It is customary that reimbursements be recommended to the owner on a monthly basis; however, it is advantageous that confirmations with the contractor occur on a weekly basis. The reason for weekly confirmation is that the quantities reported by inspectors on a daily basis are likely to be in error: a day is such a small fraction of a major project that daily measurement is inherently arbitrary. Such errors are usually self-correcting over time. For example, if a contractor were pouring concrete on part of a structure, the inspector might quantify the amount of concrete being poured directly, i.e., by adding the total quantity of concrete delivered during a given day with no compensation for waste. As the pouring of concrete on that part of the structure neared completion, the inspector might use the theoretical quantity of concrete required for that part of the structure to either eliminate the wastage or to estimate it and make corresponding adjustments. In other words, as the work progresses, the inspector can adjust his reports over several days to achieve a greater degree of accuracy. One might conclude by extension of this line of reasoning that monthly confirmations would be more accurate than weekly confirmations; however, the desirability of minimizing the scale of potential disputes between the contractor and the contract administrator militates in favor of holding to the 1-week guideline. If there are significant disagreements between the contractor and the contract administrator as to the progress of the work (and the value added to the project), it is in the interest of the owner that the scope of the disagreement be minimized and that its resolution be undertaken without delay. The 1-week confirmation seems a desirable compromise between the need for accuracy and the need for agreement. Finally, with agreed-upon confirmation in hand for the first 3 weeks of any given month, the contract administrator is well equipped to negotiate the contractor's agreement with the contract administrator's estimates of progress during the last week of that month as the last step prior to issuing his payment recommendation to the owner.

Inasmuch as these interim, or partial, payments involve a substantial amount of repetitive labor which can be undertaken at relatively low level, it seems advisable that the contract administrator develop routine procedures, i.e., *systems*, to discharge his partial payment responsibilities.

COST CONTROL

In the case of a lump-sum contract with unit prices, the cost control system will be comprised of four major parts. The first part will compensate the contractor for those parts of the work he completes on the lump-sum part of the contract in accordance with the agreed-upon lump-sum breakdown. The second part will compensate the contractor for the work he performs on the unit-price part of the contract (as described in the preceding chapter). The third part will compensate the contractor for work performed in connection with changes to the contract (see Chapters 10 and 11). The fourth part of the system will reimburse the contractor for the cost of inventoried materials and equipment on site or in approved storage areas.

Cost Control for Lump-Sum Items

The reader will recall that in Chapter 6 a typical lump-sum breakdown was suggested for the tunnel project. That illustrative lump-sum breakdown will now be employed to generate cost control gathering sheets for the tunnel project. The lump-sum breakdown separated the lump-sum part of the project into its several items of work, established a unit for each item, and estimated the number of such units as shown in Table 16-1.

TABLE 16-1   Cost Control Gathering Sheet for the Tunnel Project

Item number	Description	Quantity	Unit
1	Mobilization	—	Lump sum
2	Haul road	—	Lump sum
3	Waterline	105	Linear foot
4	Sheetpiling, west shaft	5269	Square foot
5	Sheetpiling, east shaft	6205	Square foot
6	Observation wells	2	Each
7	Excavation, west shaft	493.5	Cubic yard
8	Excavation, east shaft	635.2	Cubic yard
9	Dewatering	39	Day
10	Tunnel	126	Linear foot
11	96-in. pipe	227.67	Linear foot
12	Grouting	—	Lump sum
13	Backfill shafts	1004.9	Cubic yard
14	Riprap	—	Lump sum
15	Cleanup and demobilization	—	Lump sum

Since the tunnel project is relatively small, it is possible to state all items of work on one sheet; on a larger project, it may be advisable to list on a separate sheet only those items within the area of responsibility of a given inspector.

In order to convert the lump-sum breakdown sheet into a weekly cost control report, the contract administrator need only provide additional space on the lump-sum breakdown sheet in which to note the daily progress for each work item. He will then use the cost control sheets to calculate the payment due the contractor for each item. In order to avoid a mere copying of numbers from one sheet to another, the contract administrator should extend the cost control report to permit the dollar amounts due the contractor at the end of any given week to be calculated for each work item and then totaled on the same sheet, as shown in Figure 16-1.

While reviewing the contractor's work to assure the quality is adequate, the inspector also will note the *quantity* of work done during a particular day. That quantity of work will be noted under the item number describing it on the "Weekly Cost Control Report—Lump-Sum Items" and in accordance with the "units" for which partial payment has been agreed upon with the contractor. At the end of each week, the inspector will total the units incorporated into the work each day of the week for each item number and note that total under the Weekly Total column for that item number. He will then multiply the weekly total for each item number by the price per unit for that item number to derive the weekly total price for that item number. After doing this for each item, the inspector will add all the weekly total price items to arrive at the total weekly price (all items) at the bottom of the sheet. The inspector then turns the Weekly Cost Control Report—Lump-Sum Items over to the contract administrator's clerical staff, who check the mathematics, for ultimate incorporation into the contractor's monthly Partial Payment Request.

Cost Control for Unit-Price Items

Unit-price items should be quantified on separate summary sheets, i.e., one for each unit-price item, kept in separate folders as detailed in the preceding chapter. These data are to be transferred weekly to the monthly Partial Payment Request discussed later in this chapter. The transfer is a mere clerical function.

Cost Control for Modifications (Change Orders)

A separate file folder should be developed for each modification to the contract as detailed in Chapter 10. The folder provides a means to

WEEKLY COST CONTROL REPORT
LUMP-SUM ITEMS

PROJECT _____ PERIOD _____ TO _____

CONTRACTOR _____ REPORT NO. L.S. _____

Item No.	Description	Quantity	Unit	Units Incorporated into the Work					Weekly Total	Price Per Unit	Weekly Total Price
				(Mon)	(Tue)	(Wed)	(Thu)	(Fri)			
1	Mobilization	-	L.S.							30,000	
2	Haul Road	-	L.S.							750	
3	Water line	105	lin ft							42.85	
4	Sheetpiling, west	5269	ft³							11.85	
5	Sheetpiling, east	6205	ft³							11.85	
6	Observation wells	2	Each							500	
7	Excavation, west shaft	493.5	yd³							2.05	
8	Excavation, east shaft	635.2	yd³							2.05	
9	Dewatering	39	Day							1063.92	
10	Tunnel	126	lin ft							1211.48	
11	96-in. pipe	227.67	lin ft							209.95	
12	Grouting	—	L.S.							9043	
13	Backfill shafts	1004.9	yd³							11.77	
14	Riprap	—	L.S.							3460	
15	Cleanup & demobilization	—	L.S.							4256	

TOTAL WEEKLY PRICE (ALL ITEMS) _____

FIGURE 16-1 Weekly Cost Control Report—Lump-Sum Items.

record the administrative effort required to authorize the approval and dollar amount of each change (modification) to the contract. To this point, however, the cost control system has yet to provide a method by which to pay the contractor for such changes. Depending upon (1) the amount of time required for the contractor to complete the work of the change and (2) the method of payment for the change (as agreed upon in the change order), it is possible to pay the contractor by one of four methods. First, the contractor may be paid on a lump-sum basis if the work of the modification is completed during any given month or if no other method of payment is agreed upon in the change order. Second, the contractor may be paid on a unit-price basis if that method is stipulated in the modification. If the contractor is to be paid on a unit-price basis, the contract administrator must provide to the inspector a list of the agreed-upon unit prices and a supplemental unit-price folder to record the quantities of work completed. Third, the contractor may be paid on a time-and-material basis if the change order so provides. In such a case, the contractor should submit daily extra work orders to the inspector in order that the inspector may verify the quantities of time, labor, and equipment stated to have been provided for any given day for the work of that modification. Copies of these daily reports should be filed and tabulated by the contract administrator. The tabulated quantities should be reviewed weekly with the contractor and, once agreed upon, should be approved for payment upon receipt of the contractor's conforming monthly invoice. Fourth, in the case of a lump-sum change order which extends beyond the 1-month billing period, the contractor may be paid on a lump-sum breakdown basis. In such a case, rather than use the negotiated lump-sum breakdown costs for the project, the contract administrator would use a lump-sum breakdown derived from the details of the contractor's price proposal for the particular modification. Illustrations of all four methods follow.

Lump-Sum Modifications Most modifications (changes) to the contract will probably be of relatively short duration and of relatively low dollar amounts. These modifications, as previously stated, can be paid for when the work associated with the modification is complete. Cost control for this type of modification can be easily handled by giving the inspector a list of the modifications which have been agreed upon with the contractor or, in the case where more than one inspector is working on the project, giving the particular inspector a list of agreed-upon modifications in his area of inspection responsibility. This list, entitled "Weekly Cost Control Report—Lump-Sum Modifications," would be generated and kept current by the contract administrator or his clerical staff. (An example is shown in Figure 16-2.) The report will note the

WEEKLY COST CONTROL REPORT

LUMP-SUM MODIFICATONS

PROJECT _____   PERIOD _____   TO _____

CONTRACTOR _____   REPORT NO. MOD. _____

Change Order No.	Mod. No.	Description	Date Completed	Modification Price

TOTAL, ALL MODS. FOR PERIOD $_____

FIGURE 16-2   Weekly Cost Control Report—Lump-Sum Modifications.

data under the Change Order No. column, the Modification No. column, the Description column, and the Modification Price column when given to the inspector. When the work of the modification is complete, the inspector merely enters that date on the Date Completed line and returns the report to the contract administrator or his clerical staff. The data is subsequently transferred to the contractor's monthly Partial Payment Request, *as should be done with all modifications.*

Lump-Sum Breakdown Modifications If the agreed-upon method of payment were lump sum, but the dollar amount and time required to complete the modification were substantial, a lump-sum breakdown should be negotiated—and interim payments provided for—to facilitate cash flow to the contractor. However, modifications rarely require such intricacy. In the usual case, the contractor's lump-sum price for a modification is based upon a detailed breakdown of the major components of the work. The breakdown usually describes the item of work, the quantities involved, equipment costs, and corresponding labor costs to install the materials and any required equipment. In short, the modification has a "built-in" lump-sum breakdown. The contract administrator should merely transfer the contractor's quantities and prices to the "Weekly Cost Control Report—Modifications" as shown in Figure 16-3.

Unit-Price Modifications If the owner and contractor established that the payment for the modification was made according to the unit prices in the contractor's price proposal, the contract administrator's "Weekly Cost Control Report—Unit-Price Modifications" (Figure 16-4) should merely recite those unit prices.

Time-and-Material Modifications A fourth alternative for payment for a modification is payment on a time-and-material basis. Such an alternative would reimburse to the contractor the *cost,* not price, of the materials, equipment, and labor required to perform the work of the modification and would also provide for payment of an additional percentage of these costs to cover the contractor's overhead and a further percentage to cover his profit. (Overhead and profit percentages are usually fixed in the original contract.) As the contractor completes the work on a time-and-material modification, he submits to the inspector a tabulation of all costs incurred during a given time period, usually a day. The inspector verifies the contractor's expenditures during that time period or adjusts the reported costs (with the concurrence of the contractor), then forwards the verified sheets to the contract administrator. The contract administrator merely tabulates the totals of these

WEEKLY COST CONTROL REPORT

MODIFICATIONS

PROJECT _____

CONTRACTOR _____

PERIOD _____ TO _____

REPORT NO. MOD. _____

C.O. NO. _____

MOD. NO. _____

Price Proposal Item No.	Description	Total Quantity	Unit	Unit Incorp.						Weekly Total	Price Per Unit	Weekly Total Price
				Mon	Tue	Wed	Thu	Fri				

TOTAL PRICE FOR MOD. DURING PERIOD $ _____

FIGURE 16-3 Weekly Cost Control Report for lump-sum modifications requiring partial payment to the contractor.

WEEKLY COST CONTROL REPORT

UNIT–PRICE MODIFICATIONS

PROJECT _____

CONTRACTOR _____

PERIOD _____ TO _____

REPORT NO. _____ MOD. _____

C.O. NO. _____

MOD. NO. _____

| Price Proposal Item No. | Description | Total Quantity | Unit | Unit Incorp. | | | | | Weekly Total | Price Per Unit | Weekly Total Price |
				Mon	Tue	Wed	Thu	Fri			

TOTAL PRICE FOR MOD. DURING PERIOD $ _____

FIGURE 16-4 Weekly Cost Control Report—Unit-Price Modifications.

time period sheets, checks the weekly totals with the contractor, and recommends payment of the contractor's monthly invoice, once verified, for the modification. All such documentation should be affixed to the right-hand side of the original modification folder in order to preserve the data, an especially important consideration in view of the absence of a predetermined price for a time-and-material modification. The contract administrator's "Weekly Cost Control Report—Time-and-Material Modifications" is shown in Figure 16-5.

Given the possible multiplicity of modifications in a large project and the alternative methods of compensation for each, it seems unlikely that a single form can be devised to cover all variations. It is recommended that the contract administrator develop his own forms for modifications, using combinations of the forms proposed in this book and tabulating all modifications compensated by a given method on a separate sheet to preserve overall organization.

Once a month, all the costs developed would be totaled and figures forwarded to the owner with a recommendation that the owner pay that total amount to the contractor.

The Cost Control System for Inventoried Materials and Equipment

The reader will recall from Chapter 14 that the Inventory Control Sheet (Figure 14-1) noted, among other items, the delivery ticket number and date, a check on the fact that the material and equipment had been inspected, the vendor supplying the material and equipment, a description of the material and equipment, the exact location on the project where the equipment and material would ultimately be installed, and the storage area where they are stored. These data are gathered in the field by the inspector, as is the date the material and equipment are removed from inventory to be incorporated into the work. A suggested "Weekly Cost Control Report—Reimbursable Inventory" is shown in Figure 16-6.

As equipment and materials enter the site for storage, the contractor will so advise the contract administrator. The contract administrator will inspect the material and equipment or delegate this responsibility to one of his Inspectors should the project be large enough to warrant inspectors working under the contract administrator, the circumstance assumed here for purposes of explanation.

At this time, the required data will be recorded on the "Inventory Added" section of the Weekly Cost Control Report—Reimbursable Inventory by the inspector. At the end of each week, the inspector will turn in to the clerical staff the Weekly Cost Control Report—

WEEKLY COST CONTROL REPORT

TIME – AND – MATERIAL MODIFICATIONS

Project _____   Period _____ to _____

Contractor _____   Report No. __C.O._____

Owner _____

C.O. No.	Mod. No.	Description	Verified Time Sheet Total

TOTAL PRICE FOR ALL T&M MODS DURING PERIOD $ _____

FIGURE 16-5 Weekly Cost Control Report—Time-and-Material Modifications.

WEEKLY COST CONTROL REPORT
REIMBURSABLE INVENTORY

PROJECT _____   PERIOD _____ TO _____

CONTRACTOR _____   REPORT NO. R.I. _____

INVENTORY ADDED

Delivery Ticket No.	Delivery Ticket Date	Vendor	Description	Installed Location	Inspected By	Storage Area

INVENTORY INCORPORATED INTO THE WORK

Installed Location	Description	Approximate Percentage Installed	Installation Verified By	Date of Installation

FIGURE 16-6   Weekly Cost Control Report—Reimbursable Inventory.

Reimbursable Inventory for that week. The clerical staff will then transfer the data to the Inventory Control Sheets and will complete the remaining pertinent sections of the sheets as much as possible at that time, filling in other data, such as insurance policy numbers, as they become available. Similarly, as the inventoried material and equipment are incorporated into the work of the project, the inspector will note that fact by filling out the "Inventory Incorporated into the Work" section of the Weekly Cost Control Report—Reimbursable Inventory.

The sheet has a column to allow for a partial amount of the inventoried item to be noted should the total not be incorporated into the work at one time. (Items such as reinforcing steel quite often are not all incorporated into the work at one time.) A corresponding percentage of the value of that item will be taken off the inventory by the contract administrator's clerical staff should this situation arise.

The Installed Location and Description columns are useful in finding the material and equipment which are being taken out of inventory, since it is improbable delivery ticket numbers could be remembered. Hence sufficient care to note adequately where the material and equipment will be installed, and the description will be rewarded in time savings later.

At the end of the month, the contract administrator or the clerical staff will scan the Inventory Control Sheets, which have been kept current through data updates submitted on the Weekly Cost Control Report—Reimbursable Inventory sheets. A scan of the Delivery Ticket Date column will enable the clerk to note all items added to inventory from the date of the last review. After further checking that the other necessary requirements noted on the Inventory Control Sheet have been met by the contractor, the clerk totals these items for the month and notes that total on the "Reimbursable Inventory Summary Sheet," as shown in Figure 16-7.

Should the contractor not have met all the other requirements to allow reimbursement, the clerk should note an asterisk, or some other such mark, on the delivery ticket date to indicate, when compiling the data for the next monthly update, that the item in question was not included in the previous update.

After totaling the inventory added during the period and noting the dollar amount on the Reimbursable Inventory Summary Sheet, the clerk subtotals that amount with the dollar amount of the reimbursable inventory from the previous time period and then reviews the Date Incorporated column on the Inventory Control Sheet, which has also been updated for the period by adding to it the data from the Inventory Incorporated into the Work section of the Weekly Cost Control— Reimbursable Inventory reports for the time period of the update. The

REIMBURSABLE INVENTORY SUMMARY SHEET

PROJECT _____   PERIOD _____ TO _____

CONTRACTOR _____   REPORT NOS. RI. _____

THROUGH R.I.   _____

A.   Total Inventory at Start of Period $ _____

(+)B.   Inventory Added During The Period   _____

SUB-TOTAL $ _____

(-)C.   Inventoried Material/Equipment Incorporated into the Work During the Period   _____

SUB-TOTAL $ _____

(-)D.   Previously Paid Inventory Withdrawn From Inventory Due to Lack of Certification of Payment by The Contractor   _____

(+)E.   Previously Withdrawn Items Which Now Have Certification of Payment   _____

TOTAL REIMBURSABLE INVENTORY AT END OF PERIOD $ _____

FIGURE 16-7   Reimbursable Inventory Summary Sheet.

PARTIAL PAYMENT REQUEST

PAGE 1 OF 2

I. LUMP-SUM ITEMS

Item No.	Description	Estimated Total		Previously Expended		Expended This Period		Total Expenditure to Date	
		Quantity	Price	Quantity	Price	Quantity	Price	Quantity	Price
(1)	(2)	(3)	(4)	(5)	(6)	(7)	(8)	(9)	(10)

Column 10   Total $ _____

II. CONTRACT UNIT-PRICE ITEMS

Item No.	Description	Estimated Total		Previously Extended		Expended This Period		Total Expenditure This Date	
		Quantity	Price	Quantity	Price	Quantity	Price	Quantity	Price
(1)	(2)	(3)	(4)	(5)	(6)	(7)	(8)	(9)	(10)

Column 10   Total _____
Total contract work to date _____

FIGURE 16-8 Partial Payment Request.

PAGE 2 OF 2

$ _____

III. TOTAL REIMBURSABLE INVENTORY

IV. CHANGE ORDER WORK

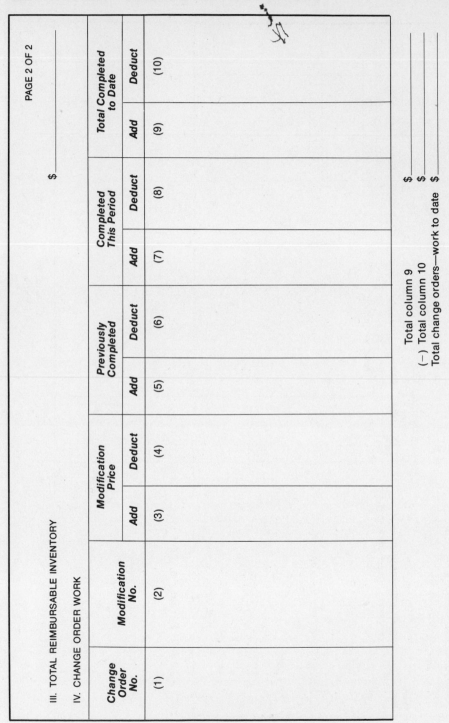

Change Order No.	Modification No.	Modification Price		Previously Completed		Completed This Period		Total Completed to Date	
		Add	Deduct	Add	Deduct	Add	Deduct	Add	Deduct
(1)	(2)	(3)	(4)	(5)	(6)	(7)	(8)	(9)	(10)

Total column 9 $ _____
(−) Total column 10 $ _____
Total change orders—work to date $ _____

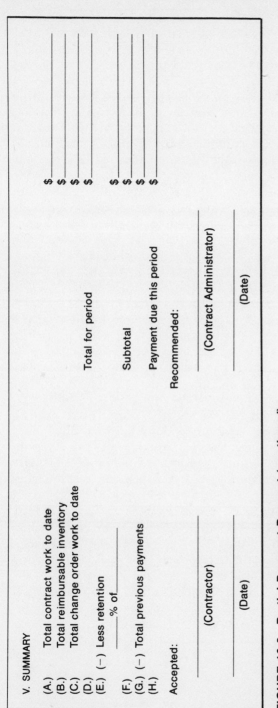

V. SUMMARY

(A.)   Total contract work to date $_____

(B.)   Total reimbursable inventory $_____

(C.)   Total change order work to date $_____

(D.)   Total for period $_____

(E.) (−) Less retention
        _____ % of _____

(F.)   Subtotal $_____

(G.) (−) Total previous payments $_____

(H.)   Payment due this period $_____

Accepted: Recommended:

_____   _____
(Contractor)   (Contract Administrator)

_____   _____
(Date)   (Date)

FIGURE 16-8   Partial Payment Request (*continued*).

clerk runs a total of the dollar value of the reimbursable inventory items which have been utilized in the work of the project and notes that total dollar amount on the Reimbursable Inventory Summary Sheet (item C) and subtracts that dollar amount from the previous subtotal on the sheet.

Next, the clerk scans the Date Paid column on the Reimbursable Inventory Summary Sheet to verify that the contractor has supplied evidence of payment to the contract administrator within the time period stipulated in the contract documents. If the contractor has done so, item D on the Reimbursable Inventory Summary Sheet will have a zero entered. If the contractor has failed to supply evidence of payment for one or more items, the dollar amount of those items will be added and the total noted for item D. The clerk will also have to mark those items on the Inventory Control Sheet so that, when verification that the contractor has paid for these items comes in, the contractor can again be given reimbursement for them. This contingency should then be accounted for by noting the dollar amount of such items after item E on the Reimbursable Inventory Summary Sheet.

The bottom figure, "Total Reimbursable Inventory at End of Period," is then transferred to the contractor's Partial Payment Request for the time period.

The Monthly Partial Payment Form

With the four necessary components for the contractor's monthly Partial Payment Request documented, the contract administrator needs a method to compile these four separate sections into one document. Many owners have their own form for the monthly partial payment to be typed on; we provide in Figure 16-8 a form of the type usually utilized. This form gives the cumulative cost to date as well as documenting current costs.

Lump-sum breakdown items are noted first on the form, the unit-price items in the contract come next, then an aggregation of the inventoried materials, and, last, the detail for each modification to the contract. In the cases of the lump-sum breakdown items and the unit-price items, the totals from the previous month for each item, the totals for each item during the month, and the cumulative total to date, are noted. The reader should have no difficulty in following the method of tabulation utilized by the form. Filling out the form merely requires aggregations of the data of the four components previously detailed in this chapter.

CHAPTER 17

THE SYSTEM FOR QUALITY CONTROL

ADMINISTRATIVE CONTROL RESPONSIBILITIES AND TECHNICAL CONTROL RESPONSIBILITIES

Chapter 1 set forth a detailed explanation of the method by which control responsibilities could be abstracted from the contract documents to serve better the needs of the contract administrator. The control responsibilities, once abstracted, may be divided into two broad groups: administrative responsibilities and technical responsibilities. Quality control in the project is created by the proper discharge of the technical responsibilities by the contractor and the monitoring and recording of proper discharge by the contract administrator.

Two important differences exist between technical control responsibilities and administrative control responsibilities. The first is that technical control responsibilities are not included in the integrated schedule for the project. The sheer numbers of technical control responsibilities in a project of any significant size would render any attempt to monitor them using the integrated schedule unwieldy. Second, unlike administrative control responsibilities, many technical matters require the conduct, monitoring, and recording of various tests. The circumstances of the project usually require that certain tests (e.g., pressure testing of field-fabricated piping systems, testing of sewers, confirmation of currents drawn by electrical equipment, and pile-driving logs) be conducted in the field and that others (e.g., compressive strength reports and aggregate soundness tests) be performed in the laboratory.

Inasmuch as this testing is, for the most part, repetitive in nature and sufficiently routine so as not to require the direct participation of the contract administrator in most cases, it seems desirable that routine procedures, i.e., *a system*, be developed by the contract administrator to promote the effective discharge of *his* responsibilities. Specifically, the quality control system should be devised so as to (1) assure that all field testing to which the contract administrator must attest is performed by the contractor, monitored by (or on behalf of) the contract administrator, and documented and attested by (or on behalf of) the contract administrator and (2) provide a method to index and file test reports and note the proper discharge of each of the technical control responsibilities of the contractor.

QUALITY CONTROL
Indexing and Filing

The quality control system is comprised of two subsystems: a subsystem to *index and file* test reports and a subsystem to record *performance* of the test, witnessing of the test, and attestation. Turning first to the subsystem for indexing and filing, the contract administrator should create a separate file for quality control. Unlike other files suggested in this book, however, the quality control file should take the form of a large, loose-leaf notebook. The first sheet in the notebook should be a general index containing a list of the technical control responsibilities transferred from the Control Responsibility Summary Sheet. Immediately following the general index, a tabbed divider should be inserted for each technical control responsibility. Immediately following each such divider, a "detailed index" sheet should appear. An example may be used to demonstrate the use of the notebook. In the case of a sanitary sewer line, it is probable that the line would be tested in sections. Accordingly, the detailed index for sanitary sewer testing should reflect the individual tests taken on each section:

SANITARY SEWER TESTS

Manhole 1 to Manhole 3   **Sheet 1**

_____

_____

_____

Manhole 3 to Manhole 6   **Sheet 2**

_____

_____

_____

Manhole 6 to Manhole 7   Sheet 3

_____

_____

_____

Etc. _____

The individual test reports would then be placed in the notebook immediately following the detailed index sheet in the order noted on the index sheet. Reports concerning electrical tests on wiring (such as meggering or high-potential tests) should similarly be inserted in the notebook following the detailed index sheet as they are performed, with the conduit designation and wire designation noted on the left-hand side of the detailed index sheet and the sheet numbers within the subsection noted on the right-hand side of the detailed index sheet.

As the project progresses, the tests for each item on the Technical Control Summary Sheet performed by the contractor and monitored and attested by the contract administrator are indexed and filed to build the quality control file. Reference to the detailed index sheet for any given technical control responsibility will readily reflect what parts of the overall responsibility have been performed to that point and, correspondingly, what items within that responsibility remain to be undertaken. For complex items such as meggering, it may be necessary to list all wires required to be meggered on the detailed index sheet and mark them as they are completed.

Recording the Performance of Tests

The focus now shifts to the second quality control subsystem: the subsystem recording performance of tests by the contractor and monitoring an attestation of tests by the contract administrator. The discharge of duties by both the contractor and contract administrator in connection with a given technical control responsibility can most easily be recorded by the contract administrator if he has prepared in advance standard forms for the various tests required within that responsibility. It should also be noted, however, that the number of potential forms in a project of substantial size could be endless and could vary widely from project to project: the data to be recorded on any such forms are determined by the provisions of the contract documents. Also, inappropriate or casually prepared forms could create unanticipated liability for the contract administrator by transferring responsibility for correct performance of the work from the contractor to himself. Accordingly, most contract administrators elect to maintain on file standard test forms which indicate the data required for given tests and which have been reviewed in advance with legal counsel from a defensive standpoint. In the event, however, that the contract administrator does not have such forms on file, he should devote sufficient time at the outset of the project to devising the forms and should submit them to legal counsel for review well in advance of the needs to use them.

A series of sample forms (Figures 17-1 to 17-5) indicating the data required for some commonly employed test reports is included. The reader is again cautioned that these forms are presented solely for purposes of illustration and that they should not be used in any project without reviews against the contract documents and review by counsel. They are presented as stimulation for thought, not substitution for thought. Each of the sample forms has three characteristics common to the others: It documents the location, date and time, and subject of the test; it records the data produced by the test; and it provides for attestation of the data as correct.

Blank, approved test report forms for each test required within each technical control responsibility should be on hand well in advance of required use. The transfer of data from scraps of paper to test reports or from dirty test reports to clean ones should be prohibited due to the possibility of error in copying and the possible liability of the contract administrator for such errors once he has attested to the correctness of the data.

Thus well before any test is required, the contract administrator's quality control notebook file should contain the general index of technical control responsibilities, the detailed indexes, and blank test report forms for each required test.

Recording the Discharge of Technical Control Responsibilities

The next step in the quality control system is notation of the contractor's actual discharge of a technical control responsibility. At some point during each weekly progress and coordination meeting (to be discussed in Part 3), the contract administrator will request that the contractor provide advice concerning his short-term schedule for the next 2 weeks. At the conclusion of the contractor's statement, the contract administrator should inquire as to what field testing the contractor contemplates in order that the contract administrator may arrange to witness and record the findings of those tests. The contract administrator or his designate, both of whom should be thoroughly familiar with the monitoring and recording of the testing to be performed, can then undertake any necessary last-minute review.

Equipment Testing
Report

GENERAL	PROJECT		FILE NO.	DATE
	CONTRACTOR		INSPECTOR	
EQUIPMENT	EQUIPMENT NAME			
	MOTOR MFR.		EQUIPMENT MFR.	
	MOTOR SERIAL NO.		EQUIPMENT SERIAL NO.	
LUBE	DATE 1ST LUBE		LUBRICANT USED (MAKE & TYPE)	
MFG. CHECK	DATE MFG. CHECK		MANUFACTURER'S SIGNATURE	
NAMEPLATE	HP	RPM	VOLTAGE	SELF (SERVICE FACTOR)
	FULL LOAD AMPS	INS CLASS	FRAME SIZE	TEMP RISE

MOTOR CONTROL	STARTER SIZE	STARTER MODEL NO.	O.L. CAT. NO. NAMEPLATE_____ ACTUAL_____	O.L. RANGE NAMEPLATE_____ ACTUAL_____
	PRE STARTUP		FULL OPERATION	
	VOLTAGE 1-2 PHASE	AMPS 1-PHASE	VOLTAGE 1-2 PHASE	AMPS 1-PHASE
	VOLTAGE 2-3 PHASE	AMPS 2 PHASE	VOLTAGE 2-3 PHASE	AMPS 2-PHASE
	VOLTAGE 3-1 PHASE	AMPS 3 PHASE	VOLTAGE 3-1 PHASE	AMPS 3 PHASE

FIGURE 17-1   Equipment testing report.

MEGGER TEST REPORT

Project _____ Date _____
Contractor _____ File no. _____
Inspector _____ Contract citation _____

Cable Data: *Circuit Data:*
Manufacturer _____   Equipment _____
Rating _____   Circuit no. _____
Insulation _____   From _____ To _____
Shielded _____   Type of service _____
Conductors _____   Length of cable _____
Size _____

Test Conditions:
Test voltage _____   Tested by _____
Voltage maintained _____   Witnessed by _____
Time maintained _____   Instrument _____
Temp. _____ Humidity _____   Serial no. _____

Test Data:

Component	*Kilovolts*	*Ohms*
ϕA to Ground		
ϕB to Ground		
ϕC to Ground		
ϕA to ϕB		
ϕA to ϕC		
ϕB to ϕC		

Notes: _____
_____
_____
_____

Test Deemed: ☐ Acceptable ☐ Unacceptable

FIGURE 17-2   Megger Test Report.

PIPE TEST REPORT

Project _____ Date _____
Contractor _____ File no. _____
Inspector _____

Location _____
Limits of test: From _____ To _____
Fluid Transported _____

Pipe size _____
Pipe material _____

Test Requirements Per:
 ☐ Contract citation _____
          or
 ☐ Code _____

Allowable loss: _____ of _____ per _____

Test Data:
Starting measurement _____ Time _____ Date _____
Ending measurement _____ Time _____ Date _____
Actual difference _____ Time _____
Projected difference _____ for a _____ Hour Period

Results Deemed: ☐ Acceptable
       ☐ Unacceptable

Computations and Comments:
_____
_____
_____
_____
_____
_____

FIGURE 17-3 Pipe Test Report.

Concrete-Filled Pipe Pile

Driving Report

GENERAL	PROJECT		FILE NO.	DATE
	CONTRACTOR		FOREMAN	
	WEATHER CONDITIONS _____ TEMP MAX _____ MIN _____		INSPECTOR	

PILE DATA	LOCATION		HAMMER, MAKE & MODEL	CUSHION BLK TYPE
	TYPE		TIP DIA _____ IN	BUTT DIA _____
	LENGTH _____ FT _____ IN	WEIGHT _____ LPS	DATE CONCRETED	VOL OF CONCRETE

PENETRATION	ELEV OF GROUND	CUT OFF ELEV	ELEV. OF TIP	PAY LENGTH

REMARKS

BLOWCOUNT

FT	NO. OF BLOWS	BLS MIN	FT	NO. OF BLOWS	BLS MIN	FT	NO. OF BLOWS	BLS MIN	FT	NO. OF BLOWS	BLS MIN
1			26			51			76		
2			27			52			77		
3			28			53			78		
4			29			54			79		
5			30			55			80		
6			31			56			81		
7			32			57			82		
8			33			58			83		
9			34			59			84		
10			35			60			85		
11			36			61			86		
12			37			62			87		
13			38			63			88		
14			39			64			89		
15			40			65			90		
16			41			66			91		
17			42			67			92		
18			43			68			93		
19			44			69			94		
20			45			70			95		
21			46			71			96		
22			47			72			97		
23			48			73			98		
24			49			74			99		
25			50			75			100		

FIGURE 17-4 **Pile-driving report of a concrete-filled pipe pile.**

Precast, Prestressed Concrete Pile

Driving Report

GENERAL	PROJECT	FILE NO.	DATE
	CONTRACTOR	FOREMAN	
PILE DATA	WEATHER CONDITIONS _____ TEMP MAX _____ MIN _____	INSPECTOR	
	LOCATION	HAMMER MAKE & MODEL	CUSHION BLOCK TYPE
PENET-TRATION	TYPE	DIMENSIONS	SPLICE DATA
	ELEV. OF GROUND	CUT OFF ELEV	ELEV. OF TIP	PAY LENGTH

FT	BLOWS FT / NRG MIN	FT	BLOWS FT / NRG MIN	FT	BLOWS FT / NRG MIN	FT	BLOWS FT / NRG MIN	FT	BLOWS FT / NRG MIN	FT	BLOWS FT / NRG MIN	FT	BLOWS FT / NRG MIN	FT	BLOWS FT / NRG MIN	FT	BLOWS FT / NRG MIN
100		130		160		190		220		250		280		310			
1		31		61		91		21		51		81		11			
2		32		62		92		22		52		82		12			
3		33		63		93		23		53		83		13			
4		34		64		94		24		54		84		14			
5		35		65		95		25		55		85		15			
6		36		66		96		26		56		86		16			
7		37		67		97		27		57		87		17			
8		38		68		98		28		58		88		18			
9		39		69		99		29		59		89		19			
110		140		170		200		230		260		290		320			
11		41		71		1		31		61		91		21			
12		42		72		2		32		62		92		22			
13		43		73		3		33		63		93		23			
14		44		74		4		34		64		94		24			
15		45		75		5		35		65		95		25			
16		46		76		6		36		66		96		26			
17		47		77		7		37		67		97		27			
18		48		78		8		38		68		98		28			
19		49		79		9		39		69		99		29			
120		150		180		210		240		270		300		330			
21		51		81		11		41		71		1		31			
22		52		82		12		42		72		2		32			
23		53		83		13		43		73		3		33			
24		54		84		14		44		74		4		34			
25		55		85		15		45		75		5		35			
26		56		86		16		46		76		6		36			
27		57		87		17		47		77		7		37			
28		58		88		18		48		78		8		38			
29		59		89		19		49		79		9		39			

FIGURE 17-5 Precast, prestressed concrete pile-driving report.

(Date) _____

(Contractor) _____
_____
_____

Attn: _____

                                    Re: (Project Title) _____
                               Subject: Test Report Transmittal
                                  File: _____

Gentlemen:

Attached is a copy of the test report for (Type and Location of Test)
which was conducted on ____(Date)____.

This test is deemed   ☐ Acceptable

                       ☐ Unacceptable

Very truly yours,

Contract Administrator

cc: Design Engineer
    Quality Control File

FIGURE 17-6 Transmittal of test report.

The test procedures required pursuant to the contract documents should be rigidly adhered to, and the test forms should be filled out neatly, accurately, and in considerable detail. In the event it becomes necessary to deviate from a prescribed test procedure, the contract administrator should contact the design engineer to obtain information concerning acceptable variations to the test to accommodate field conditions. The information provided by the design engineer should be treated as a clarification to the contract with appropriate notation on the test report itself. Should the variation create a substantial cost saving for the contractor, the contract administrator should invoke the customary modification or change order procedures to pass the saving on to the owner.

It seems worthy of mention that field tests and laboratory tests either meet the requirements of the contract documents as to both procedures and results or they do not. A test which "nearly" meets the required standards and results has no contractual meaning. The contract administrator who accepts the results of such a test does so at his peril.

In the event that a test—by either procedures employed or results obtained—fails to meet the requirements of the contract, the contract administrator should so advise the contractor at the earliest practical time in order to allow him to make the necessary corrections to his testing procedures or to his work and to schedule another test. The contract administrator should also advise the contractor of all tests which are acceptable as to both procedures and results in order that the contractor may file his copy of the test report and acceptance by the contract administrator.

Figure 17-6 is a standard letter for transmission of test reports to the contractor, with a copy to the design engineer. Copies of these letters and the original test report should be filed in the contract administrator's quality control file. Upon completion of the last test report with attestation as to satisfactory procedures and results, the contract administrator's quality control file will be complete. At this point, the contract documents may require, or the owner may request, that a copy of all test data be provided to the owner.

PART THREE

MONITORING OF CONTROLS

In Part 1, the contract was dissected, then rearranged so as to permit establishment by the contract administrator of the necessary devices to control the project. Part 2 was concerned with the creation of systems (e.g., status sheets, standard forms, and standard letters) to facilitate administration. Part 3 will discuss and illustrate the ways in which the operating systems can be monitored by the contract administrator to promote the timely discharge of contractual responsibilities.

The most important tools for monitoring are "system status reports" and meetings of contract participants. The status report for any system summarizes the current status of transactions within the system, points out deficiencies in the contractual performance of one or more participants, and advises deficient performers of the need to upgrade their efforts. Meetings, on the other hand, are initiated by the contract administrator to facilitate coordination of multiparticipant efforts and to further investigate deficient performances which have not been resolved through status reports.

The format for discussion of these two tools will be examination of the respective systems set forth in Part 2. The chapters of Part 3 will be organized according to three distinct, but related, dimensions of the systems discussed in Part 2. Chapters 18 through 21 are concerned primarily with project *cost,* Chapters 22 and 23 with *scheduling,* and Chapters 24 and 25 with project *quality.*

CHAPTER 18

MONITORING OF MODIFICATIONS

In Part 2, a system for the processing of changes to the contract (i.e., modifications) was presented (see Chapter 10). This system provided for complete processing of individual modifications. This chapter presents methods by which the system developed in Part 2 can be effectively implemented and monitored. This will be achieved by addition of the following components to the modification system: (1) a Modification Summary Sheet, (2) a letter of exception to the contractor related to his price or credit proposal for the modification in question, (3) similar letters of exception to the design engineer related to his estimate of the price or credit for a particular modification, (4) a written status report for modifications to be issued to both the contractor and the design engineer, and (5) meetings between all parties involved in the modification procedure to overcome differences which are encountered during the process.

Once all issues concerning a given modification have been resolved, the modification should be incorporated in a change order (the subject of Chapter 19).

MODIFICATION SUMMARY SHEETS

A Modification *Status* Sheet (Figure 10-1) for an individual modification was developed in Part 2. This status sheet is intended to be affixed to the left-hand side of the modification file folder. It notes the status of an individual modification at any given time relative to all actions required for the entire process. The contract administrator could ascertain the status of all modifications for the project by referring to each status sheet in each modification file folder. He will find, however, that with slight additional effort—transferring the data from the status sheet to a *summary* sheet—a more expedient method of determining the status of all modifications to the contract can be generated such that they can be determined at a glance.

The "Modification Summary Sheet" is nothing more than a reiteration of the individual Modification Status Sheets. The top of the Modification Summary Sheet should identify the project, the owner, the engineer, and the contractor by means of the normal headings. The body of the summary sheet should recite on a single line the data provided by the status sheet, together with a brief description of the modification and the dollar amounts of the engineer's estimate and the contractor's price proposal. (Actually, two lines for each modification should be provided to allow for revised submittals of each item in the process.) Figure 18-1 is an example of the Modification Summary Sheet, so generated. The reader will note that by adding the dates on the summary sheet (just as is done on the status sheets), the contract administrator can quickly find the source and duration of delays in the process. For example, if the contractor is not submitting his price on credit proposals for modifications on a timely basis, all the dates to the left of the Contractor's Price Proposal Received column will be filled in, but the dates under that column itself will be blank. Further, by reference to the dates entered in the column immediately to the left (Contractor's Price Proposal Requested), the contract administrator knows the period of time during which the contractor has been lax in submitting his price proposals. Once all the columns are filled in with dates except the column furthest right, entitled Change Order No., the contract administrator himself is reminded that he must incorporate the modification into a change order.

LETTERS OF EXCEPTION

Sources of Disagreement

During the routine review of the contractor's price and credit proposals for modifications to the contract, it is probable that the contract administrator will take exception to certain items. The general categories of such exceptions are:

1. Failure of the contractor to include the entire scope of work of the modification in his price proposal.

Such matters as not giving a credit on contractual work deleted by the modification while giving a price for added work of the same modification, not including a price for all the work identified in the modification, or not giving credit for all the work deleted by a modification would fall into this general category.

2. A discrepancy in the contractor's quantity takeoff for the work of the modification as compared to the engineer's estimate for the modification.

These items are mere errors in taking off quantities for the work or credit required, rather than omitting them altogether as in the case of errors in the scope of work.

3. A discrepancy between the prices the contractor proposes for the work items or one or more of the work items included in the modification as compared to the engineer's estimate for the cost of that, or those, work items.

This is probably the most difficult exception to resolve since the contractor may be working with his historic costs for such items while the engineer may be using average costs for his estimate. Often, the final resolution of such discrepancies requires the work be done on a time-and-material basis if other prices cannot be successfully negotiated with the contractor.

4. Discrepancies between the method by which the contractor derives the total cost for his price proposal and the method stipulated in the contract documents.

Restatement of lengthy contract provisions would be required to afford a concrete example; however, matters such as the contractor's overhead and profit markups are a typical problem. If the contract were to provide that the contractor might add 20 percent for overhead and profit to his price proposal for a modification and he were to submit his price proposal by subtotaling all his costs, then adding 10 percent for overhead, again subtotaling his price, and adding another 10 percent for profit. By using this system the contractor would be adding a total of 21 percent for overhead and profit, not the 20 percent total allowed in the contract.

Suggested Letters

In any event, as the contract administrator routinely reviews the contractor's price proposals, and he observes any discrepancy between the contractor's proposal and the engineer's estimate, he should resolve on

MODIFICATION SUMMARY SHEET

PROJECT _____

CONTRACTOR _____

OWNER _____

ENGINEER _____

				(1)	(2)	(3)	(4)	(5)
					Owner's Permission to Proceed		Engineer's Concurrence	
Modifi- cation No.	Description	Amount of Engi- neer's Cost Esti- mate	Amount of Con- tractor's Price Pro- posal	Date Modifi- cation Issued	Date Re- quested	Date Re- ceived	Date Re- quested	Date Re- ceived
1								
2								
3								
4								
5								
6								
7								
8								
9								
10								
11								
12								
13								
14								
15								

FIGURE 18-1   Modification Summary Sheet.

(6)	(7)	(8)	(9)	(10)	(11)	(12)	(13)	(14)
Date Engineer's Estimate of Cost Received	Date Revised Drawings or Verbal Description Received	Contractor's Price Proposal		Date Contractor's Price Proposal Reviewed	Owner's Acceptance		Date Letter of Intent Sent to Contractor	To Change Order No.
		Date Requested	Date Received		Date Requested	Date Received		

his own or in conjunction with the design engineer the source of the error for items such as the scope of work, quantity takeoff, or price and advise the erring participant, requesting that the discrepancy be overcome by letter. Simple statements such as the following should suffice:

> Review of your Price Proposal for Modification No. 3 to your Contract on the above referenced Project indicates a possible error on your part related to the quantity of concrete required.

> Please review the quantity of concrete required and, if an error has been made, resubmit your Price Proposal with necessary revision to those quantities.

The tone of the letter should not be dictatorial or absolute, for the participant seemingly in error may prove to be correct.

A letter taking exception to the price of an item included in the contractor's price proposal which is substantially higher than the engineer's estimated price for that item should advise the contractor of the problem and tell him to be prepared to defend or revise his price in a forthcoming meeting. An example follows:

> Review of your Price Proposal for Modification No. 5 to your Contract on the above referenced Project indicates a unit-price for installation of formwork which is substantially higher than the price normally expected for this type of work.

> Review your cost for this item and either resubmit your Price Proposal if an error has been made or be prepared to advise us in the next scheduled Modification Meeting of the circumstances which require this price to be as stated.

Letters or memoranda of exception to the design engineer would follow the same line as those sent to the contractor. These letters would advise the design engineer of discrepancies between his estimates and the contractor's price proposals and ask him to review his estimate in light of the discrepancy and to either issue a revised estimate or to be prepared to justify his estimate in a forthcoming modification meeting with the contractor.

MODIFICATION STATUS REPORT

It has been suggested that periodic meetings of the contractor, the design engineer, the contract administrator and, possibly, the owner may be required to resolve differences related to the final price or credit for a modification. These meetings will be greatly facilitated by the contract administrator's advice to all participants who are to atttend the meeting of the status of all modifications approximately 1 week in advance of the date of the meeting. If the contract administrator reminds the other participants of what they must do about a week in advance, most of it will normally be done. In addition, such a report requires that the contract administrator himself complete work requiring his action prior to issuing the status report so that he is always current and the burden of required action shifts to the other participants.

The Modification Status Report should include a statement concerning each action noted to be required on the Modification Summary Sheet:

Column 1: Date Modification Issued   If there is a known modification to be issued but the design engineer has been dilatory in generating the necessary paperwork, a statement should be inserted on the Modification Status Report as follows: "Design engineer to issue the modification."

Column 2: Owner's Permission to Proceed Requested   If the contract administrator has delayed requesting the owner's permission to proceed, he should immediately fill out the standard letter developed in Part 2, issue it, and fill in the date. Hence no standard verbiage for this occurrence is required on the Modification Status Report.

Column 3: Owner Permission to Proceed Received   If the owner's permission has not been received, the standard verbiage would be, "Awaiting owner's permission to proceed."

Column 4: Engineer's Concurrence Requested   If the design engineer initiated the modification, the same date as the first column, Modification Initiated, will be filled out. If a participant other than the design engineer initiated the modification, the date the design engineer's concurrence was requested should be entered. If the contract administrator, upon review of the summary sheet, finds he has not requested the engineer's concurrence for a modification initiated by another party to the contract, he should fill out the standard letter generated in Part 2 and request that design engineer's concurrence, then fill in the date. Hence no standard verbiage is required for the Modification Status Report.

Column 5: Engineer's Concurrence Received   If the engineer's concurrence to initiate a modification has not been received—and hence the column is blank—the standard verbiage for the Modification Status Report would be, "Engineer's concurrence required to initiate the modification."

Column 6: Engineer's Estimate of Cost Received If this is the first blank column, proceeding from left to right, the standard verbiage for the Modification Status Report would be, "Awaiting engineer's estimate of cost."

Column 7: Revised Drawings or Verbal Description Received If this is the point in the process at which the modification has stopped and, therefore, the engineer has not transmitted to the contract administrator the necessary drawings or verbal description of the scope of work for the modification, the standard verbiage entered should be, "Awaiting revised drawings or verbal description of the modification from the engineer."

Column 8: Contractor's Price Proposal Requested If this is the first blank column going from left to right on the Modification Summary Sheet, the contract administrator has not requested the price proposal from the contractor although he has all the concurrences and data required to do so. Hence he should immediately fill out the standard letter developed in Part 2 to request the contractor's price proposal and fill in the date. No standard verbiage would be required for the Modification Status Report.

Column 9: Contractor's Price Proposal Received If the price proposal has not been received, i.e., if this is the first blank column, the standard verbiage to be entered should be, "Awaiting contractor's price proposal."

Column 10: Contractor's Price Proposal Reviewed If the contractor's price proposal has been received but exceptions to it have been found, the contract administrator should place a checkmark in the space for the date and transmit to the contractor a letter noting the exception to the price proposal, then note the date on the *second* line under Price Proposal Requested. The standard verbiage in such a case would be, "Contractor's revised price proposal requested." The other possibility is that the contractor's price proposal is acceptable. If this is the case, the contract administrator should issue the standard letter requesting the owner's acceptance of the modification if he has not already transmitted it. The standard verbiage for the Modification Status Report should be, "Awaiting the owner's acceptance of the modification."

If no revised price proposals are required of the contractor, the second line for each modification need not be filled out. If revised price proposals are required, the price proposal request, receipt, and review go through a second cycle.

Column 11: Owner's Acceptance Requested   As previously noted, no standard verbiage is required for this column because if the contract administrator has not previously requested the owner's acceptance of the modification, he would do so while generating the Modification Status Report.

Column 12: Owner's Acceptance Received   If this is the first blank column for the modification, the standard verbiage to be entered would be, "Awaiting owner's acceptance of the modification."

Column 13: Letter of Intent Sent to Contractor   If the standard letter of intent generated in Part 2 and sent to the owner to sign as the indication of its acceptance of the modification has been received signed by the owner, but has yet to be transmitted to the contractor, the contract administrator should do so immediately by means of the standard letter developed in Part 2 and should enter the date on the report.

Column 14: To Go into Change Order   If transmittal has occurred but the formalizing change order has not been issued (as would be apparent if column 14 remains blank), the standard verbiage should be, "To go into change order." Once a modification has been incorporated in a change order, the standard verbiage should be "In change order no. __."

The reader will note the only entry required of the contract administrator in the Modification Status Report is, "To go into change order," because change orders are generally issued at monthly intervals and it might be to the advantage of the contract administrator to wait for the period to end before issuing the change order. On the other hand, if the time intervals between modification meetings and the Modification Status Report and the change order generation can all be 1 month, the time to generate the monthly change order would be the time at which the Modification Status Report is generated; therefore, no item would be waiting for the contract administrator's action.

In summation, the Modification Status Report is generated by the contract administrator monthly 1 week before the scheduled modification meeting, by review of the Modification Summary Sheets for the project and by "triggering" certain standard verbiage as illustrated in Figure 18-2.

STANDARD MODIFICATION STATUS REPORT

(Date) _____

(Contractor's Name) ____

(Contractor's Address) ____

Attn: _____

                           Re: (Project Title) ____

          Subject: Modification Status
                  Report #_____

             File: _____

Gentlemen:

Our records indicate the following status to modifications to your contract
on the above referenced Project as of the date of this letter:

Mod. No.   Status

  1   (Standard Verbiage as per Mod. Summary Sheet)
  2   (Standard Verbiage as per Mod. Summary Sheet)
  3   (Standard Verbiage as per Mod. Summary Sheet)
  4   (Standard Verbiage as per Mod. Summary Sheet)
  5   (Standard Verbiage as per Mod. Summary Sheet)
  6   (Standard Verbiage as per Mod. Summary Sheet)
  7   (Standard Verbiage as per Mod. Summary Sheet)
  8   (Standard Verbiage as per Mod. Summary Sheet)

The next Modification is scheduled for ___(time)___ on (Date) at (place).

Be prepared to submit data required by your firm as noted above at that
time.

Very truly yours,

_____
Contract Administrator

cc: Owner
    Design Engineer
    Mod. Meeting File

FIGURE 18-2 Modification Status Report.

By sending copies of the Modification Status Report to the design engineer and owner, the contract administrator advises them of the modifications in which they may be delaying the process.

The standard verbiage, as in Figure 18-3, for each modification number across from the modification number on the status report depends on the point at which the process has stopped for that modification. That point is readily discernible from a glance at the Modification Summary Sheet.

MODIFICATION MEETINGS

Meetings to discuss and resolve problems related to modifications should be held at prearranged times each month with the contractor or, in the case of a project with multiple prime contractors, each prime contractor. By so doing, the contract administrator will keep the administrative effort flowing smoothly, and a forum will be established within which discrepancies between the contractor's price proposals and the engineer's estimates can be resolved.

In continuous preparation for these meetings, the contract administrator will issue a Modification Status Report to the contractor 1 week before each meeting and will, as he routinely reviews the contractor's price or credit proposals, issue letters of exception to those proposals as required. These two administrative efforts should form the agenda for the modification meetings.

The atmosphere in the meeting should be cordial, with a feeling of mutual respect between the participants. The same limits as given for the progress and coordination meetings (see Chapter 25) should be followed for the modification meetings. The contract administrator should chair the meeting. He should have a pad to record agreements reached in the meeting. Starting with the first modification, he should read the Modification Status Report—modification number and status—and ask the participant which action is required (as noted on the Modification Status Report) when that action will be forthcoming. He should obtain a date from that participant on which the participant promises to submit the required action and note it on his pad after the modification number.

If there is a dispute related to the contractor's price proposal, it would have been noted in a letter of exception to the contractor and engineer, and it should be resolved between them with the contract administrator acting as referee. If full resolution cannot be obtained in the meeting, further constructive action aimed at resolving it at or before the next modification meeting should be agreed upon. Such action might include the possibility of a revised price proposal by the

Column		Standard Verbiage for the Mod Status Report
1) Mod Initiated	-	"Design Engineer to Issue the Mod"
2) Owner's Permission to Proceed Requested	-	None.
3) Owner's Permission to Proceed Received	-	"Awaiting Owner's Permission to Proceed"
4) Engineer's Concurrence Requested	-	None.
5) Engineer's Concurrence Received	-	"Engineer's Concurrence Required to Initiate the Mod"
6) Engineer Estimate of Cost Received	-	"Awaiting Engineer's Estimate of Cost"
7) Revised Drawings/Verbal Description Received	-	"Awaiting Revised Drawings/Verbal Description of the Mod from the Engineer"
8) Contractor Price Proposal Requested	-	None.
9) Contractor's Price Proposal Received	-	"Awaiting Contractor's Price Proposal"
10) Contractor's Price Proposal Reviewed	-	"Contractor's Revised Price Proposal Requested" - or - "Awaiting Owner's Acceptance of the Modification"
11) Owner's Acceptance Requested	-	None.
12) Owner's Acceptance Received	-	"Awaiting Owner's Acceptance of the Mod"
13) Letter of Intent sent to the Contractor	-	None.
14) Incorportated into Change Order	-	"To go into Change Order #_____" - or - "In Change Order # _____"

FIGURE 18-3   List of standard entries for Modification Status Report.

contractor, a revised estimate by the engineer, or field measurements. Should this procedure fail, the contract administrator might be required to change the method of payment for the modification from lump sum to unit price or time and material.

After each modification is reviewed in the meeting, the date of the next meeting should be set. The contract administrator should then compile the minutes of the meeting and issue the minutes to all participants.

The entire cycle should then be repeated for the next month.

CHAPTER 19

MONITORING OF
CHANGE ORDERS

The change order is, as noted in Part 2, the legal document by which changes to the scope, price, and, possibly, completion date of the project are made with the mutual consent of the parties to the contract. A modification (or a number of modifications) upon the completion of the modification process are documented in a change order and, upon execution of the change order by signature of the parties to the contract, the modifications become "official" changes to the contract.

The monitoring effort by the contract administrator for the change order system is dependent upon the size of the project, the type of contract (e.g., single general contractor, multiple primes, etc.) and, possibly, the number of projects the contractor is handling simultaneously.

CHANGE ORDER SUMMARY SHEETS

As in the case of the modification system, the Change Order Summary Sheet (Figure 19-1) can be derived from reorganizing the data on the Change Order Status Sheet (Figure 11-3). Eight items comprise the change order system. First, the change order must be generated. The other seven items appear on the Change Order Status Sheet:

1. Date change order is sent to the contractor

2. Date change order is received from the contractor

3. Date change order is sent to the engineer

4. Date change order is received from the engineer

CHANGE ORDER SUMMARY SHEET

PROJECT TITLE _____

OWNER _____

CONTRACTOR _____

ENGINEER _____

C.O. No.	Mods. Included	Sent To Cont'r	Rec'd Fm Cont'r	Sent To Eng'r	Rec'd Fm Eng'r	Sent To Owner	Rec'd Fm Owner	Executed Copies Sent
1								
2								
3								
4								
5								
6								
7								
8								

FIGURE 19-1 Change Order Summary Sheet.

(Date) _____

(Owner, Engineer or Contractor)

(Address) _____

_____

Attn: _____

Re: (Project Title)

Subject: Change Order #____

File: _____

Gentlemen:

Our records indicate the subject Change Order was transmitted to your office for signature on _____(date)_____ .

Advise us should you not have received this Change Order or if you have concern related to signing it.

Very truly yours,

Contract Administrator

cc: Change Order File

FIGURE 19-2   Change order transmittal follow-up.

5. Date change order is sent to the owner

6. Date change order is received from the owner

7. Date copies of the executed change order are sent to all participants

Each of these seven items will be noted on the columns of the Change Order Summary Sheet. In the case of a single project being monitored by the contract administrator, it may be easiest merely to add the seven columns to the right-hand side of the Modification Summary Sheet rather than to generate an additional piece of paper. We shall assume, however, the contract administrator desires to have a separate Change Order Status Sheet. The project title, contractor's name, owner's name, and engineer's name are entered as a heading to the Change Order Summary Sheet.

A horizontal line is provided for each change order to trace its progress as the columns are completed.

The first column on the left-hand side of the Change Order Summary Sheet records the number of the change order: the numbers should be entered in numerical order. The second column notes the number of the modification incorporated into the change order number to the left. The next seven columns note the dates the items of correspondence identified were sent to, and received from, the contractor, engineer, and owner.

At least once a month, the contract administrator should review the Change Order Summary Sheet. Any change orders which have not been received within a reasonable period of time from the participant to whom they were transmitted for signature should be noted and a standard letter similar to Figure 19-2 should be transmitted to that party.

Figure 19-2 and the standard letters of transmittal generated in Part 2 will allow for rapid processing of the change order system.

At the same time the contract administrator reviews the Change Order Status Sheet, he should also review the Modification Status Sheet and generate a change order for all modifications that have undergone the modification process during the month.

CHAPTER 20

MONITORING
OF CLAIMS

In Chapter 1, contractual duties involving more than one participant in the construction process were shown to constitute control responsibilities, and it was noted that the assertion and disposition of contractor claims was one such multiparticipant duty. The establishment of a system for handling claims was discussed in detail in Chapter 9. This chapter will set forth methods by which the contract administrator may monitor the effective investigation and resolution of claims which have met the minimum requirements of the contract.

MONITORING TECHNIQUES

The two most effective monitoring techniques are Claim Status Reports and claim meetings. The effective use of each enhances the value of the other in moving the project smoothly to a successful conclusion.

Claim Status Reports

At a predetermined frequency, a copy of a status report for all claims should be sent to each participant. The best frequency for a given project would vary with the number of claims acknowledged to date and the rate at which they are being generated and resolved; however, experience and good practice suggest that this summary of claims should be sent to each participant at least once per month.

It is usual that three participants (other than the contract administrator) will be involved in the disposition of a claim: the contractor, the engineering design group, and the owner. The Claim Status Sheet developed in Chapter 9 and bound into the left side of the folder maintained for each claim will provide the contract administrator with an immediate update concerning the status of that claim, if his file entries have been properly maintained. Generation of a status report for individual claims can then be achieved by reference to previous Claim Status Sheets and the minutes of previous claim meetings. A status report based upon the sample claim provisions set forth in Chapter 9 would be similar to Figure 20-1.

The reader will note that the entries in the status report require action by some participant other than the contract administrator; this is a typical situation inasmuch as the contract administrator's performance seldom determines the merit of a claim.

In most cases, the contract administrator can properly and effectively discharge his own responsibilities for contract administration by reviewing the folder for each unresolved claim on a weekly basis. If the contract administrator diligently maintains a monthly schedule for the issuance of Claim Status Reports, his diligence will act as a safeguard against occasional laxity in weekly reviews because the monthly Claim Status Report cannot be issued until the contract administrator's folders have been put in order.

In addition to the formal Claim Status Report, it may be a good idea for the contract administrator to occasionally prod other participants to act between the monthly reports by oral or speed-memo communications. However, any important interim communications should be timely and fully documented.

Claim Meetings

The second major monitoring technique for claims is the use of carefully planned claim meetings. Like the status reports, claim meetings should also be scheduled at predetermined frequencies—probably not less often than once per month. Each meeting should be held 7 to 10 days after the participants receive their copies of the Claim Status Report. This delay will provide sufficient time for each participant to prepare himself to speak to those matters noted in the report to be his responsibility. Properly constituted, the monthly Claim Status Report can constitute the agenda for the meeting.

The contract administrator must constantly bear in mind that he best serves his own interests and those of his employer, the owner, by conducting himself in claim meetings in the highest professional manner, i.e., by striving to remain impartial and analytical. Admittedly, maintaining this balance and objectivity may be quite difficult for the contract administrator given his "employment" by the owner and the personal differences which naturally occur among participants in a

To: File   Date: 6/6/80
FM: Contract Administrator   File: 123.456
Subject: Jones Project   cc: Contractor
         Claim Status Report   Engineer
                                           Owner

The status of Claim to the above referenced project, after the Claim
Meeting No. 3 of 6/6/80, is as follows:

Claim No. 1   -   Claim deemed invalid. Contractor to issue a
                  Claim Withdrawal Letter.

Claim No. 2   -   Resolved by Change Order No. 3.

Claim No. 3   -   Claim deemed valid. Engineer to issue a
                  Contract Modification.

Claim No. 4   -   No resolution, Engineer to review Corres-
                  pondence File to ascertain the date of the HVAC
                  Shop Drawing Submittal.

Claim No. 5   -   No resolution. Contractor to advise Engineer of
                  his rationale by which Contract Section 12
                  stipulations do not apply.

Claim No. 6   -   No resolution. Contract Administrator to issue
                  a Proceed Letter to the Contractor and the
                  Contractor is to provide time and material data
                  as work progresses should the Claim be deemed
                  valid at a later date.

     The next Claim Meeting has been scheduled for 9:00 a.m.,
July 8, 1980 in the Contract Administrator's Field Office on the site
of the above referenced Project.

FIGURE 20-1   Claim Status Report.

major construction project. A useful perspective for the contract administrator may be to equate his role in the claim meeting to that of an arbitrator in a civil case. Most contractors honestly believe in the validity of their claims; similarly, most design professionals honestly believe that the contractors could have avoided the situation giving rise to the claim and that, therefore, the claim is improper. The contract administrator has the difficult but inescapable duty to use his best efforts to forge from these disparate views a resolution acceptable, if not satisfactory, to the concerned participants. Although tactics and procedures to be employed in the claim meeting are beyond the scope of this book, experience teaches that face-to-face discussion by the participants involved and the objective, expert contributions of the contract administrator will settle the great majority of the claims in an equitable and effective manner.

There are four possible resolutions of a claim upon its merits:

1. The claim is determined to be valid, and a modification is issued to compensate the contractor for the amounts claimed.

2. The claim is determined to be invalid, and the contractor verifies his assent to the determination by executing some document to that effect.

3. The participants reach an impasse concerning the validity of the claim, and the matter is deferred for negotiation at the completion of the contract.

4. The participants proceed immediately to arbitration or litigation.

A determination that a given claim is valid constitutes the final entry in the claim folder for that claim, and a project modification is then issued to provide reimbursement to the contractor in accordance with the claim. On the other hand, should a contractor become convinced that his claim is invalid, the contract administrator should advise him to submit a claim withdrawal letter for that claim. A simple written statement to that effect should suffice:

> _____ (Contractor's Legal Name) hereby withdraws its Claim No. __ in connection with _____ (description of contract). Said Claim is attached and made a part of this withdrawal.

In the event of an impasse, the participants will usually agree to defer negotiation of the claim until completion of the contract. Most well-drawn contract documents contain a clause which requires the contractor to submit a waiver of claims and liens prior to final payment as well as a clause which provides for retention by the owner of a percentage of the funds payable to the contractor until the satisfactory completion of the project (including due execution of the waiver). These two clauses equip the contract administrator with a powerful tool in subsequent negotiations of unresolved claims. The contractor, desiring to obtain retained funds ostensively payable to him as soon as possible in order to reduce his costs of borrowing, may become increasingly conciliatory in the negotiation of claims as the prospect of receiving retainage grows nearer. In short, the prospect of receiving the retainage and the projected costs of not receiving it may cause the contractor to become more receptive to the contract administrator's arguments concerning an equitable resolution of the claim.

The final alternative resolution of a claim upon its merits is arbitration or litigation of the claim in accordance with the terms of the contract as supplemented or, in some cases, overridden by existing laws, rules, and regulations. In the event of arbitration or litigation, the role of the contract administrator changes from that of arbitrator to that of expert witness for his client, the owner. Typical support activities in this situation might include a review of the provisions of the contract with the design group and the owner's litigation counsel, review and control of documents associated with the claim, and experienced counsel as to the merits of combat or settlement in regard to the success of the project itself.

In summary, to effectively monitor the claims systems developed in Part 2, the contract administrator should:

1. Review the claim folder status sheet for each claim once per week to discharge his own responsibilities and to prod other participants through verbal or speed-memo communications to discharge their claim-processing responsibilities.

2. Issue monthly Claim Status Reports to all participants.

3. Hold monthly claim meetings (following distribution of the reports) to provide a forum in which claims proper in form can be objectively resolved upon their merits.

4. Negotiate unresolved claims at the completion of construction contracts at a point where proposed resolutions become more economically attractive to the contractor without constituting avoidable economical duress; and assume a role supportive of the owner if the claim becomes the subject of arbitration or litigation.

CHAPTER 21

PARTIAL PAYMENT REQUESTS AND FINANCIAL STATUS REPORTS

Should reflect draw down

In Chapter 16, it was pointed out that one key responsibility of the contract administrator in most projects is determination of the value added to the project during given time periods in order to accommodate the cash-flow obligations of the owner and the cash-flow requirements of the contractor. The contractor's cash-flow needs are usually met through issuance by the owner of interim funds called "partial payments" once such payments have been determined by the contract administrator to be due pursuant to the contract.

From time to time, the owner and the contract administrator may also wish to know the financial status of the entire project to a given date or point of construction. These Financial Status Reports can be developed from the documents which underlie the partial payments.

This Chapter will address the expeditious compilation, preparation, and transmittal of information required to implement the cost controls discussed in Chapter 16.

PARTIAL PAYMENTS

Interim payments to the contractor usually result from the contract administrator's submittal to the owner of a document called a "Partial Payment Request," shown originally in Figure 16-8. Compensation due the contractor for a given period, as set forth in the Partial Payment Request, is usually categorized as follows:

1. Work completed on the lump-sum part of the contract (as detailed in the negotiated lump-sum breakdown—see Chapter 6)

2. Work completed on unit-price items (as detailed in the contractor's bid prices for these Items—see Chapter 15)

3. Reimbursable inventory (as verified by the contract administrator's system for inventory control—see Chapter 14)

4. Work completed on modifications as agreed upon in fully executed change orders (see Chapters 10 and 11)

Assuming that each of the above-mentioned systems has been kept current, generation of a Partial Payment Request requires only transfer and tabulation of available data, confirmation that the contractor agrees with the data, and transmittal of the request to the owner.

The specific form of a Partial Payment Request in a given project will be directly dependent on the terms of the contract for that project. In general, however, a Partial Payment Request (Figure 16-8) will include the items described below. The method for transfer of data and calculations to complete the Partial Payment Request follows.

Lump-Sum Items   The first four columns are copied from the lump-sum breakdown negotiated by the contract administrator and the contractor. Columns 5 and 6 are copied from the totals shown in columns 9 and 10 from the previous Partial Payment Request. If this is the first Partial Payment Request for the contractor, the totals are, of course, zero. Columns 7 and 8 are transferred from the contract administrator's cost control system for lump-sum items. Columns 9 and 10 are the totals of columns 5 and 7, and 6 and 8, respectively. The prices in column 10 are totaled at the bottom of the Lump-Sum Items section of the Partial Payment Request.

Unit-Price Items   Columns 1 through 4 are copied from the bid documents for the project. Columns 5 and 6 are taken from columns 9 and 10 of the previous Partial Payment Request. All other columns are tabulated by the same method employed for the lump-sum breakdown. The totals for column 10 for lump-sum and unit-price items are then calculated.

Reimbursable Inventory   The total reimbursable inventory payable at the cutoff date for the Partial Payment Request is transferred from the contract administrator's reimbursable inventory system.

Change Order Work   The change order number by which the modification was approved by the owner and contractor is noted in column 1. The modification number for the particular change to the contract as documented is entered in column 2. It should be noted that more than one modification may be concluded in one change order. Hence this detail is required. Columns 5 and 6 are copied from columns 9 and 10 of the previous Partial Payment Request. Since a modification documents all changes to the contract which may add to the cost of the contract, deduct from the contract price, or have no change to the contract price, two columns, one for additions to the contract price and one for deductions from the contract price, are required. In the event the modification has no effect on the contract price, a zero can be entered into either column. Columns 7 and 8 are taken from the cost control system for change orders for the time period of the Partial Payment Request. Columns 9 and 10 are the totals of columns 5 and 7, and 6 and 8, respectively. When all data are entered onto the partial payment form, columns 9 and 10 are totaled separately. Then column 10 is subtracted from column 9 to give the total additional cost incurred for change orders during the time period of the Partial Payment Request. If the deductions from the contract have a larger total than the additions to the contract, a negative sign is entered before the dollar amount of the difference.

Summary   The total contract work to date, i.e., the total expenditure to date for lump-sum items plus unit-price items, is entered on line A. The total reimbursable inventory is copied from section III of the Partial Payment Request and entered on line B. The total change work to date from section IV is entered on line C. Lines A, B, and C are then totaled on line D. The retention percentage which is noted in the contract documents as applicable is noted on line E, and the dollar amount of line D is multiplied by that percentage and entered at the end of line E. Line F is the result of the subtraction of line E from line D. Line G is entered from the previous Partial Payment Request, if any: it would have been line F on that previous request. Line G is subtracted from line F and entered on line H. This is the dollar amount due the contractor for work done during the time period of the Partial Payment Request.

The Partial Payment Request for the month is then reviewed with the contractor. As previously stated (see Chapter 16), total dollar amounts for each section of the Partial Payment Request are agreed upon weekly with the contractor; hence there should be little or no differences in what the contractor expects to be paid and what line H indicates he should be paid. Should corrections be required due to errors on the part of the contract administrator, these corrections would be made, of course. Once the contractor has agreed to the dollar amounts and quantities in the contract administrator's draft of the Partial Payment Request, the request is typed, signed by the contractor and contract administrator, and then forwarded to the owner for payment by a standard letter such as in Figure 21-1.

(Date) _____

(Owner) _____

(Address) _____

Attn: _____

                                    Re: (Project Title)____

                          Subject: Partial Payment Request #___

                             File: _____

Gentlemen:

Attached, please find the subject Partial Payment Request for the time period _____ to _____. Compensating the (Contractor's Name) for work complete during that time period on the above referenced Project.

Very truly yours,

_____
Contract Administrator

cc: Contractor
    Engineer

FIGURE 21-1 Transmittal of partial payment request.

FINANCIAL STATUS REPORT

It is customary to advise the owner periodically as to the overall financial status of the project. If the time interval agreed upon with the owner for this Financial Status Report is by the month, much of the data can be taken directly from the Partial Payment Request. For their own purposes, contract administrators may wish to tabulate these data monthly, irrespective of the owners' requirements to promote the contract administrators' respective reviews, in order that the contract administrators review the overall financial status of their projects at least once a month and thus stay up to date.

The Financial Status Report notes costs to date, probable costs to complete the project, and financial exposure for claims. It requires that the contract administrator, with his firsthand knowledge of the project, make a number of estimates which should become increasingly accurate as the project nears completion. Beginning contract administrators may not be experienced in the making of such estimates, but it is likely that no one else could do better; the contract administrator is the closest to the project.

The contract administrator should give his best estimate. If there is uncertainty in his mind as to the dollar amount of the various estimates he must make, he should include in his estimate a contingency to cover this uncertainty so that the dollar amount of the estimate is not exceeded in actuality. He should not be afraid to advise the owner of "bad news": it is better to advise the owner as soon as possible of possible overruns in the contract amount to afford the owner adequate time to procure the additional funds. This is not to say that estimates should be grossly high. If the owner does procure additional funds for expected overruns and the overruns are substantially less than expected, the owner loses the time value of the funds procured based on the contract administrator's estimate. There is simply no inexpensive alternative to the methodical, painstaking preparation of estimates.

The Financial Status Report should follow a format similar to Figure 21-2 and should be filled out as follows.

Heading   Reports should be numbered in chronological sequence. The normal heading items are the project title; names of the contractor, owner, and engineer; and the date of the data which went into the report.

Lump-Sum Contract Amount   This amount, i.e., the dollar amount the contractor bid on the lump-sum part of the contract, will be the same for all Financial Status Reports for a particular contract on a particular project.

FINANCIAL STATUS REPORT NO. ____

PROJECT _____

CONTRACTOR _____

OWNER _____

ENGINEER _____

DATE _____

I. LUMP-SUM CONTRACT AMOUNT $ _____

II. UNIT-PRICE VARIATIONS

(1) Item No.	(2) Description	Contract		Expended to Date		Total Estimated to Complete		(9) Estimated Overrun	(10) Estimated Underrun
		(3) Quantity	(4) Price	(5) Quantity	(6) Price	(7) Quantity	(8) Price		

(A) Total contract price $ ___

(+) (B) Total estimated overrun $ ___

(C) Subtotal $ ___

(−) (D) Total estimated underrun $ ___

(E) Total estimated price of unit-price items (Should equal column 8 total) $ ___

III. MODIFICATION TO THE CONTRACT

(A) Total dollar amount of modification in change order $ ___

(B) Total dollar amount of pending modifications $ ___

(C) Total known modifications $ ___

FIGURE 21-2 Financial Status Report.

IV. PENDING CLAIMS

Claim no. (1)	Description (2)	Amount (3)

Total amount of outstanding claims $ _____

V. SUMMARY

(A) Totals of sections I, II, III, and IV $ _____

(B) Overrun/underrun % of contract

$[I + II + III + IV] \div [I + II(A)]$ _____ %

                                  _____ %

FIGURE 21-2 Financial Status Report *(continued)*.

Unit-Price Variations The first four columns—item number, description, contract quantity, and contract price—are taken from the contractor's bid for the unit-price items. These figures will also be the same for each Financial Status Report for a particular contract on a particular project. Columns 5 and 6 are taken from the contractor's Partial Payment Request for the period ending coincident with the date of the Financial Status Report. Column 7 is the contract administrator's best estimate of the total quantity of each unit-price item which will be required, including that quantity already expended, to complete the project. (As stated previously, this estimated quantity should become increasingly accurate as the project proceeds and should contain an adequate contingency in the first phases of the project.) Column 8 is the corresponding dollar amount for the estimated quantities noted under each of the unit-price items in column 7. Should the dollar amount of column 8 be larger than the estimated dollar amount of column 4, the difference should be entered in column 9. Should the dollar amount of column 8 be less than that of column 4, the difference should be entered in column 10.

Column 4, the estimated contract price for each unit-price item, is totaled and the figure entered on line A. This number will remain the same for all Financial Status Reports. The total of column 9, estimated overruns, is entered on line B, and a subtotal of lines A and B is calculated and entered on line C. The total of column 10, estimated underruns, is entered on line D and subtracted from line C to provide the entry for line E, which is the estimated cost to complete all unit-price items in the contract as of the date of the Financial Status Report.

Modifications to the Contract The entry for line A of section III is taken from the contract administrator's modification system (see Chapter 10). It is the total dollar amount of all modifications which are included in fully executed change orders. In the case of lump-sum modifications, the agreed-upon lump-sum price is utilized; in the cases of unit-price modifications and time-and-material modifications, the engineer's estimate of the total price of the modifications is utilized in arriving at the total price of all modifications in the change order. Line B is also taken from the contract administrator's modification system. It is the total of the engineer's estimate of all types of modifications which have not been put into change orders as of the date of the Financial Status Report. Line C is the total of lines A and B.

Pending Claims Section IV of the Financial Status Report is taken from the contract administrator's claim system (see Chapter 9). Each unresolved claim, as of the date of the Financial Status Report, is listed with the dollar amount claimed for each by the contractor. The total dollar amount for all outstanding claims is then entered at the bottom of section IV.

Summary The lump-sum contract amount from section I, the total estimated price of unit-price items, the total known modification price, and the total amount of outstanding claims are then added, and that total is entered on line A. The corresponding percentage of overrun or underrun to the contract amount can then be formed by dividing the sum of sections I, II, III, and IV by the total of section I plus line II(A). A dividend greater than 1 would indicate an overrun, a dividend less than 1 an underrun. The differences between the dividend and unity will be the percentage of overrun or underrun.

CHAPTER 22

MONITORING OF CASH-FLOW CURVES

The cash-flow curve for a project is derived from the contractor's schedule and the negotiated lump-sum breakdown prices (see Chapters 4 and 6). Unit-price items, modifications, and claims are usually omitted from the cash-flow curve on smaller projects in order to allow a comparison of what was originally intended to what is actually happening. On large projects, with a computer available, it would not be a difficult problem to include unit-price items and modifications in the cash-flow curve for the project; for purposes of illustration and clarity, however, these items will be omitted.

MONITORING TECHNIQUES

The example of the cash-flow curve given in Part 1 was somewhat independent of weather conditions. Hence it followed the theoretical cash-flow curve quite closely. Since the project cash-flow curve to be reviewed here will follow the contractor's schedule, it will include weather considerations. If the project under consideration involved outside work in an area where cold temperatures and snow would reduce productivity of the workers in the winter, one might expect to find a cash-flow curve similar to Figure 22-1.

The early phases of the project indicated by Figure 22-1 would probably not be unduly affected by the first winter season inasmuch as productivity would be low and much of the work of the project (e.g., submittal of shop drawings, mobilization) would occur somewhat independent of the weather. Productivity would be lowered during the second winter when most of the work would be occurring in the field

291

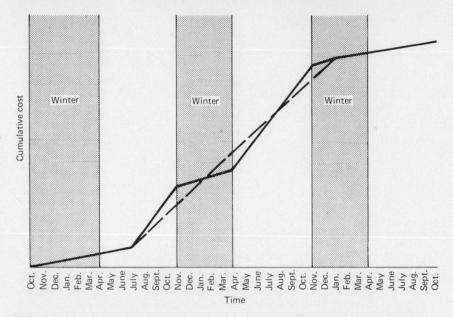

FIGURE 22-1   Sample cash-flow curve recognizing weather constraints.

and would be weather-dependent. The completion and low-productivity stages of the project would occur during the third winter and would be largely unaffected by weather conditions.

It may be useful to turn to an illustrative project relatively independent of weather conditions. (The contract administrator should, however, be aware that the cash-flow curve may not always closely follow the theoretical curve. The reason for the deviation should be ascertained.) It will also be assumed that the project has a single prime contractor. Figure 22-2 represents the cash-flow curve for the project.

Each month as the Partial Payment Requests are finalized, the contract administrator will note the total cumulative lump-sum contract work completed by the cutoff date of that Partial Payment Request on the same paper as the scheduled cash-flow curve (taken from the contractor's schedule and the negotiated lump-sum breakdown prices.) In this manner, he will generate the actual cash-flow curve for the project. As long as the actual cash-flow curve for the project lies to the top or the *left* of the scheduled cash-flow curve for the project, the project can be considered *ahead* of schedule. This does not mean, however, that every item of work which is being undertaken is ahead of schedule. It means that when considering all the construction activities which have taken place—some of which may be ahead of schedule and some of which may be behind schedule—the aggregate of those construction activities

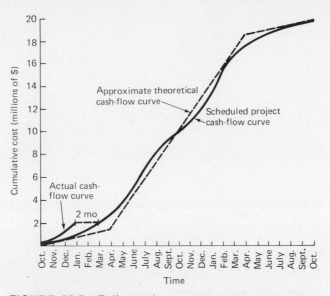

FIGURE 22-2 Estimated schedule status from comparison of actual cash-flow curve to scheduled project cash-flow curve.

is generating cash flow at a rate higher than anticipated. One activity of high cost may be ahead of schedule while all other activities are behind schedule, but value is being incorporated into the work of the project at a rate more rapid than originally scheduled.

If the actual cash-flow curve is below or to the right of the scheduled cash-flow curve, the project should be considered *behind* schedule. The same cautions as noted above are also applicable in this situation; i.e., not every item of construction may be behind schedule, but the aggregate of all items is behind schedule.

The slope of the cash-flow curve indicates the productivity rate during a month in dollars per month: the steeper the slope, the higher the productivity rate. Figure 22-3 indicates a situation in which the project is ahead of schedule (i.e., the actual cash-flow curve lies to the left of the scheduled cash-flow curve), but the productivity rate which has occurred over the past 2 months (as recorded on the actual cash-flow curve) is less than the anticipated productivity rate as indicated by the slope of the scheduled cash-flow curve. Hence although the project still is approximately 2 weeks (i.e., ½ month) ahead of schedule, unless the productivity rate experienced on the project over the last 2 months is increased in the next month, the project will fall behind schedule.

Should such a situation arise on a project, the contract administrator should review the individual items of construction which comprised

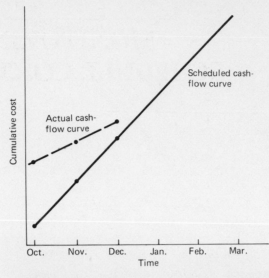

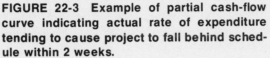

FIGURE 22-3 Example of partial cash-flow curve indicating actual rate of expenditure tending to cause project to fall behind schedule within 2 weeks.

the work undertaken over the past 2 months as well as the work projected for the next month on the project schedule. After review, the contract administrator should understand which of the scheduled items of work are not meeting the productivity rate originally scheduled. The lack of productivity could then be brought up in the next progress and coordination meeting (the subject of Chapter 25), the contractor's attention drawn to the situation, and his proposed method of overcoming the problem solicited.

On a small project, it would probably become apparent from cursory examination of the project schedule that the project was falling behind schedule, but on a large project, with dozens of activities going on at the same time, the timeliness or untimeliness of performance might be far less clear.

The plotting and review of the scheduled and actual cash-flow curves can be of major assistance in determining the overall schedule performance for the large project by rapidly indicating the overall status of the project and indicating upcoming problems. When the curves are used in conjunction with the project schedule, the reasons for problems are usually quite easy to locate. Contract administrators who utilize these tools regularly will become increasingly sophisticated at measuring the actual progress of major projects.

CHAPTER 23

MONITORING OF SCHEDULE CONTROLS

In Chapter 7, creation of an Integrated Schedule Sheet (Figure 7-1) was discussed and illustrated in detail. This integrated schedule elaborated the contractor's schedule for the project by notation of administrative requirements of the contract administrator at the times at which they were required to occur so as not to delay the construction efforts of the contractor. Two lines were provided for each construction task identified by the contractor and scheduled as an individual-line item. On the first of these two lines was noted the length of time which the contractor estimated that the item would require. The second line was reserved for subsequent entry of the time actually spent by the contractor on that task. Finally, the contract administrator superimposed upon the line, or "bar," representing the contractor's time estimate, the lump-sum breakdown price negotiated between the contract administrator and the contractor for that item.

In Part 2, a cost control system was devised to permit the contract administrator to quantify the amount of work performed by the contractor for interim payment purposes. One of the documents of that system, the Weekly Cost Control Report—Lump-Sum Items (Figure 16-1), provided space for notation by the contract administrator of the contractor's several identified construction tasks, the total quantities of materials and labor required to complete those tasks, the units by which those quantities could be measured, and the agreed lump-sum breakdown price per unit. The Weekly Cost Control Report—Lump-Sum Items also provided space for notation by the contract administrator of the number of units completed each day by the contractor for each task.

Just as the data developed in the integrated schedule permitted the systematization embodied in the Weekly Cost Control Report—Lump-Sum Items, the Weekly Cost Control Report provides the contract administrator with the information necessary to monitor the contractor's performance relative to his announced schedule. The ultimate purpose of this monitoring is indirect schedule control by the contract administrator on behalf of the owner. Although direct control of the construction schedule is a matter within the exclusive domain of the contractor and one which contract administrators dominate at their peril, contract administrators can serve well the interests of their clients by exerting appropriate indirect influence upon the progress of the project. In private-sector projects, for example, the owner provides capital for the project in anticipation of a return on investment. In most cases, the return will not be obtained until the project is sufficiently complete to generate that return. The late completion of the project would create a dual negative effect for the owner: tying up the owner's invested capital, without return, for a period longer than anticipated and reducing the amount of the return by the time value of money during the delay. Extended delays could render the entire project unprofitable. In the case of public projects, where the ultimate goal is service to the public rather than financial gain, the need for indirect schedule control is more subtle but equally real. Tax money has been allocated to the project to provide a public betterment. If the public project is truly worthwhile, it follows that there is a real value in providing to the public the benefit of the project at the earliest practicable time, i.e., within the period established by the contractor's schedule. In either private or public projects, the contract administrator serves well the interests of his client by effecting indirect schedule control for one other important reason. If the project substantially overruns the date of completion set forth in the contract documents or negotiated pursuant to the contract, it is likely that the contractor will have expended greater sums than anticipated at the commencement of the project. The consequent reduction in profit or, worse, the contractor's actual loss of money on the project will usually lead to an attempt by the contractor at recoupment of losses through claims against the owner. Always a burden to the owner and contract administrator, claims become especially frustrating when the contractor fails to complete the work on time through no fault of others. In short, although the contract documents usually provide that matters of project scheduling are within the exclusive province of the contractor, the contract administrator and the owner have strong interests in influencing indirectly the pace of the work. This chapter will explain the effective creation and use of that influence within the confines of the contract documents.

THE CREATION AND USE OF INDIRECT SCHEDULE CONTROL

Of the myriad means of indirect control available to the contract administrator on a major project, some, such as the exertion of financial duress upon the contractor, are, in our judgment, unacceptable both as a matter of principle and as a disservice to the long-term interests of the project. Situations of economic duress often arise as follows: the contractor may fail to meet the time expectations of the contract administrator by ignoring the contract administrator's suggestions that additional crews be added. The contract administrator then punishes the contractor by delaying monthly partial payment recommendations, with a consequent delay in ultimate payment to the contractor. Such tactics are always dangerous and can be disastrous. They lay the owner open to a claim for the time value of the delayed funds; moreover, even when used occasionally, they establish a feeling of animosity between the contractor and the contract administrator in which retribution, rather than cooperation, can become the order of the day. In extreme cases, these two participants can become so preoccupied with combat that they lose sight of the importance of the project itself. Any tactic which, in the hands of the contract administrator, can cause either the contract administrator or the contractor to lose the clear focus of the quality of the project is unprofessional; it is a disservice to the owner's interests and should be avoided at all costs.

Timely Performance by the Contract Administrator

In our experience, the best methods to effect indirect schedule control are those which assist the contractor in achieving the shared goal of timely completion rather than those which assert the contract administrator's authority or punish the contractor for failing to complete the project on schedule. Of the several acceptable techniques of indirect schedule control, the foremost is that the contract administrator do everything within reason to clear the way administratively in order that the contractor may proceed in an orderly manner with the construction efforts. The contract administrator's guiding principle in this regard should not be to avoid all administrative encumbrances, for the contract documents nearly always impose substantial administrative burdens, and the contract administrator takes the contract documents as he finds them; rather, the goal the contract administrator should establish is to avoid all undue hindrance to the contractor within the boundaries of the contract documents. The contract administrator who defines control responsibilities at the outset of the project, carries the control responsibilities forward into the integrated schedule, issues letters to the contractor in advance of required submissions, provides for rapid processing of the submissions through systematization, and works to maintain a courteous, constructive relationship throughout the project not only can achieve great personal satisfaction but creates greater time consciousness and cooperation in the contract. In our experience, many contractors are not administratively adept or inclined and appreciate appropriate facilitation by the contract administrator when offered constructively.

Progress and Coordination Meetings

A second indirect technique for schedule control is the progress and coordination meeting, the subject of Chapter 25. In these routine weekly meetings, the contractor's short-range schedule, i.e., items of work to be undertaken within the 2 weeks following the meeting, are reviewed in detail and coordinated with other project participants. A 2-week projection of construction activity should be a simple matter for the contractor: a contractor unable to schedule work that far in advance would seem headed for problems far more serious than failure of performance in any given project. The meeting provides a forum for discussion in order that everyone concerned may learn the contractor's plans for the next 2-week period. Knowing that he will be requested to provide a 2-week schedule each week, the contractor will likely allocate sufficient time to consider in advance what to undertake during that period. This is, of course, the key to remaining on schedule: sufficient planning by the contractor greatly increases the probability that activities will occur as intended. The contractor should also be requested during the progress and coordination meeting to advise those present of any long-range schedule problems which the contractor foresees or that have occurred since the last meeting. Long-term matters such as late delivery dates for equipment and materials can, if foreseen and communicated to the appropriate participants, usually be obviated. Such long-range inquiries also cause the contractor to look beyond the immediacies of the short-range period, with the result that the scenario of the overall project remains in clear focus.

The Contractor's Schedule

Another common, but effective, indirect schedule control technique is the posting of the contractor's schedule in the room designated for the progress and coordination meeting. The reader will recall that each scheduled item of construction was accorded two lines on the contractor's schedule; the first line indicated what the contractor projected to be the time of completion for each item and the second line was reserved for notation by the contract administrator of the contractor's actual progress. Thus designed, the schedule readily illustrates in which areas, if any, the contractor is falling behind, and prominent display of the schedule will serve to communicate the status of each construction item to concerned participants and stimulate the necessary discussion. Furthermore, the contract administrator has at his disposal information concerning the productivity rates anticipated by the contractor in arriving at his schedule and thus knows—and should advise the contractor of—the variance between the contractor's anticipated and actual productivity. In the event of substantial variances, the contract administrator should inquire of the contractor how the contractor intends to meet his schedule given these lower-than-projected productivity rates. Such constructive inquiries are clearly more beneficial to the contract administrator—and thus the owner—than an arbitrary demand that the contractor add crews, a measure which could easily occasion expense for the owner and liability for the contract administrator.

Targeted Production

The next suggested indirect schedule technique follows directly from the foregoing discussion. The contract administrator should consider setting targeted production for the major components of the project undertaken by the contractor at any given time. For example, if the project requires incorporation of 20,000 yd^3 of concrete and the contractor has scheduled that activity to occur over a period of 20 weeks, the contract administrator should inquire weekly as to how many cubic yards had been poured during the preceding week and should keep a running total of the amount poured. Thus if the contractor had poured 500 yd^3 during the first week, 500 yd^3 during the second week, and 1000 yd^3 during the third week, it would be clear to both the contract administrator and the contractor that the contractor was 1000 yd^3 behind his own schedule. If this effort on the part of the contract administrator seems somewhat elementary, it is nonetheless highly effective: most contractors are possessed of pride sufficient that they would find discomfort, absent good reason, in reporting week after week that they had not accomplished what they had agreed to accomplish. The contract administrator's role in this situation is to remind the contractor of his announced schedule in a matter-of-fact manner, then to elicit from the contractor a statement of targeted goals which, if met, would allow the contractor to regain compliance with his schedule. On the other hand, a contractor who is meeting the schedule or has successfully regained compliance with his schedule after falling behind earlier in the project should nonetheless be asked to report the status of his efforts for important reasons: first, the contractor should be "rewarded" for his compliance by having the opportunity to let all project participants know about it; second, this pleasant moment during the progress and coordination meeting will serve to reinforce the contractor's attentiveness to timely performance. The contract administrator's strategy should be to use the report on one major project component—be the report remedial or positive—as a lead-in for questions to the contractor concerning the next major component of the project as it appears on the schedule, e.g., steel erection following pouring of concrete, even where, from a scheduling standpoint, the two activities overlap.

The Cash-Flow Curve

Another effective indirect schedule technique involves conspicuous display of the cash-flow curve. The reader will recall that the cash-flow curve was generated using the contractor's schedule and the lump-sum breakdown. It is suggested that an enlarged copy of the cash-flow curve be placed on the wall of the room in which the progress and coordination meeting is held. As monthly partial payments are made to the contractor, the contract administrator should reflect the amounts of these payments on the cash-flow curve in a color different from those previously used on the chart, thus generating the actual cash-flow diagram for the project. If the actual cash-flow diagram falls above the anticipated cash-flow diagram on the chart, the contractor is receiving money faster than anticipated and has the additional benefit of the time value of that money. It may also indicate that he is ahead of schedule. On the other hand, if the anticipated cash-flow curve falls above the actual cash-flow curve, the contractor is not earning money as rapidly as anticipated and is losing the time value of that money. This should serve as an indicator that the contractor may have problems paying his suppliers in the future and that he may have fallen behind schedule. Another benefit of using the probability-based cash-flow curve is that it overcomes the common mistake of assuming that the contractor will regain his schedule during the last quarter of the project. The schedule usually indicates a somewhat relaxed program of work during the last quarter, and the natural and common defense of the contractor who has fallen behind schedule is that he will again meet the schedule during this period. The probability is that the contractor will be unable to regain his schedule during that period, and blithe assumptions at this

·point are one of the major causes of late project completion. Close examination by the contract administrator of the components which went into the cash-flow curve may also explain why, in some cases, the contractor may be achieving the targeted goals of the major components of the project but nevertheless remains behind schedule; usually this phenomenon occurs where the major components have relatively low unit costs. This exercise is also a good method to make the contractor aware of the actual productivity for construction items too small to be considered targeted goals. This can easily be done by returning to the data from which the cash-flow curve was originally generated with reference to a period beginning 2 months before the current month and ending 2 months after the current month. For example, the integrated schedule might state six construction items for each of the 5 months in question. Each item should be plotted on a vertical line, the length of each item on the line being in proportion to the dollar amount scheduled to be expended on that item. This graph should be created for each month of the 5-month period on a single chart, with a distance scaled between the months. The top of each item should then be connected with a line running from left to right, and the areas beneath this new line and between the vertical lines should be colored with different colors. Figure 23-1 is an example of this cash-flow breakdown. Although the chart is a mere recital of information derived from the integrated schedule, it presents the information contained in the integrated schedule more vividly and, therefore, may be of greater value in discussions with the contractor.

Marking of Plan and Profile Sheets

An effective indirect schedule control technique is the marking of the component lines of plan and profile sheets (from the contract documents) as completed by the contractor. For example, on a sewer line project, the contract administrator would display the plan and profile sheet on the wall of the room used for the progress and coordination meetings. As the contractor installs the sewer pipe from one station at the beginning of the day to another station at the end of the day, the progress for that day would be traced on the profile sheet with a unique color and it would be dated. Thus the contractor's daily progress is recorded each day on the contract drawing sheets themselves. The use of different colors for consecutive days and especially vivid colors for days of exceptionally high or low productivity creates a clear picture of daily achievement. In the case of a plant or building project, the contract administrator could employ the same basic approach with some

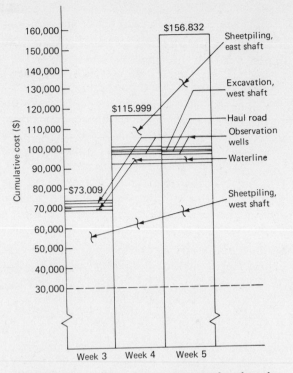

**FIGURE 23-1 Bar chart representing break-
down of components of cash-flow curve.**

adjustments. The project drawings could be overlayed with colored
transparent sheets, each color indicating a different operation, i.e., red
for excavation, green for foundations, blue for superstructure, orange
for roofing and siding, etc. In using this indirect schedule control technique, the contract administrator should take great pains to declare in
writing to the contractor that the color or marking of given lines or
areas in no way indicates the contract administrator's acceptance of the
quality or *conformance* of the work in place, for those matters await the
outcome of testing procedures and closer inspection and are subject to
the limitations set forth in the contract administrator's agreement for
services and in the contract documents. Carelessness on the part of the
contract administrator at this point could result in the colored markings being characterized by the contractor as an admission by the contract administrator on behalf of the owner that the marked sections of
the work have been properly completed, a situation which could produce extensive expense to the owner and extensive liability to the
contract administrator.

SUMMARY

The variety of proper and effective indirect schedule control techniques available to the contract administrator is practically limitless; the purpose of this chapter has been to suggest a few basic techniques which contract administrators can adapt to their own style and objectives. Moreover, each project is unique and requires an individualized approach given the physical characteristics and personalities involved.

Notwithstanding the best efforts of the contract administrator, however, situations may be encountered in which the contractor fails to respond either to the foregoing basic stimuli or to those which the contract administrator has devised for the project in question. The usual result is that the gap between scheduled performance and actual performance widens to the point that the contract administrator becomes concerned about the fate of the project in the hands of the contractor in question. The contract administrator's first obligation is to keep the owner continually advised of the gap in order that the owner may make an informed decision whether to place the contractor in default and risk litigation or to bear the loss of the potential financial advantages of finishing on time. Whatever the owner's decision, the contract administrator will have performed the duties of documentation both in his efforts to stimulate the contractor and in his reports of contractor deficiencies to the owner. Also, the consistent, analytical approach of the contract administrator in invoking the indirect schedule controls will not be lost upon most contractors, who realize that a detailed and regular record is being made against them should they fail to respond to the stimuli. A contractor whose performance is made easier by the organized and administrative approach of the contract administrator at the outset of the project, whose progress is regularly monitored and discussed in progress and coordination meetings, and whose failures of timely performance are both discussed and documented will likely realize both the benefits of timely performance and the costs of schedule failure. Although the contract administrator's role in controlling the schedule must be indirect, the contract administrator has considerable power, the wise use of which can determine the success of the project without unduly threatening the contract administrator himself.

CHAPTER 24

MONITORING OF
QUALITY CONTROLS

During the review and dissection of the contract, the contract administrator developed one or more Control Responsibility Summary Sheets (see Chapter 1). Control responsibilities were subsequently divided into two groups: administrative and technical (see Chapter 17). Technical control responsibilities (usually drawn from the materials and performance sections of the contract) differ from their administrative counterparts in three important respects:

- They, unlike most administrative control responsibilities, usually require direct interaction between the contractor and the contract administrator.

- They require positive action of the *contractor* in (1) providing, for review by the design engineer, data received from vendors and suppliers which confirms the suitability of materials and equipment proposed to be incorporated into the project and (2) performing field tests to confirm the quality of work in place.

- They require positive action of the *contract administrator* in (1) witnessing test procedures and confirming results, (2) recording results, and (3) confirming the conformance of tests to contractual standards.

By discharging his duties related to technical control responsibilities, the contract administrator fulfills a substantial portion of his responsibilities for project quality control.

This chapter will consider methods by which the contract administrator can most effectively monitor the quality of labor and material components during and after incorporation into the project. Thorough study and diligent application of these methods will permit contract administrators to meet their obligations without undue commitments of time and expense.

SUBMITTALS BY CONTRACTORS

In Chapter 13, it was noted that both contracts and custom often require that the contractor submit to the design engineer data concerning proposed material and equipment at the time the contractor requests approval of the manufacturers and vendors proposed to furnish them. The nature and scope of these data are governed by the specific terms of each contract and may be comprised of shop drawings, samples, test data, or other information. The design engineer usually reviews the submittal and, when satisfied that both the manufacturer or vendor and the material or equipment are consistent with the terms of the contract, communicates approval to the contractor through the contract administrator.

It is also customary that the design engineer transmit copies of all such data to the contract administrator once the manufacturer or vendor itself has been approved. As these data are received by the contract administrator, they should be reviewed and filed: a separate file folder should be prepared for each section of the contract requiring such submittals. Once all necessary approved data for a given section of the contract documents has been received by the contract administrator, the contract administrator should note that the technical control responsibility of the contractor has been fulfilled by highlighting the applicable line on the Control Responsibility Summary Sheet. In this manner, the contract administrator can rapidly scan the Control Responsibility Summary Sheet periodically to determine outstanding technical responsibilities.

It is normally the design engineer's duty to extract outstanding submittals required from the contractor for this type of a technical control responsibility; it is the contract administrator's responsibility either to prevent incorporation of nonaccepted materials or equipment into the work of the project or to advise the contractor that he is doing so at his own jeopardy.

It is beyond the scope of this book but nevertheless worthy of mention to state that good design engineering practice would include periodic transmittal to the contractor of a listing of outstanding items which either have not been submitted by the contractor for the design engineer's review or have been submitted and found unacceptable by the design engineer and, hence, require resubmittal, utilizing a different supplier or vendor or a different type of material or line of equipment from the original supplier or vendor, by the contractor. A copy of such a listing to the contract administrator would provide the contract administrator with a ready checklist for comparison to nonhighlighted entries on the Control Responsibility Summary Sheet and with a basis upon which to note problems that may occur if the acceptance of the material or equipment is not obtained in time to meet the project schedule. If the design engineer periodically reminds the contractor of his outstanding submittals, the responsibility for not having the materials and equipment available by the time they are required in the project schedule can usually be laid to the contractor, with the possible result that some subsequent delay claims can be overcome.

The progress and coordination meetings (the subject of Chapter 25) provide a forum for discussion between the design engineer and the contractor concerning problems which might be experienced in the acceptance of the contractor's proposals by the design engineer.

This class of technical control responsibility is noted on the integrated schedule or, in the case of larger projects, on a critical-path-method (CPM) schedule and, hence, the time by which it must be completed is known.

FIELD TESTING

The discussion now turns to those technical control responsibilities which require field testing by the contractor. As previously stated (see Chapter 17), these control responsibilities do not always lend themselves to insertion into an integrated schedule. Of course, in larger projects, monitored by CPMs, they could be scheduled. We have chosen to employ the progress and coordination meeting to establish dates for testing between the contractor and contract administrator in an example.

Chapter 17 included discussion of a method by which this type of technical control responsibility could be culled from the Control Responsibility Summary Sheets to form the general index of the loose-leaf quality control notebook. From this general index, a subindex was developed for each control responsibility in a particular materials and performance section of the contract documents. Blank test report forms of the type required were then inserted behind the subindexes. As the schedule dictates and the contractor confirms he is ready, the tests are performed and the blank forms completed. Completion of all the tests required by a particular section is indicated by a fully filled-out subindex. Once this has been accomplished, the contract administrator highlights the applicable item on the general index. Reference to items not

Closeout propert

highlighted in the general index readily makes apparent those subindexes for which there are items not yet tested for acceptability. Review of the subindex indicates which detailed tests have not been completed. The contractor can then be reminded in the progress and coordination meeting of any outstanding tests, should he not request them himself, and a date can be agreed upon to perform the tests. The contractor is notified, as previously stated in Chapter 17, upon the completion of each test. Upon completion of all testing—normally at the end of the project—copies of the quality control notebook can be distributed to participants requiring them.

This concludes discussion of tests prescribed explicitly by the contract and distilled through the Control Responsibility Summary Sheets. However, there are other requirements which, although not "captured" on the sheets, nevertheless are critical to the ultimate quality of the project. These requirements can usually be met by application of the "best standard practices" of the construction industry, i.e., customary, rather than contractual, field inspection.

An example may be helpful: Project specifications usually do not require a "test" to confirm proper installation of reinforcing steel in a reinforced concrete structure. These specifications would, however, either detail the tolerances for such an installation or make reference to specification from an independent organization which does give such detail in a published code. The contract administrator and his inspection staff must be aware or make themselves aware of these best standard practices and, during their routine inspection of the work as it is being performed, either satisfy themselves that the contractor is properly discharging his responsibilities in this regard or take exception to the contractor's practices. If the contract administrator is satisfied the contractor is properly installing the components of the project, no action is normally required other than to note that impression. If, however, the contract administrator is not satisfied with the contractor's performance, he should so notify the contractor by letter. Liability can accrue to the contract administrator if he is incorrect or if his letter is not properly composed. Hence the letter should not instruct the contractor as to how to do the work; this is the contractor's province and, if stipulations outside the contract documents are imposed on him, he would have a legitimate right to extra compensation if he could show that the stipulation occasioned added costs.

The letter should follow the guidelines below:

1. Note the particular action with which the contract administrator is concerned and its exact location.

(Date) _____

(Contractor) _____

_____

Attn: (_____)

Re: (Project Title)

Subject: Conduit Spacing

File: _____

Gentlemen:

Conduit presently being installed for the future second floor, floor slab in the Electrical Room in the Operations Building, is not properly spaced.

Section MP-3.01 of the Contract Documents for the above referenced Project provides, in pertinent part, as follows:

"Conduits to be installed in structural concrete shall have a clear distance between them equal to, or greater than, four times the outside diameter of the larger of the two conduits."

Take all necessary and proper action to discharge your contractual obligation in regard to this situation.

Very truly yours,

(Contract Administrator)

FIGURE 24-1 Advice of defect or deficiency.

2. Make reference to the applicable section of the contract or applicable code which indicates the action to be unacceptable.

3. Instruct the contractor to meet the requirements of the contract or applicable code.

4. Do not instruct the contractor as to *how* to meet the requirements of the contract.

Figure 24-1 is a typical letter. Should the contractor, upon receipt of a letter such as that used in the example, wish confirmation by the contract administrator that the contractor's newly proposed method of overcoming the problem would be acceptable, such confirmation should be given where merited, with the clear, written understanding that the method of overcoming the problem is being proposed by the *contractor*, not the contract administrator.

All letters of exception to the contractor should be reviewed in the progress and coordination meeting. Once they are so reviewed, they should be entered in the minutes of the meeting and should remain in the minutes until it has been confirmed that proper remedial action has been completed. When proper remedial action has been completed, the minutes of the next meeting should so note, and the item should be dropped from following minutes.

Careful adherence to the methods set forth in this chapter will enable contract administrators to monitor effectively the operation of their quality control systems without inviting liability through undue incursions upon prerogatives reserved to contractors.

CHAPTER 25

THE PROGRESS AND COORDINATION MEETING

It is essential in any construction project that an atmosphere be created and maintained in which key participants can communicate freely within the limitations established by applicable contracts. Our experience suggests that such an atmosphere may best be created by the contract administrator through organization of project meetings (called "Progress and Coordination Meetings") at uniform, predetermined time intervals during the course of the project. Properly undertaken, these meetings can create a forum in which participants can both provide information and pose questions. Progress and coordination meetings also afford the contract administrator a medium through which to coordinate the activities of the various participants, review the progress of construction with them, and advise them of any concerns relative to their activities. In this atmosphere of open, but defined, communication, the prospect of major misunderstandings which could impair the progress or quality of the project itself is minimized.

Given that the interests of owners and other project participants are always potentially in conflict and that meetings present inescapable opportunities to exert influence, contract administrators should take the opportunity to tailor progress and coordination meetings so as to serve best the interests of the owners. Effective planning of these meetings requires considerable forethought. The remainder of this chapter will be addressed to the various matters which the contract administrator may wish to consider in planning the meetings.

TECHNIQUES

It should be observed at the outset that each construction project is unique. Variations in numbers of participants, types of construction, and the personalities involved from project to project means that the contract administrator cannot be content to develop one "boiler-plate" style and structure for the progress and coordination meetings; rather, the contract administrator must constantly reconsider the needs of each project at its various stages to assure that the progress and coordination meetings are best serving the owner's interests at that time.

Attendance

The number of participants attending the progress and coordination meetings will depend upon the type of contract, the size of the contract, and the desires of the owner. At a minimum, however, each meeting should be attended by a representative of the contractor who possesses decision-making authority, a representative of the design engineer, and the contract administrator. Also, it is usually advantageous to have a representative of the owner in attendance. This representative may elect to participate actively in the meeting or merely to observe. In the event of active participation, the contract administrator will be well advised to review in advance with the representative all matters which could reasonably be anticipated to arise during the meeting in order to permit coordination between the owner and the contract administrator. The contract administrator will also be well advised to undertake a similar advance review with the representative of the design engineer. Each prime contractor in the project should be represented by one person with decision-making authority. If any prime contractor states a desire to have one or more major subcontractors under that contractor's jurisdiction attend, this should be permitted. It is reasonable to expect that multiple prime contractors and their respective subcontractors might undertake premeeting planning similar to that undertaken by the contract administrator: such intercontractor planning poses no threat in itself to the contract administrator, but the contract administrator should be and remain aware that advance coordination may have taken place.

Channels of Communication

The contract administrator should always bear in mind that the purpose of the progress and coordination meetings is *channeled*, rather than random, communication. These channels of communication are established by the contract documents, and the interests of the project will thus be served by keeping communication within those channels. For example, the interests of the project would not be served if the contract administrator, an agent of the owner, were to issue an order directly to a subcontractor; indeed, such an action might well found an action by the bypassed contractor based upon the contract administrator's interference with the contractor's subcontractual arrangement. The purpose of the progress and coordination meetings is to further the smooth and effective completion of the project; that result will best be achieved if each participant performs his designated contractual role. The role of the contract administrator is to coordinate the activities required of the various participants as set forth in the contract documents.

It should not be expected that all questions or problems can be resolved during the meeting. Those questions and problems which can be resolved should be resolved, but many will require substantial research. The contract administrator's responsibility is to promote resolution without undue delay.

The meeting should be held with formality sufficient to maintain the proper decorum, but each participant should be encouraged to speak openly whenever possible. An open exchange of information and requests for information is essential if the participants are to discover subtle problems which might impair the success of the project.

Personalities

Given the varied, and sometimes conflicting, interests of the participants in a construction project, it is quite possible that arguments will develop during a meeting and that, over the course of a substantial project, certain animosities may develop between participants. Although the contract administrator is virtually powerless to control the likes and dislikes of others, the contract administrator can exert a significant influence by remaining analytical and objective at all times; the contract administrator can claim no excuse for becoming argumentative or hostile. Generally speaking, the greater the tendency of meeting participants to become hostile, the greater should be the degree of formality with which the meetings are conducted. A natural and sincere degree of humor in such situations may be helpful in easing tensions.

The Meeting Site

Progress and coordination meetings should be held in relatively comfortable surroundings. The meetings should occur in the contract administrator's office or field trailer on site or in the owner's facilities on site. It should not occur in the contractor's facilities. In our experience, this "home-turf" advantage confers an important psychological benefit to the owner; since it is inevitable that the benefits of location and style of meeting will accrue to some participant, it is the duty of contract administrators to do all they reasonably and ethically can to place those benefits at the disposal of the owners. It is critical that the meeting room contain a table large enough for all participants in order to convey a feeling of equality of viewpoints. It is also useful to provide facilities in the room for coffee and other beverages. Another important consideration is seating arrangements. Inasmuch as the meeting will occur on the contract administrator's turf, the contract administrator and the owner will be able to choose their seats before anyone else arrives. Although seating strategy varies with the shape and size of the meeting room, the contract administrators should generally attempt to place themselves diagonally across the table from the door, in a corner, and next to the telephone. In this position, the contract administrator can see everyone and everything without turning and can control telephone calls to or from the meeting room. The design engineer should sit opposite the contract administrator, and the owner's representative should be seated midway between the two and facing the door. Once these positions have been established during the first three or four meetings, the participants will gravitate to their respective seats through habit.

Visual aides—including, at a minimum, the integrated schedule and cash-flow curve—should be on the wall behind the main body of the contractors. Should discussion related to these matters be required, anyone can easily walk to them. Finding a reason to use these materials can be most helpful in overcoming hostility during the meeting.

Documentation and Conduct of the Meeting

The contract administrator should document each progress and coordination meeting with written minutes. Properly taken, these minutes will form the basis of the agenda for the next progress and coordination meeting. The minutes should first identify the chronological number, date and time, and location of the meeting. For example: "The 23d Weekly Progress and Coordination Meeting for the _____ project was held at __ P.M. on June 20, 1982, in _____'s office at the project site."

The second paragraph of the meeting minutes should state the names and titles of all persons in attendance together with the name of the firm that each represents.

The third paragraph should note all items which arose during the "short-range schedule review," i.e., all project activities which are scheduled to occur within 2 weeks of the meeting. In establishing this short-range schedule, the contract administrator should lead the discussion by referring to the project schedule and asking the appropriate contractor questions concerning the status of each schedule item. In most cases, the contractor will be sufficiently familiar with these short-term items so as to provide an adequate reply during the course of the meeting. If the contractor anticipates problems with any given item which could be resolved by action or approval of another participant, the meeting provides the vehicle to resolve those problems by direct communication. By restricting the short-range schedule review to those items scheduled to occur within 2 weeks of the meeting, the contract administrator can maintain a list of manageable proportions which addresses only those matters requiring immediate attention.

As the short-range schedule review progresses, the contract administrator should note on his pad all such problems as identified by the contractor. One method of notation employed successfully by us is as follows: When any participant raises a problem, the contract administrator should draw a small box at the left-hand side of the paper, then leave a space of approximately 2 in., then draw another box. Beneath these entries, the contract administrator should record a summary of the problem. Between the two boxes, the contract administrator should enter the name of the participant who must answer the problem or question presented. Once the contract administrator confirms that the participant who must answer the question or problem has been advised of the question or problem (either in the progress and coordination meeting or later), the second box should be marked with an "x"; once the contract administrator confirms that the participant has actually answered the question or problem, the first box should be marked with an "x." This technique provides the contract administrator with an effective means of reviewing the status of all questions and problems raised during the progress and coordination meeting while providing a list of items to be noted in the minutes of the meeting. An example may help illustrate the best use of the technique: A contractor might state during a progress and coordination meeting that the contractor's concrete design mix had yet to be reviewed by the design engineer and that the contractor was scheduled to make the first concrete pour within 2 weeks of the meeting. The contract administrator would make the following notation:

☐ Design Engineer ☐ transmit review of the General Contractor's concrete design mix

If the design engineer was in attendance at the progress and coordination meeting, mere verbal assurance by the design engineer acknowledging the request would permit the contract administrator to mark the second box with an "x." Once the review of the concrete design mix was transmitted to the general contractor with a copy to the contract administrator, the contract administrator could mark the first box and be assured that no further action would be required of him relative to that item.

After reviewing the short-range schedule with each contractor and recording all problems and questions raised by the contractors (or statements by the contractors that no such problems existed), the contract administrator should ask the contractors whether they have questions or problems related to the timing of construction items which are scheduled to occur more than 2 weeks after the meeting. All such questions and problems which can be answered by one of the participants present should be resolved during the meeting and recorded by the contract administrator for inclusion in the minutes. All problems and questions which cannot be resolved during the meeting should be handled with the "box technique" described above.

The contract administrator's next step in conducting the progress and coordination meeting should be an item-by-item review of the minutes of the last progress and coordination meeting. Many of these items will have been answered either during the time period between the last and present meetings or during the early stages of the meeting; others will remain to be resolved. Unresolved matters should be addressed at this time, and the minutes of the meeting should reflect that such items either were resolved during the meeting or remain outstanding. The contract administrator will be well advised to adhere strictly to the rule that no item should ever be dropped from the meeting minutes until it has been resolved.

Following the review of questions or problems from the minutes of the previous meeting, the contract administrator should move systematically around the table (either clockwise or counterclockwise), asking each participant if there are other matters for discussion. Any matters so raised should be treated by the contract administrator using the box technique. Once all other participants have had the opportunity to speak, the contract administrator should address matters of concern to him. The contract administrator should advise the appropriate participant of questions or problems noted by the contract administrator since the last meeting which require some administrative or technical action to correct.

SUMMARY

The progress and coordination meeting is perhaps the contract administrator's most effective device in promoting controlled and constructive communication between participants. Given the importance of this method of dispensing and receiving information, it is essential that the contract administrator plan and conduct the meeting carefully in order to best serve the interests of the owner and of the project itself.

Alan N. Culbertson, a graduate of Edinboro State College of Pennsylvania and the Syracuse University College of Law, is an attorney admitted to practice in New York and Pennsylvania. He has served for several years as internal counsel to a large international engineering consultant.

Donald E. Kenney is a graduate of the University of Illinois and a licensed professional engineer. He has been active in construction-related matters for more than thirty years. In addition to having owned a construction firm, he has worked as a tradesman and has held key contract administration positions with large manufacturers. For several years, he has served as a contract administrator for a major engineering consultant. Articles by Mr. Kenney have been published in various trade journals.